The Double Black Box

The Double Black Box

*National Security, Artificial Intelligence, and
the Struggle for Democratic Accountability*

Ashley S. Deeks

OXFORD
UNIVERSITY PRESS

OXFORD
UNIVERSITY PRESS

Oxford University Press is a department of the University of Oxford.
It furthers the University's objective of excellence in research, scholarship,
and education by publishing worldwide. Oxford is a registered trade mark of
Oxford University Press in the UK and in certain other countries.

Published in the United States of America by Oxford University Press
198 Madison Avenue, New York, NY 10016, United States of America.

Library of Congress Cataloging-in-Publication Data
Names: Deeks, Ashley S., author.
Title: The double black box : national security, artificial intelligence,
and the struggle for democratic accountability / Ashley S. Deeks.
Description: New York : Oxford University Press, 2025. | Includes bibliographical references and index.
Identifiers: LCCN 2024039819 | ISBN 9780197520901 (hardback) |
ISBN 9780197520925 (epub) | ISBN 9780197520918 (updf) |
ISBN 9780197520932 (online)
Subjects: LCSH: National security—Law and legislation—United States. |
Artificial intelligence—Law and legislation—United States. |
Government accountability—United States.
Classification: LCC KF4850 .D44 2025 | DDC 343.73/01—dc23/eng/20240828
LC record available at https://lccn.loc.gov/2024039819

DOI: 10.1093/9780197520932.001.0001

Printed by Marquis Book Printing, Canada

Note to Readers
This publication is designed to provide accurate and authoritative information in regard to the
subject matter covered. It is based upon sources believed to be accurate and reliable and is intended
to be current as of the time it was written. It is sold with the understanding that the publisher is not
engaged in rendering legal, accounting, or other professional services. If legal advice or other expert
assistance is required, the services of a competent professional person should be sought. Also, to
confirm that the information has not been affected or changed by recent developments, traditional
legal research techniques should be used, including checking primary sources where appropriate.

*(Based on the Declaration of Principles jointly adopted by a Committee of the American Bar
Association and a Committee of Publishers and Associations.)*

You may order this or any other Oxford University Press publication by visiting the Oxford
University Press website at www.oup.com.

MIX
Paper | Supporting
responsible forestry
FSC
www.fsc.org FSC® C103567

Contents

PART II. UNPACKING THE DOUBLE BLACK BOX

Acknowledgments

This book has benefited from very helpful thoughts, comments, critiques, and support from friends and colleagues, including David Abramowitz, Jocelyn Aqua, Tess Bridgeman, Danielle Citron, Rebecca Crootof, Laura Dickinson, Kristen Eichensehr, Jack Goldsmith, Duncan Hollis, Margaret Hu, Leslie Kendrick, David Kris, Marty Lederman, Daragh Murray, Mitt Regan, Rich Schragger, Alissa Starzak, Paul Stephan, Edward Swaine, and the team at Lawfare. I also thank participants in workshops and colloquia at New York University, George Washington University, William & Mary, and University of Virginia Law Schools. For excellent research assistance, thanks to Manal Cheema, Jacqueline Dejournett, James Harper, Niki Hendi, Chris Kent, and Katherine Krudys. And I am so grateful for the support of my husband, Mike Flowers; my son, Tate; and my mother, Susan.

Many other people commented on articles that I subsequently incorporated in revised form into this book. These earlier articles are *Checks and Balances from Abroad*, 83 U. CHI. L. REV. 65 (2016); *Intelligence Communities, Peer Constraints, and the Law*, 7 HARV. NAT'L SECURITY J. 1 (2016); *Predicting Enemies*, 104 VA. L. REV. 1529 (2018); *The Judicial Demand for Explainable AI*, 119 COLUM. L. REV. 1829 (2019); *Machine Learning, Artificial Intelligence, and the Use of Force by States*, 10 J. NAT'L SEC. L. & POL'Y 1 (2019) (with Noam Lubell & Daragh Murray); *Secret Reason-Giving*, 129 YALE L.J. 612 (2020); *Secrecy Surrogates*, 106 VA. L. REV. 1395 (2020); and *Will Cyber Autonomy Undercut Democratic Accountability?*, 96 INT'L L. STUD. 646 (2020). The content of these articles, as well as several blog posts, has been shortened and revised for the book. In addition, the book contains much new material.

Introduction

The President sits in the Situation Room with members of her Cabinet. They have assembled to make a final decision about whether to initiate a drone strike against someone they believe to be a senior member of al Qaeda. The Secretary of Defense briefs the others in the room about the information that the Department of Defense (DOD) has compiled. Using advanced facial recognition software, he notes, the Department is 90% certain that the individual in question is al Qaeda's third most senior operative, even though the enhanced image he puts on the screen is so hazy that the Cabinet members can't identify him when shown the still frame.[1] Further, the Secretary tells the President, a different Defense Department machine learning algorithm that was trained on huge volumes of telephonic data indicates that the operative is very likely to lead an attack against the U.S. embassy in Algiers in the coming week. A third algorithm has predicted that, based on his pattern of life, there is an 87% chance he'll be alone in a particular house tomorrow. The CIA Director chimes in: "If we kill him, the U.S. intelligence community believes—based on our algorithms—that there is a 62% probability that it will take al Qaeda at least six months to replace him."

"How do you know all of this?" the President asks. "Our algorithms made these predictions," the Secretary replies, "and we trust them." What the Secretary knows is that DOD's facial recognition software can identify subjects at a higher rate of accuracy than humans can. He also knows that other machine learning algorithms used by his Department and the various agencies in the intelligence community are making predictions about individuals' identities, locations, and behaviors based on connections that humans would take years to find, using millions of data points on which the engineers have trained the systems. The computer's predictions rely on the quality of information from sensors, electronic surveillance, and models—things that the President and his senior advisers cannot see and

---

[1] Ben Woods, *Facial Recognition Can Identify You Even If Your Face Is Blurred*, WIRED (Aug. 8, 2016).

may not fully understand.[2] Yet the President may authorize the Defense Department to kill this alleged senior al Qaeda member based on these algorithmic recommendations, especially if the situation requires an immediate decision. And the Defense Department might decide to use an autonomous drone swarm that, once launched, requires no further human involvement in executing the operation. Because these types of operations are classified, we—the American people—likely would not know that the Defense Department has these types of machine learning algorithms at its disposal, or that the President has ordered the killing on the basis of predictions made by algorithms, or that the Defense Department is using autonomous drones to perform the mission.

Imagine a few other scenarios: an AI system that "systematically misclassifies civilian construction workers carrying pipes as hostile insurgents with rocket launchers."[3] Or an autonomous defensive cyber tool that mistakenly attributes a cyberattack on the U.S. electrical grid to Russia and responds against the Russian electrical grid, severely escalating bilateral tensions. Or consider a decision by U.S. Special Operations Command to release a deepfake video of North Korean leader Kim Jong Un declaring war on South Korea, which triggers an exchange of missiles on the Korean peninsula.

Although these scenarios are fictional, machine learning algorithms are everywhere today, in products as diverse as driverless cars, Amazon and Netflix recommendations, Google Translate, and medical diagnostics. Even some actors in the criminal justice system now rely on predictive algorithms to help them assess how dangerous certain people are, with the goal of making sounder judgments about whom to keep in custody and about how dangerous certain physical locations are, so that police departments can allocate their resources more efficiently. To oversimplify, a machine learning algorithm is a computer program that improves its knowledge or performance with experience.[4] Programmers "train" machine learning systems by exploiting large amounts of data in a particular category—movies, X-rays, photos of cats, or weather. The systems process the information and "learn"

---

[2] Richard Danzig, *Technology Roulette*, CTR. FOR NEW AM. SECURITY 16 (June 2018) ("Human decisionmakers are riders traveling across obscured terrain with little or no ability to assess the powerful beasts that carry and guide them.").

[3] These are modified scenarios drawn from Sydney J. Freedberg Jr., *Why a "Human in the Loop" Can't Control AI: Richard Danzig*, BREAKING DEFENSE (June 1, 2018).

[4] PETER FLACH, MACHINE LEARNING: THE ART AND SCIENCE OF ALGORITHMS THAT MAKE SENSE OF DATA 3 (2012) (emphasis omitted).

which characteristics or factors are helpful in predicting outcomes. When presented with a new example, the algorithm can offer a statistical, data-driven prediction about how likely it is that this new example will have particular characteristics, such as a cancerous tumor. These systems can make sense of huge volumes of data and do so much faster than humans can.

Like companies, the U.S. government has been drawn to the promise of artificial intelligence (AI) and machine learning (ML) tools. We are starting to understand the ways in which civilian executive agencies such as the Social Security Administration and the Securities and Exchange Commission are deploying AI/ML to adjudicate benefits cases and focus their enforcement efforts.[5] These tools hold real promise for enhancing accuracy, fairness, and speed, and—perhaps—for reducing human bias. However, scholars, ethicists, and technologists have articulated a litany of concerns and challenges that AI/ML pose as well. For example, it is possible to inadvertently embed biases in the algorithms. It is often difficult to understand how advanced ML algorithms reach their conclusions, which is why many refer to those algorithms as "black boxes." Sometimes algorithmic developers significantly overclaim what their AI/ML tools can achieve.[6] And users may too readily accept the machine's recommendations, even when their own experiences suggest that the machine is wrong, which undermines the effectiveness of human oversight.[7]

The use of AI/ML algorithms in the administrative state is complicated and raises a host of important issues that the Executive, Congress, and the federal courts must work hard to resolve in the coming decades. This book, however, is about an even thornier challenge: the use of AI/ML algorithms to protect U.S. national security. U.S. national security and homeland security agencies are using more of these algorithms every day, raising fundamental questions about how the U.S. public can ensure that its government only adopts and uses these tools in a way that reflects the values and virtues of a democracy. These questions are hard not simply because it is difficult to decide when, whether, and how to use AI, but also because so much national

---

[5] Danielle Citron & Frank Pasquale, *The Scored Society: Due Process for Automated Predictions*, 89 Wash. L. Rev. 1 (2014); David Freeman Engstrom & Daniel Ho, *Algorithmic Accountability in the Administrative State*, Ctr. for Study of the Admin. State (Nov. 15, 2019).

[6] *See* Inioluwa Raji et al., *The Fallacy of AI Functionality*, 2022 ACM Conference on Fairness, Accountability, and Transparency (June 2022), Seoul, Republic of Korea.

[7] *See* Kate Goddard et al., *Automation Bias: A Systematic Review of Frequency, Effect Mediators, and Mitigators*, 19 J. Am. Med. Info. Ass'n 121 (2012).

security activity takes place behind the veil of classification and because the geopolitical stakes of national security decisions are very high.

Many of the leading voices on AI in the United States are urging the United States to move forward with alacrity. For instance, the National Security Commission on AI (NSCAI), set up by Congress, argues that the United States must do what it takes to retain its technological advantages in the AI competition with China and to responsibly use AI to defend democracies.[8] In the NSCAI's words, "AI is going to reorganize the world. America must lead the charge."[9] More recently, some of the NSCAI's members issued a more sharply worded report that argued, "Absent targeted action, the United States is unlikely to close the growing technology gaps with China" and will fall behind in developing critical AI tools.[10]

Notwithstanding this hard-charging approach to AI, the NSCAI recognizes that the competition between the United States and China is a "values competition," and it urges the United States to "work with fellow democracies to . . . advance democratic norms to guide AI uses so that democracies can responsibly use AI tools for national security purposes."[11] Both of these approaches seem reasonable: the United States should continue apace to develop national security AI tools, but in doing so must make sure that it preserves its values. The hard question remains: How will we—the public—know whether it is doing so?

Let's assume that actors within the U.S. Defense Department and the intelligence community fully intend to follow the seven or eight basic norms that most agree are requisites for responsible AI—norms such as reliability, governability, and accountability.[12] How can we know if they are following through on those intentions? What if they confront a new, highly classified national security threat that causes them to revisit those basic norms? What legal and moral guidelines will they use to decide whether and how to use AI to handle the new threat? These types of questions are real, and they are pressing. The United States made some poor legal, policy, and operational

---

[8] Eric Schmidt & Bob Work, *Final Report* 11, National Security Comm'n on AI (2019).

[9] *Id.* at 14.

[10] Eric Schmidt et al., *Mid-Decade Challenges to National Competitiveness*, Special Competitive Stud. Project (Sept. 2022).

[11] Schmidt & Work, *supra* note 8, at 2 (Letter from the Chair and Vice Chair).

[12] U.S. Department of Defense, *DOD Adopts Ethical Principles for Artificial Intelligence* (Feb. 24, 2020); Office of the Director of National Intelligence, *Principles of Artificial Intelligence Ethics for the Intelligence Community* (2020); North Atlantic Treaty Organization, *Summary of NATO's Autonomy Implementation Plan* (last updated Oct. 13, 2022); European Commission, *Ethics Guidelines for Trustworthy AI* (Apr. 8, 2019).

decisions in secret after the September 11 attacks, even as those inside the government were acting with good intentions to protect the country. The rise of AI amid broader geopolitical tensions with China, Russia, and Iran triggers similar pressures to protect the United States, even at high costs.

This book makes six arguments. First, governments are introducing AI/ML and autonomy into their national security operations today. This means we are at a key inflection point, both for setting expectations around the world for what responsible uses of AI look like and for setting granular rules and standards for the U.S. government. Second, there is rough consensus (especially in the United States, including inside the U.S. government) about what basic principles AI/ML should follow. Signs are favorable regarding the government's commitment to the ethical and responsible use of AI (as reflected in recent DOD and intelligence community policies). But these policies are written at a high level of generality, and it matters a lot how these principles cash out in specific cases.

Third, and critically for this book, much of the use of national security AI/ML will happen in secret. This secrecy, coupled with the opaque nature of the AI/ML tools themselves, will significantly complicate democratic oversight, including in the United States. I term this the "double black box" problem. We have already seen the U.S. government adopt uses of AI that, when they come to light, turn out to be tools that the public rejects. Although U.S. officials generally are competent and well-intentioned, we should not leave the executive branch (or private sector actors that sell the government AI/ML tools) entirely to their own devices in deciding what types of AI systems to develop and deploy.

Fourth, we will need to rely heavily on both the traditional set of actors that check and balance classified executive policymaking—Congress, the courts, executive branch lawyers, inspectors general, and whistleblowers—and on alternatives to these traditional surrogates to ensure that the U.S. government complies with the public law values of legality, competence, accountability, and justification. These actors will need to be creative about how to do so and will bear an antecedent burden of educating themselves about AI tools and their pathologies. Fifth, it is very unlikely that the full set of states pursuing advanced AI will agree on new, binding international rules to regulate those tools, but the United States is potentially well aligned with European and other allies to develop AI tools that are palatable to democratic populations. This group should band together to create appropriate norms and tools that comport with their own values, regardless of what

AI/ML tools countries such as China and Russia adopt. Finally, there is no one silver bullet to address the double black box problem. We must pursue many avenues simultaneously.

A. The National Security Black Box: Traditional Checks and Balances

At the heart of national security decisions lies a paradox: these decisions are among the most consequential that any government can make but are very difficult for democratic publics to oversee because they often are classified. In the United States, the constitutional checks and balances that we canonize are seriously weakened in the national security setting. In theory, Congress and the courts should serve as counterweights to and checks on executive decision-making, drawing on the Madisonian theory that ambition will check ambition.[13] And, to be sure, there are laws on the books that regulate certain areas of U.S. national security activity. Further, we have created mechanisms by which limited numbers of congressional committees and federal judges oversee the Executive's activities in classified settings, so that national security secrets can stay secret. These congressional members and judges serve as surrogates for us, the broader public, which generally does not and should not have access to government secrets.

In practice, though, Congress faces significant difficulties when it seeks to learn about the substance of and rationales behind the Executive's military and intelligence decisions. The Executive has the first-mover advantage over Congress: the President is commander-in-chief and head of the executive agencies that collect intelligence, engage with foreign officials, and develop and execute U.S. foreign policy. The Executive controls the levels of classification of documents and can assert that certain national security programs are too sensitive to share with Congress.[14] Members of Congress generally have fewer political incentives to challenge executive programs than we might like

---

[13] THE FEDERALIST No. 51, at 322 (James Madison) (Clinton Rossiter ed., 1961) ("Ambition must be made to counteract ambition.").

[14] For a 2023 example of such claims, see White House, *Statement from President Joe Biden on H.R. 2670, National Defense Authorization Act for Fiscal Year 2024* (Dec. 22, 2023) ("Certain provisions of the Act . . . would require the President and other officials to submit reports and plans to committees of the Congress that will, in the ordinary course, include highly sensitive classified information . . . . The Constitution vests the President with the authority to prevent the disclosure of such highly sensitive information in order to discharge his responsibility to protect the national security.").

because many of those programs are targeted not at their constituents but at foreign governments, companies, and nationals. Insufficient levels of congressional staffing and the difficulty in acquiring relevant technical expertise further complicate the ability to provide robust legislative oversight.

The courts generally fare even worse than Congress in their ability to serve as robust checks on the Executive's national security decisions, even when those decisions may be unlawful. Courts are necessarily reactive: they can only hear cases that plaintiffs choose to bring. Further, the Executive is often very reluctant to make classified information available to courts (other than the court that oversees foreign intelligence surveillance). Third, courts tend to defer to the Executive's intelligence or military decisions and its arguments about the harms that could flow from litigating certain cases, because courts are worried about their own technical incapacity and lack of democratic accountability. And, like Congress, courts worry about reaching decisions that might result in national security harms. As a result, even when plaintiffs try to use the courts to challenge executive decisions, the courts often rely on a range of doctrines, including the political question doctrine and the state secrets privilege, to avoid wading into the Executive's intelligence and military activities and issuing decisions on the merits.[15]

Although it may sound counterintuitive, the Executive itself has created structures and procedures that help check some of the dysfunction that secrecy creates. These include agency general counsels' offices, privacy and civil liberties offices, and professional responsibility offices. It is in the DNA of executive national security lawyers to urge their policy clients to comply with the law, even if they interpret the law in a way that gives the Executive ample flexibility. These lawyers can help minimize the scope of any legal violations that may occur, even when the legal challenges arise in classified settings.[16] Interagency processes themselves can serve as important checks on individual agencies. For example, the National Security Council (NSC) within the White House can serve as an internal battleground whereby an agency not engaged in a particular planned operation can learn about the operation and question its wisdom or legality. The NSC's structure takes advantage of the fact that different executive agencies may have different perspectives about what the law permits and what policies will best advance

---

[15] Ashley Deeks, *Secrecy Surrogates*, 106 VA. L. REV. 1395, 1417–18 (2020).
[16] Ashley Deeks, *The Substance of Secret Agreements and the Role of Government Lawyers*, 111 AM. J. INT'L L. 474 (2018).

U.S. national security. Likewise, the Executive frequently requires its officials to give reasons for decisions, even in secret; secret reason-giving can impose systemic checks on national security decision-making while improving the quality of those decisions.[17] Finally, Congress has created two groups of actors inside the Executive to identify violations of law or policy, and which have access to classified information: inspectors general and the Privacy and Civil Liberties Oversight Board.

The last set of traditional "checks" on the Executive are whistleblowers, leakers, and journalists. Whistleblowers are people inside the government who follow procedures set out in statute to convey their concerns about waste, fraud, abuse, or other illegalities that they observe.[18] However, because these statutes are not very user-friendly and the agencies have ways to penalize whistleblowers, especially in the national security context, this process often fails to work as intended.[19] Leakers are government officials or contractors with access to classified information who engage in unlawful releases of classified information, often to journalists. Good journalists can curate and contextualize the contents of the leaks, thus introducing the information into the public conversation. Although leaking can impose serious costs on U.S. national security and often is a crime, many have concluded that the system needs to periodically tolerate leaks, even as it sometimes prosecutes leakers.[20] It is a haphazard and risky way to oversee government secrecy, however, and therefore cannot serve as a consistent, robust check on the government.[21]

---

[17] Ashley Deeks, *Secret Reason-Giving*, 129 YALE L.J. 612 (2020).

[18] I use "whistleblower" to mean someone who attempts to reveal evidence of executive waste, fraud, abuse, or illegality by following statutorily created channels. *See, e.g.*, Whistleblower Protection Act of 1989, Pub. L. No. 101-12, 103 Stat. 16 (codified as amended in scattered sections of 5 U.S.C.); Whistleblower Protection Enhancement Act of 2012, Pub. L. No. 112-199, 126 Stat. 1465; Intelligence Community Whistleblower Protection Act of 1998, Pub. L. 105-272, 112 Stat. 2396, 2413–17; Defense Contractor Whistleblower Protection Act, Pub. L. 114-261, 130 Stat. 1362. I use "leaker" to mean someone who reveals classified information to a journalist with the expectation of anonymity. *See* RAHUL SAGAR, SECRETS AND LEAKS 202–03 (2013).

[19] *See* David Pozen, *The Leaky Leviathan: Why the Government Condemns and Condones Unlawful Disclosures of Information*, 127 HARV. L. REV. 512, 527 (2013) (noting that in the national security context whistleblowers "play a marginal role").

[20] *See, e.g.*, JACK GOLDSMITH, POWER AND CONSTRAINT: THE ACCOUNTABLE PRESIDENCY AFTER 9/11, at 218 (2012) ("There are costs and benefits to national security from both secrecy and disclosure."); Pozen, *supra* note 19.

[21] Neal Katyal, *Stochastic Constraint*, 126 HARV. L. REV. 990, 1003 (2013).

B. Alternative Checks on the Executive

In short, the two primary constitutional actors meant to check the Executive face serious hurdles to ensuring that it is adhering to the law and pursuing effective and desirable policies, and leakers offer only a stochastic (and usually unlawful) solution. As a result, we have started to rely on a diverse set of additional—though also unpredictable—actors to try to understand what the Executive is doing and to identify and challenge problematic policy and operational decisions. These alternative actors include technology and cybersecurity companies with which the Executive shares classified information; U.S. states and localities that are grappling with threats from new technologies that are similar to those the federal government faces; and foreign allies who undertake joint military and intelligence operations with the United States.[22] Call these our nontraditional secrecy surrogates.

Even with these additional checks, many decry the enduring "black box" nature of national security decision-making and the ability of U.S. citizens to constrain the Executive as (or before) it makes poor policy choices or undertakes illegal actions. After all, this is what we are really worried about when the government acts in secret: that it may be acting unlawfully or making ill-conceived policy choices, that officials can avoid having to justify their decisions to external actors, and that it is particularly hard for us to hold our government officials accountable for those errors. These worries are exacerbated by the perception that the Executive today has accrued an overwhelming amount of power.

C. The AI Black Box

Against the backdrop of this national security "black box"—whose workings are powerful, hidden, and complex—consider what happens when we introduce advanced technologies into the picture. The U.S. National Security Agency, the Central Intelligence Agency (CIA), and the Departments of Defense and Homeland Security reportedly have begun to deploy sophisticated algorithms involving AI/ML to bolster their decision-making and

---

[22] *See* Deeks, *supra* note 15; Ashley Deeks, *Intelligence Communities, Peer Constraints, and the Law,* 7 Harv. Nat'l Security J. 1 (2016); Ashley Deeks, *Checks and Balances from Abroad,* 83 U. Chi. L. Rev. 65 (2016).

operations. For example, the Department of Defense is using AI-powered computer vision tools to identify threatening activities—and ultimately potential targets—among thousands of hours of drone footage.[23] Cyber operations are increasingly driven by AI, raising the possibility that autonomous U.S. cyber tools could clash with a foreign adversary's autonomous cyber tools and escalate into an armed conflict without an affirmative human decision to produce that result.[24] And the idea of lethal autonomous weapon systems that use force against individuals without meaningful human oversight looms in the background of every discussion about military AI.

It is understandable why the Defense Department and the intelligence community are turning to AI tools: the tools can increase the accuracy of government prediction and decision-making, decrease decisional biases to which humans are vulnerable, and enhance decisional speed. Further, two of the foremost U.S. adversaries, China and Russia, are actively pursuing AI in military settings. Many military and intelligence algorithms will not be hugely risky: that is, they are unlikely to result in physical harm to humans or lead to serious foreign policy tensions. But some will. Algorithm-driven decision-making raises thorny questions about the algorithms' transparency and accuracy, the values embedded in the algorithms, and which specific actors to hold accountable for algorithmic national security decisions. Because it is frequently difficult to understand how AI algorithms reach their conclusions, people refer to these algorithms as "black boxes"; users and even programmers generally cannot access the algorithms' internal processes.[25] It is very difficult to learn how an algorithm weighted different factors to reach its recommendations because most AI tools do not produce reasons for their outputs. Further, unlike traditional military technology, these systems can learn and change over time. As a result, the use of AI to advance U.S. national security efforts will render "black box" national security choices even more opaque—not only to the public and people targeted by the government's national security actions but also to those we rely on to provide checks on the Executive and to the very people inside the executive branch who must make these national security decisions. That is, the widespread and growing

---

[23] Daisuke Wakabayashi & Scott Shane, *Google Will Not Renew Pentagon Contract That Upset Employees*, N.Y. TIMES (June 1, 2018).

[24] *See* Maggie Miller, *NATO Prepares for Cyber War*, POLITICO (Dec. 3, 2022); PAUL SCHARRE, ARMY OF NONE: AUTONOMOUS WEAPONS AND THE FUTURE OF WAR 222 (2018).

[25] *See, e.g.*, Tom Simonite, *AI Experts Want to End "Black Box" Algorithms in Government*, WIRED (Oct. 18, 2017) (discussing AI algorithms as "black boxes" that are "opaque to outside scrutiny").

use of AI to advance national security has the potential to create a "double black box."

D. The Double Black Box

What does this mean as a practical matter? It means that the range of actors who serve as surrogates for the U.S. public—who already seek, and sometimes fail, to check the Executive in the national security space—will have an increasingly hard time doing so. If it is already difficult for congressional committees to gain access to sensitive military operations, how—once they do gain access—can those committees understand whether the Executive's AI systems comport with our laws and values? How will our secrecy surrogates know what levels of risk and error the Executive decides to tolerate, including for systems that implicate people's life and liberty? Will the Executive retain power to override machine-generated decisions and, if so, when and how?[26] Is it feasible for the Executive to do so when states start to fight wars at hypersonic speeds? To bring us back to the opening hypothetical scenario, how well must the President and her advisers understand the machine learning systems on which they are basing life-and-death decisions? And how can the public be confident that it should trust both the systems and the people relying on the systems to act responsibly in our name? These, then, are the core questions that this book asks: How do we hold the executive branch accountable for its use of AI in national security settings? And how can we (collectively) ensure that it is adopting only safe, transparent, and reliable AI in its secret activities, especially where AI's operations are opaque even to its users?

U.S. national security officials, including military actors, make mistakes in warfare and intelligence analysis today. Why should we worry in particular about AI mistakes? As this book will explain, the difficulties that Congress and other overseers have today in identifying unlawful executive activities will be amplified by the challenges of understanding whether the use of a particular AI tool is lawful. The difficulty in obtaining enough information from the Executive to evaluate whether a given national security policy

---

[26] *See* Greg Allen, *DOD Is Updating Its Decade-Old Autonomous Weapons Policy, But Confusion Remains Widespread*, CSIS (June 6, 2022) (noting that DOD's policy does not require a human in the decision cycle).

choice is effective will be compounded by how hard it is to assess the reliability of AI recommendations and predictions that inform that choice. The
difficulty in deciding who to hold accountable for a particular flawed policy
will be amplified by the challenge of determining who is responsible for significant algorithmic errors. And the ease with which the Executive can avoid
defending its national security decisions by invoking classification limits will
be amplified by the nontransparency and inexplicability of the AI algorithms
it uses.

The use of AI tools to deeply inform and sometimes initiate U.S. military
and intelligence operations places governmental decision-making at an even
greater distance from the U.S. public than it already stands. This is particularly problematic at a time when large groups of people have come to distrust
the government—whether it is people who distrust local police departments
or people who believe that the bureaucracy is out of touch with those suffering from the pandemic's aftermath and economic hardships. The government is supposed to work for us, these actors remind us, and a government
that makes its decision-making even harder for the public to understand and
scrutinize is a government that undercuts that ideal.

We can identify and start to address these challenges without knowing
precisely what each AI tool will look like or which settings the government
may use it in. Some think tanks and congressionally mandated independent
commissions have called for the use of AI in line with "American values."[27]
But there are widely disparate views about what those substantive values are
and how to translate them into policy choices. Is an aggressive pursuit of lethal autonomous weapons to create a robust deterrent against China consistent with American values, even if we don't plan to use those weapons in
the near term? Should the CIA decline to train its algorithms on data given
to it by autocracies that systematically violate their citizens' liberty and privacy? Should the U.S. intelligence community deploy "deepfakes" that interfere with foreign elections or the decision-making of adversarial foreign
governments? It will be difficult for Congress to pass statutes that contain
specific rules of the road for DOD and the intelligence community (IC) on
these kinds of issues as they begin to adopt AI—though there may be some
narrow areas where realistic substantive regulation is possible.

[27] Schmidt & Work, *supra* note 8.

E. Public Law Values

A more fruitful way to approach this problem is to consider what we expect from and value in the executive branch—attributes that we sometimes refer to as "public law values." The relevant subset of public law values in the AI context includes expectations that the Executive will (1) comply with the law; (2) make competent and rational decisions; (3) be accountable for the decisions that it has made; and (4) be prepared to justify those decisions to an appropriate set of actors.[28] It may be hard to decide whether a given military use of AI tools complies with "American values"; it will be easier to assess whether the Executive's decision to use those tools complies with these public law values, which have a more neutral valence.[29] People may disagree about whether substantively to prioritize security or liberty, for instance, or about how willing the United States should be to use force abroad, but they likely will agree that their government should act lawfully, rationally, and accountably.

The national security black box challenges these public law values. The need for secrecy in many military and intelligence operations makes it easier for the Executive to avoid a free flow of information inside the government, which can decrease the quality of decision-making. Secrecy also makes it easier for the Executive to conceal incompetence and unlawful acts after the fact.[30] It is more difficult to know who made which decision inside the

[28] See Jody Freeman, *Private Parties, Public Functions and the New Administrative Law*, 52 ADMIN. L. REV. 813, 818–19 (2000) (listing "openness, fairness, participation, consistency, rationality, impartiality, and accessibility of judicial review" as well as accountability and legality as public law values); Michael Taggart, *The Province of Administrative Law Determined?*, in THE PROVINCE OF ADMINISTRATIVE LAW 1, 3 (Michael Taggart ed., 1997) (defining public law values to include openness, participation, accountability, honesty, and rationality); Kristen Eichensehr, *Public-Private Cybersecurity*, 95 TEX. L. REV. 467 (2017) (citing accountability, transparency, due process and fairness, security, and privacy as public law values relevant to cybersecurity operations); Deeks, *supra* note 15 (discussing legality, competence, good policy decisions, and the need to justify policies to actors outside the government); Daphna Renan, *Presidential Norms and Article II*, 131 HARV. L. REV. 2187, 2226 (2018) (identifying a "core structural commitment of a considered, fact-informed presidential decision"); Note, *Subdelegation by Federal Administrative Agencies*, 12 STAN. L. REV. 808, 811 (1960) ("[I]t is reasonable to assume that Congress intends to create agencies that will function competently, efficiently and fairly.").

[29] *Cf.* Ashley Deeks, *An International Legal Framework for Surveillance*, 55 VA. J. INT'L L. 291, 295 (2015) (arguing that a focus on procedural norms for surveillance will allow states to avoid contentious discussions about personal privacy). *See also* K. Sabeel Rahman, *Reconstructing the Administrative State in an Era of Economic and Democratic Crisis*, 131 HARV. L. REV. 1671, 1697 (2018) (reviewing JON MICHAELS, CONSTITUTIONAL COUP (2017)) ("Michaels argues that part of the value of the administrative process is that it provides a procedure and a structure through which to manage conflicts over substantive values.").

[30] *See* Mark Fenster, *The Opacity of Transparency*, 91 IOWA L. REV. 885, 900 (2006).

executive branch, and it is therefore harder to know how to assign blame and sanction wrongdoers. And it is persistently hard for the Executive to disclose enough information to foster trust among the public without revealing so much information that it undercuts our security.[31]

The algorithmic black box may threaten those same public law values.[32] Algorithmically driven decisions can complicate the question of who exactly made the decision (the programmer, the adopter, the end user?) and as a result may diffuse the responsibility of any one person for a mistaken decision. There is a real risk that algorithms will be trained on poor, incomplete, or biased data, which will produce faulty predictions, and it is difficult—though not impossible—to repeatedly test and verify weapons that use ML to "learn" over time. There are likely to be fewer policymakers and lawyers involved at the front end in developing these systems, even though the presence of a diverse group of people as the tools are built could help ensure the systems' legality and rationality. It will be very hard for the public to identify the extent to which the military and intelligence community are even using AI for decision-making. Finally, at least at first blush, AI systems themselves tend to render the decision-making process opaque, not transparent.

Further, as a structural matter, the use of national security AI has the potential to alter the power dynamics *within* the U.S. executive branch itself. Important checking and balancing take place within the rough-and-tumble of the "interagency process." Those who work for agencies that are developing and using classified AI tools will be better postured to understand their contents and proposed uses than those who work for agencies that do not use those tools, which makes it harder for the full set of U.S. values to be represented and defended in interagency conversations. The same point holds for other internal executive branch checks, such as inspectors general and lawyers who engage in interagency work. Even within a single agency, the use of AI tools may create power shifts. An increased reliance on AI will empower the computer scientists who create the tools at the expense of policy

---

[31] A possible counterexample is the policy shift that the United States undertook in the wake of the Snowden leaks, after which the Director of National Intelligence created a website and DNI and CIA leadership began to give public speeches.

[32] Researchers producing a report for the Administrative Conference of the United States considered this issue while reviewing a range of government algorithms, most of which were not national-security focused. David Engstrom et al., *Government by Algorithm: Artificial Intelligence in Federal Administrative Agencies 7*, Admin. Conf. of the United States (Feb. 2020) ("A crucial question will be how to subject such tools to meaningful accountability and thus ensure their fidelity to legal norms of transparency, reason-giving, and non-discrimination."). This problem becomes more acute in the national security space.

officials and lawyers who lack that skill set. The interagency processes that presidential administrations have developed to promote public law values in executive decision-making will need to adjust to this coming shift in internal power dynamics.

F. How Do We Crack the Double Black Box?

This book's focus on ensuring that the U.S. process of deciding to use, build, and deploy AI systems reflects public law values means that many of its proposed solutions focus on institutional design and process, rather than the contents or parameters of the algorithms themselves.[33] Process and substance are deeply intertwined, though: if we can ensure that the Executive complies with our public law values, it is more likely to produce substantively reliable and legally defensible algorithms. Unless we find a set of satisfactory answers to the questions raised earlier—how do we hold the executive branch accountable for its use of AI in national security settings and how can we be sure that it is adopting only safe, transparent, and reliable AI?—we will end up with a national security state that is less responsive to its citizens, harder to hold to account for serious errors, operated by an ever-shrinking set of players, and setting precedents that we may not want other countries to follow.

A key theme of this book is that ensuring executive compliance with public law values will require diligence by a wide range of actors. We will need to rely on our traditional surrogates, especially the congressional committees that oversee the military, intelligence community, and diplomats. But we will also need to rely on our nontraditional secrecy surrogates, including foreign allies and U.S. technology companies. Front-end input will be important. By virtue of how machine learning algorithms work, it will be critical to ensure early policy and legal input into whether to use a machine learning algorithm at all in a given context and what kinds of data and parameters that algorithm should use (or avoid). This will be particularly challenging when the government purchases AI tools (including large language models) from the private

---

[33] *See* JON MICHAELS, CONSTITUTIONAL COUP: PRIVATIZATION'S THREAT TO THE AMERICAN REPUBLIC 65 (2017) ("[T]he best we can hope for is precisely what the administrative separation of powers provides: a structure that helps harmonize, accommodate, and cycle among leading, but conflicting, administrative values" such as promoting expertise, civic participation, or presidential control).

sector with the goal of adapting them to national security work. Drawing from Lawrence Lessig's seminal early insight that "code is law," there is important work for lawyers to do to introduce legal guardrails into the code that helps produce national security outcomes.[34]

A second theme relates to the way in which the government's use of AI could actually improve the surrogates' ability to oversee the government's national security activities. For example, absent AI tools, individual soldiers must make unilateral decisions in the heat of battle. AI tools that provide decisional support to militaries, if developed correctly, will allow legal and ethical input from a range of interagency actors at the front end because important decisions about the tools' parameters will be made early in the development process, before the fighting starts.[35] Further, AI tools may facilitate the work of secrecy surrogates themselves by helping intelligence committee staffers identify important themes in executive branch reporting, for example, or enabling journalists to make connections among unclassified data from disparate sources to identify government misconduct. A third theme relates to transparency: the national security Executive should be radically transparent with the public about the virtues and challenges of national security AI and its plans to address those challenges.

The book emphasizes the U.S. legal system and U.S. domestic law, rather than international law, although international law and norms generally serve as important standards against which we measure the U.S. public law value of "legality." U.S. public law values are consistent with the liberal democratic values held by NATO partners, Japan, South Korea, Australia, and other like-minded states. If the United States successfully works through the challenges posed by the double black box and develops AI tools that reflect U.S. public law values, it seems likely that its approach will shape the international actions and expectations of a range of states, either because they find the U.S. approach worth emulating or because they acquire AI tools that the United States has developed.

---

[34] LAWRENCE LESSIG, CODE AND OTHER LAWS OF CYBERSPACE (1999); CURTIS BRADLEY, HISTORICAL GLOSS AND FOREIGN AFFAIRS: CONSTITUTIONAL AUTHORITY IN PRACTICE (2024) (describing political branch decision-making on national security issues as creating the law in this area).
[35] Ashley Deeks, *Coding the Law of Armed Conflict: First Steps, in* THE FUTURE LAW OF ARMED CONFLICT (Matthew Waxman & Thomas Oakley eds., 2022).

G. Assumptions

The book makes a number of assumptions. First, even though a core tenet of this book is that it is imperative for a democracy to impose checks on secret executive branch activities, this is not because U.S. officials act with malicious intent or gross incompetence as a matter of course. They do not. The vast majority of executive officials care about ethics and laws. But history is rife with examples that remind us that the government can drift off course.[36] Secrecy diminishes a number of standard checks on the behavior of government actors, individually and collectively, which can facilitate sloppiness, groupthink, and other confounding habits. Therefore, this book assumes not that national security officials are ill-intentioned but that they suffer from the same set of cognitive biases that we all suffer from and that become heightened in an operating environment infused with secrecy. The book also assumes that, without external pressures to do otherwise, the government will default to a posture of preferring not to discuss publicly its approaches to difficult questions posed by the use of AI tools, even where those questions do not implicate classified information.

Second, the book envisions a relatively predictable pace of development of AI, based on current trends. It does not assume that any states today are close to achieving "artificial general intelligence": AGI, if and when it occurs, will change the international and domestic political, legal, and cultural landscapes dramatically. Instead, it anticipates that advances in AI will continue along current lines, with improvements every year in the accuracy of AI's predictions, its ability to detect anomalies, and the autonomous capabilities of military and intelligence systems.

Third, even if some or most of the AI tools considered in this book never come to full fruition, the goal of this book is to present useful ways to analyze and grapple with the ever-shifting set of national security black box problems that will arise in the future. Whether one views national security AI as qualitatively different from other technologies or sees it as simply the next step on the technology continuum, the dilemmas that arise from AI's use in classified settings—and the tools we use to respond to these dilemmas—can inform a range of other problems that arise when democratic governments act in secret.

---

[36] *See* STEPHEN DYCUS ET AL., NATIONAL SECURITY LAW 514–19, 612–13 (7th ed. 2020) (discussing unlawful, rogue, or failed intelligence community activities).

Fourth, the book assumes that existing domestic policy tensions in the United States—and in some European states—about how heavily to rely on national security AI will continue. At present, a range of policymakers in Congress and inside the executive branch, as well as some outside commentators, want the United States to push ahead aggressively to remain at the forefront of AI development. This group is motivated by the idea that the United States must maintain a qualitative edge in military and intelligence AI to preserve its geopolitical position, particularly against China and Russia. Others, including some high-profile technologists, want the United States to proceed cautiously, fearing that AI may lead to abuses of privacy and bodily integrity, subvert existing domestic and international laws, lower the barriers to resorting to international force, and dehumanize armed conflict.[37] If China tomorrow reveals that it has successfully embedded AI tools and high levels of autonomy in most of its weapons, weapon systems, and military command and control systems, today's balance of views likely would tip heavily toward the former group. But for now, these two sets of views are in some equilibrium, and indeed, a key U.S. goal should be to move ahead on AI systems in a way that is both robust and careful.

H. Existing Literature

To date, much of the domestic legal writing about AI has focused on how AI can defeat due process requirements, make biased recommendations, and violate individuals' privacy. On the international front, legal scholars are concerned about whether and how AI tools can comply with the laws of armed conflict, whether there is a way to maintain accountability for use of the tools, and whether states must maintain some type of meaningful human control over weapons that use AI. Political scientists are focused on how AI will affect the great power competition between the United States and China. Little has been written, however, about the ways that AI's characteristics affect the ability of actors outside (and inside!) democratic states, including the United States, to oversee, check, and challenge executive national security activities. Some scholars have offered thoughtful prescriptions for legislatures

---

[37] At the start of the Cold War, Clinton Rossiter worried that liberal democracies were not up to the task of doing battle with totalitarian systems such as the Soviet Union's because they were committed to playing by "Queensberry Rules" that would limit how far they would go to fight the enemy. CLINTON ROSSITER, CONSTITUTIONAL DICTATORSHIP 5, 17 (1948).

to develop laws to guide the use of AI[38]—but they assume full visibility by policymakers and companies into what projects are underway and therefore assume that the public will be able to weigh in on AI using our standard democratic tools. Yet secrecy will erect significant hurdles to ensuring that the U.S. government, and a range of other democratic governments that are pursuing national security AI, only develop AI tools that their publics can be proud of.

I. Overview of the Chapters

This book has two parts. Part I lays out the problem: the existence and implications of the growing double black box in national security. Chapter 1 sets forth the foundational problem in national security: most U.S. national security operations take place within a black box into which few non–executive branch actors have visibility. Drawing on standard accounts of public law values, it illustrates why U.S. national security structures and processes make it hard to ensure that the Executive is acting lawfully, rationally, and accountably, even with a range of traditional and nontraditional checks on executive activity. Chapter 2 explains the latest turn in national security law: the increased use of AI/ML and autonomous systems within homeland security, defense, and the intelligence community to make predictions and recommendations that will deeply inform national security activities. It provides a brief description of what machine learning and AI are and, using real-world examples, illustrates why some of the systems that the Department of Homeland Security, DOD, and the IC are pursuing have features of an AI black box.

Chapter 3 draws together the threads from Chapters 1 and 2, showing why a "double black box" lurks on national security's horizon: the problems posed by the national security black box will be exacerbated by the growing use of AI tools. It argues that the nature of AI means that both the traditional and nontraditional checks on the Executive will have an increasingly difficult time playing their roles, which poses significant challenges for a government that is trying to maintain the confidence of its citizens. It then uses

---

[38] JAMES BAKER, THE CENTAUR'S DILEMMA: NATIONAL SECURITY LAW FOR THE COMING AI REVOLUTION (2021).

the prospect of autonomous cyber tools as an illustration of how the double black box will manifest itself.

Part II turns to solutions, exploring ways to reduce the opacity of the double black box. Most of these proposed solutions focus on domestic processes, though a few employ existing relationships between the United States and its democratic allies. Chapter 4 revisits the traditional checks on the Executive discussed in Part I and offers ways for those actors to make incremental progress chipping away at the double black box. Chapter 5 does the same for our nontraditional checks. Chapter 6 asks what role, if any, international law can play in addressing some of the concerns raised by the double black box. After all, states have long used international law as a tool to regulate their collective behavior, reduce tensions among adversaries, and articulate and enforce agreed-upon norms. It offers a pessimistic evaluation, however: in today's conditions, international fora and international law will only be effective in curbing states' uses of problematic AI in limited circumstances. Nevertheless, there are some bilateral and multilateral steps that the United States and its allies could take to ameliorate these problems. In general, though, this pushes the question back into the domestic arena and toward efforts to improve the capacity of our secrecy surrogates to understand and judge the Executive's national security AI-related choices. The conclusion summarizes.

PART I
THE PROBLEM

1

The National Security Black Box

A. Overview

U.S. national security practices have long been a black box. U.S. counterterrorism practices in the years following the September 11 attacks serve as a recent and robust example.[1] Especially between 2001 and 2006, the U.S. government conducted a range of highly classified military and intelligence operations against al Qaeda and, to a lesser extent, the Taliban. The U.S. government perceived the United States as facing an unprecedented threat and concluded that it needed to employ a host of novel and controversial tools in order to defeat further similar attacks. Many of these programs tested or crossed the outer limits of the law. The government kept these programs highly classified not only to advance operational security but also to avoid legal controversies that would have quickly arisen if the government had made the programs public.

The United States used a range of tools to detain, interrogate, and target members of al Qaeda. First, the United States used renditions to transport detainees from one country to another, where the receiving state sometimes tortured them. Second, the CIA opened several "secret sites" in foreign countries, at which CIA employees held and interrogated high-value al Qaeda detainees, using harsh interrogation techniques and preventing the International Committee of the Red Cross from visiting them. Third, the United States began in 2002 to target and kill members of al Qaeda in regions such as Yemen and Pakistan, which were not then areas of active military hostilities. Fourth, the United States transferred hundreds of individuals to a detention facility at Guantanamo Bay Naval Base with the expectation that those detainees would not be able to file habeas corpus petitions in U.S. courts.

These programs eventually came to light. Some were revealed through leaks. Some became public through a combination of journalists' and foreign

---

[1] This section is drawn from Ashley Deeks, *Predicting Enemies*, 104 VA. L. REV. 1529 (2018).

citizens' investigations, as when "plane spotters" recorded the flight patterns of small aircraft that seemed to mirror suspected CIA rendition paths. In some cases, affected individuals gained access to federal court and sued to challenge their detention or treatment. In yet other cases, the government altered its own policies *sua sponte*, as when the government closed the CIA's secret sites and transferred the detainees to Guantanamo. Regardless of how these programs came to light, each proved highly controversial once made public and reminded many commentators that national security secrecy— the national security black box—can serve to conceal programs that the public does not support.

This chapter explains why the executive branch's national security operations are generally less regulated and harder to oversee than other governmental activities, which is a problem for democratic systems such as the United States and many of its allies. First, states perceive national security threats as existential and are often reluctant to use either domestic law or international law to tie the hands of the agencies that protect their people against those threats. Second, large swaths of a state's national security activities—such as fighting wars or spying on adversaries—take place overseas. Because they are happening outside the country, these activities are less likely to infringe on their citizens' rights, which means the public is less concerned about how their government conducts those operations, at least until something goes wrong.[2] Third, and critically, many national security activities are classified, which makes it harder for a state's legislature and courts to shape the Executive's decisions and conduct public—or even nonpublic—oversight. Yet using legislation to shape policy on the front end and conducting oversight on the tail end are the key ways by which the United States ensures in other policy areas that the Executive is acting consistent with U.S. public law values, including legality, competence, accountability, and the expectation of justification.

This chapter will first explore why the national security Executive is so empowered.[3] It then will explain the constitutional checks on the national

---

[2] The government may also miscalculate public support for particular national security choices. Some studies examining public sentiment about torture in the eight years following the September 11 attacks suggest that more than half of the U.S. public did not support its use. *See* Paul Gronke et al., *U.S. Public Opinion on Torture, 2001–2009*, 43 POLIT. SCI. & POLITICS 437 (July 2010).

[3] The U.S. executive branch is not the only government that sometimes declines to disgorge information to its legislature about national security activities. *See* Intelligence and Security Committee of Parliament, *Press Release* (2017) (discussing the Committee's difficulty obtaining information about a U.K. drone strike on an individual in Syria).

security Executive, including checks from Congress and federal courts, but also from certain actors within the Executive itself and from leaks of government information. It will argue that even with those checks, much that happens inside the national security arena remains a black box to outside observers. However, there are a burgeoning set of nontraditional checks on the Executive as well. These nontraditional secrecy surrogates help chisel away at the black box nature of national security in different areas of national security operations. The chapter will show how all of these actors can help reduce the opacity of the black box but cannot eliminate it.

B. The Dominance of the National Security Executive

In the U.S. system, Congress possesses the constitutional authority to declare war. These days, it uses statutes called Authorizations for the Use of Military Force (AUMFs) to do so—and it passed two of them in the early 2000s. The first was the 2001 AUMF, passed on September 18, which authorized the President to use all necessary and appropriate force against those who committed the September 11 attacks and those who harbored the attackers. The second was the 2002 AUMF, which authorized the President—then George W. Bush—to use force in Iraq against Saddam Hussein. More than twenty years later, both statutes are still on the books. The Executive has used these AUMFs as the basis for using force against a much wider set of actors than Congress originally intended. Indeed, the public does not know the full list of groups that the Executive believes to be covered by the 2001 AUMF, and at some points many members of Congress did not know either. Further, Congress has been unable to repeal those AUMFs, even though President Joe Biden affirmatively supported the repeal of the 2002 AUMF.

What is going on? Can this seemingly puzzling situation teach us anything about the national security black box? As this chapter will show, this example illustrates the dominance of the national security Executive over military operations, its use of secrecy to expand its authorities, the pathologies of Congress related to the use of force, and the quietude of the judicial voice in this area.

1. The Executive's Structural Advantages

It is beyond cavil that the executive branch has accreted vast amounts of power to itself in the national security space. The President sits at the pinnacle of the full set of intelligence agencies—the nineteen entities known collectively in the United States as the "intelligence community" (IC). He also serves as the commander-in-chief of the military. The Secretaries of Defense, Homeland Security, and State, as well as the Attorney General, serve at his pleasure. Of course, the same thing is true for a wide range of administrative agencies, and many of the same trends visible there—particularly the steady growth of the administrative state since the 1950s[4]—have arisen in the national security agencies as well. The Defense Department employs approximately 2.9 million people, including active duty servicemembers and civilians.[5] It hires many contractors as well: in 2020, it obligated $420 million under federal contracts.[6] The intelligence community is also huge. In 2010, reporters found that approximately 854,000 people working on intelligence, counterterrorism, and homeland security held top-secret clearances.[7] For fiscal year 2023, Congress appropriated $71.7 billion to the National Intelligence Program.[8] In other words, Congress has enabled the sprawl and depth of these agencies, both by enacting organic statutes and appropriating funds annually.[9]

These statistics illustrate how big the national security apparatus has become, but they don't explain why it happened. The key reason is structural: Alexander Hamilton famously remarked that housing powers in a unitary Executive provides the advantages of "[d]ecision, activity, secrecy, and dispatch."[10] Each of those features is critical to ensuring the country's defenses. Someone must gather diplomatic, military, and other intelligence;

---

[4] Susan Dudley, *Milestones in the Evolution of the Administrative State*, 150(3) DAEDALUS 33 (Summer 2021).

[5] U.S. Dep't of Defense, *About*.

[6] Heidi Peters, *Defense Primer: Department of Defense Contractors*, CONG. RES. SERV. (Jan. 17, 2023).

[7] Dana Priest & William Arkin, *A Hidden World, Growing Beyond Control*, WASH. POST (July 19, 2010).

[8] Dir. of Nat'l Intel., Press Release, *DNI Releases Appropriated Budget Figure for 2023 National Intelligence Program* (Oct. 30, 2023).

[9] *See, e.g.,* 50 U.S.C. § 3034 (establishing the responsibilities and authorities of the Director of National Intelligence); 50 U.S.C. §.3036 (same for CIA).

[10] THE FEDERALIST NO. 70, at 403 (Alexander Hamilton) (Isaac Kramnick ed., 1987). In 1936, the Supreme Court reiterated the Executive's advantages when it described "the very delicate, plenary and exclusive power of the President as the sole organ of the federal government in the field of international relations." United States v. Curtiss-Wright, 299 U.S. 304 (1936).

use that intelligence to inform a coherent and timely decision-making process; develop plans of action; and order experienced actors to execute those plans in the field. In today's world, only the Executive is suited for that. Only the Executive has the volume of personnel, continuity of staffing, and expertise; the ability to create the necessary foreign policy, military, and intelligence infrastructure overseas (in the forms of embassies and military bases); and a structure that funnels difficult choices up to a single decision maker. Congress and the courts would fail terribly at these tasks.

The Executive has certain other institutional advantages that allow it to bolster these powers. For one, it has a first-mover advantage that can make it difficult for Congress to unwind the Executive's choices. Once the President has ordered U.S. troops to deploy overseas to fight an armed conflict, for instance, members of Congress are often loathe to criticize that deployment or defund those forces for fear of looking unpatriotic. That is, the Executive has placed Congress on its back foot. Second, because significant portions of the U.S. IC's operations take place overseas and are directed against foreign nationals, it is less likely that members of Congress will hear complaints by constituents about abuses or missteps by the IC. Those on the receiving end of any abuses that occur are usually not U.S. citizens and are far away from the power centers in Washington.

Third, an influential office within the Justice Department—the Office of Legal Counsel (OLC)—interprets the law in a way that generally favors executive power and seeks to protect executive prerogatives against encroachment by the other branches.[11] OLC's opinions assume the character of law within the Executive. One prominent line of opinions relates to war powers. OLC has concluded that the President can resort to force overseas without congressional authorization if it is in the U.S. national interest and the amount of force would not constitute "war in a constitutional sense."[12] This is a capacious interpretation of the Constitution, but it serves as the modus vivendi of U.S. war powers today because Congress has been unable to displace it by statute. Further, the Executive can narrow the constraints contained in certain statutes by using signing statements that announce how the President intends to interpret certain statutory provisions and set out his constitutional

[11] Curtis Bradley & Trevor Morrison, *Historical Gloss and the Separation of Powers*, 126 HARV. L. REV. 411, 414–15 (2012). *See also* Dep't of Justice, *History of Refusals by Executive Branch Officials to Provide Information Demanded by Congress* (Dec. 14, 1982) (stating that presidentially mandated refusals to disclose information to Congress are not unprecedented).

[12] *See, e.g.*, Memorandum from Assistant Attorney General Steven A. Engel to Counsel to the President, *April 2018 Airstrikes Against Syrian Chemical-Weapons Facilities* (May 31, 2018).

views. Congress has no equivalent to OLC, though some have proposed that it develop one,[13] and though Congress can frame its wishes in committee reports, it does not issue formal "counter-signing statements" that contest the constitutional arguments that the President's own signing statements make.

It is impossible to fully understand the Executive's powers in a vacuum, without understanding the weaknesses of countervailing pressures from the other branches. However, before turning to the role of other branches in the national security space, it is important to understand how secrecy magnifies the Executive's structural advantages.

2. How Secrecy Strengthens the Executive

In addition to the President's structural dominance over national security policy and actions, he also sets the rules for classifying and declassifying government information related to national security policies, intelligence, military activity, and foreign policy. This ability to use and regulate secrecy amplifies the Executive's powers and can even conceal the extent to which it arrogates power to itself.

Presidential administrations have asserted—and the other two branches have agreed—that the President has the constitutional power to classify information, and that Congress and the courts have limited power to shape the President's actions here. The Supreme Court repeatedly has stated that the President's "authority to classify and control access to information bearing on national security . . . flows primarily from this Constitutional investment of power in the President and exists quite apart from any explicit congressional grant."[14] Several recent presidential administrations have reiterated this point in signing statements. For instance, President George W. Bush objected to certain provisions of the Intelligence Reform and Terrorism Prevention Act because, in his view, they impeded certain presidential prerogatives related to classification.[15] His signing statement noted, "Several provisions of the Act . . . purport to regulate access to classified national security information. The Supreme Court of the United States has stated that the President's authority to classify and control access to information bearing

[13] Saikrishna Prakash, The Living Presidency (2020); William Ford, *What Might a Congressional Counterpart to the Office of Legal Counsel Look Like?*, Lawfare (May 17, 2022).

[14] Dep't of the Navy v. Egan, 484 U.S. 518, 527 (1988).

[15] P.L. 108-458 (2004).

on national security flows from the Constitution and does not depend upon a legislative grant of authority. The executive branch shall construe such provisions in a manner consistent with the Constitution's commitment to the President of the executive power, the power to conduct the Nation's foreign affairs, and the authority as Commander in Chief."[16]

Presidents since President Eisenhower have memorialized the classification power and process in executive orders (EOs).[17] The current classification EO identifies which officials can classify information; what standards they must meet to classify information as "top secret," "secret," or "confidential"; how long information can remain classified; which reasons for classification are inappropriate; how to declassify information; and when agencies may establish "special access programs" that are particularly sensitive.[18] It also creates several internal bodies that can review and oversee agency classification and declassification decisions.

Congress occasionally enacts statutes that relate to classification or declassification, but it generally only requires the Executive to review certain documents with an eye toward declassification, rather than mandating that the Executive declassify specific documents. In the 2015 USA Freedom Act, for instance, Congress required the Executive to conduct a declassification review of each order or opinion by the Foreign Intelligence Surveillance Court (FISC) that contains a "significant construction or interpretation" of the law.[19] It did not mandate that the Executive declassify any given order, however. Congress's most important statute related to the release of government information is the Freedom of Information Act (FOIA), but that statute allows the government to withhold from release information that is properly classified and is authorized under the classification EO to be kept secret in the interest of national defense or foreign policy.[20] And although both the Senate and the House of Representatives have established procedures by which they themselves can disclose classified information that they possess when they deem it to be in the public interest, neither body appears to have ever done so.[21] (Individual members may leak information, though.)

---

[16] Statement on Signing the Intelligence Reform and Terrorism Prevention Act of 2004, 2004 Pub. Papers 3118, 3119 (Dec. 17, 2004).

[17] See Exec. Order No. 10501, Safeguarding Official Information in the Interests of the Defense of the United States (Nov. 5, 1953).

[18] Exec. Order No. 13526 (Dec. 29, 2009).

[19] USA FREEDOM Act of 2015, Pub. L. No. 114-23, 129 Stat. 279, § 402 (2015).

[20] 5 U.S.C. § 552(b)(1).

[21] Jennifer Elsea, *The Protection of Classified Information: The Legal Framework*, CONG. RES. SERV. (May 18, 2017).

In a 2016 report to the President, the Information Security Oversight Office at the National Archives noted that the U.S. government made 52.8 million derivative classification decisions in fiscal year 2015 and 55.2 million in fiscal year 2016.[22] Critiques about the extent to which the government overclassifies information are well-rehearsed. However, neither the Executive nor Congress has made much progress in reducing the overclassification problem. The Executive, in particular, has few incentives to do so; even if it did, issues like this play second fiddle to the urgent, substantive policy problems that the Executive confronts daily.

None of this extensive secrecy would pose a particular issue if the Executive were forthcoming with its coequal branches about the substance of the classified information. It is not, however. The Executive has a range of reasons to resist sharing information with Congress and the courts. Some are not surprising. For example, the Executive treats some of its activities as highly compartmentalized and fears that information about those activities could leak any time it shares beyond a small circle of people. Even though Congress enacted a statute requiring the Executive to keep it "currently and fully informed" about significant intelligence activities,[23] the Executive failed to inform Congress about CIA programs that explored sending teams overseas to kill terrorists, about the CIA's destruction of videotapes of detainee interrogations, and about the CIA's role in a shoot-down of a missionary flight in Peru.[24]

In addition, by declining to be forthcoming about what its national security agencies are doing, the Executive can postpone or avoid certain criticisms about its policy choices or operations.[25] The post–September 11 U.S. counterterrorism practices discussed at the start of the chapter are a good example. By keeping these operations highly classified, the Executive was able to continue operations that it knew would be controversial without needing to justify their effectiveness or legality to Congress.

Perhaps not surprisingly, given the President's control over intelligence and military information, classification decisions, and policy execution, a robust body of literature on government secrecy bemoans this greatly unequal

---

[22] Nat'l Archives, Information Security Oversight Office, 2016 Report to the President 3–5 (2017).

[23] 50 U.S.C. § 3091.

[24] Scott Shane, *Intelligence Bodies Faulted on Disclosure*, N.Y. TIMES (Nov. 18, 2010).

[25] Richard Fontaine & Loren DeJonge Schulman, *Congress's Hidden Strengths: Wielding Informal Tools of National Security Oversight*, CTR. FOR NEW AM. SECURITY (July 30, 2020) ("Too many interviewees for this report cited a culture of holding Congress at arm's length and treating legislative overseers simply as adversaries.").

distribution of national security power. Critics worry that secrecy enables the Executive to undertake legally or politically problematic policies in our name without our knowledge and conceal mistakes or abuse. Although some of the critiques of the U.S. national security state breathlessly overstate the intentionality of Executive missteps, there are—as just shown—kernels of truth in each of these precepts. It therefore is worth bearing down on the core reasons why we worry about government secrecy.

C. Challenges to Public Law Values

In an ideal world, we would not need to worry about the significant imbalance between the Executive's power on the one hand and Congress's and the courts' powers on the other. The Executive's acts would always be beyond reproach, and there would be no need to oversee its activities, whether public or secret. As James Madison famously remarked, "If men were angels, no government would be necessary. If angels were to govern men, neither external nor internal controls on government would be necessary."[26] But we do not live in an ideal world, and the public should be interested in, if not concerned about, what the Executive does behind closed doors. After all, past practice has given occasion to worry. To give a few examples outside the September 11 context, the CIA and FBI famously ran amok in the 1960s and 1970s, compromising many citizens' civil liberties; Presidents John Kennedy, Lyndon B. Johnson, and Richard Nixon spied on political adversaries; and the Reagan administration violated the law during the Iran-Contra episode.

Put affirmatively, we want our government to act consistent with public law values such as legality; consistency, rationality, and competence; accountability; and justification.[27] There are a host of ways in which

---

[26] THE FEDERALIST No. 51, at 322 (James Madison) (Clinton Rossiter ed., 1961).

[27] See Jody Freeman, *Private Parties, Public Functions and the New Administrative Law*, 52 ADMIN. L. REV. 813, 818–19 (2000) (listing "openness, fairness, participation, consistency, rationality, impartiality, and accessibility of judicial review" as well as accountability and legality as public law values); *id.* at 819 ("Private actors are not just rent-seekers that exacerbate the traditional democracy problem in administrative law; they are also regulatory resources capable of contributing to the efficacy and legitimacy of administration."); Michael Taggart, *The Province of Administrative Law Determined?, in* THE PROVINCE OF ADMINISTRATIVE LAW 1, 3 (Michael Taggart ed., 1997) (defining public law values to include openness, participation, accountability, honesty, and rationality); Kristen Eichensehr, *Public-Private Cybersecurity*, 95 TEX. L. REV. 467 (2017) (citing accountability, transparency, due process and fairness, security, and privacy as public law values relevant to cybersecurity operations); Ashley Deeks, *Secrecy Surrogates*, 106 VA. L. REV. 1395 (2020) (discussing legality, competence, good policy decisions, and the need to justify policies to actors outside the government).

government secrecy can obscure government dysfunction—that is, activities that run afoul of those values. Executive misuses of secrecy fall into four main categories: *concealing legal violations; concealing poor policy choices or incompetence; eliding accountability for errors;* and *avoiding the need to justify its decisions to an appropriate set of actors.* There are a host of legitimate reasons why the Executive classifies information; no democracy could abolish government secrecy entirely. But the possibility and history of misuse makes government secrecy a persistent and thorny challenge.

Concealing legal violations. First, and perhaps most importantly, secrecy is a problem when the Executive uses it to conceal the unlawfulness of its acts.[28] Such actions might include spying on domestic political enemies,[29] engaging in assassination attempts,[30] or transferring individuals to foreign governments to face torture.[31] Even if a program is not patently illegal, the Executive may employ secrecy to preserve programs that are legally tenuous, such as the National Security Agency's (NSA's) warrantless wiretapping of individuals in the United States connected to al Qaeda. An Executive that fails to comply with the Constitution or statutes is acting as an unfaithful agent. But if secrecy conceals those abuses, it is impossible for the principals—members of the public—to hold it accountable.

Concealing poor policy choices or incompetence. Relatedly, the government may use secrecy to conceal policies that the public would condemn if it knew about them, even if the policies were not illegal per se. Take President Donald Trump's phone call with Ukrainian President Volodymyr Zelensky. A range of officials who heard the call were troubled by its contents, including President Trump's suggestion that he would withhold military aid to Ukraine unless and until it agreed to investigate Hunter Biden's relationship with a Ukrainian company. At least one of these officials decided to relocate the call transcript to a highly classified system where it would be unlikely

---

[28] ROBERT M. PALLITTO & WILLIAM G. WEAVER, PRESIDENTIAL SECRECY AND THE LAW 7 (2007) (discussing how the President's ability to operate in secret prevents Congress and the courts from determining his "constitutional and statutory conformance").

[29] *See* David Law, *A Theory of Judicial Power and Judicial Review,* 97 GEO. L.J. 723, 745 (2008). As Kiewiet and McCubbins put it, "The essence of the problem is that resources or authority granted to an agent for purposes of advancing the interests of the principal can be turned against the principal." D. RODERICK KIEWIET & MATHEW D. MCCUBBINS, THE LOGIC OF DELEGATION: CONGRESSIONAL PARTIES AND THE APPROPRIATIONS PROCESS 26 (1991).

[30] Lynne Duke, *Regime Change Assassin? Easier Said Than Done,* WASH. POST (Aug. 24, 2005) (describing U.S. attempts to assassinate Castro, Lumumba, and Trujillo).

[31] Comm'n of Inquiry into the Actions of Canadian Officials in Relation to Maher Arar, *Report of the Events Relating to Maher Arar* 13–14 (2006) (discussing decision by U.S. officials to send Arar to Syria, where he was interrogated and tortured).

to leak. For many, this incident reflects a paradigmatic problem with government secrecy: actors in the Executive can employ it as a tool to avoid politically embarrassing or legally problematic revelations or to conceal a self-enriching act.

Further, the government may deploy secrecy when it wants to conceal incompetently executed,[32] empirically wrong,[33] or insufficient[34] intelligence, analysis, or operations. Indeed, the current executive order on classification states that executive officials may *not* classify information "in order to conceal violations of law, inefficiency, or administrative error; [or] to prevent embarrassment to a person, organization, or agency . . . ."[35] The fact that the executive order contains this language indicates that this misuse of secrecy has occurred in the past and requires a specific prohibition to address it.[36] Secrecy can also cause problems ex ante, rather than merely serve as a tool for abuse ex post. That is, executive secrecy can prevent obvious incompetence, empirical errors, or shirking from coming to light as policies develop, because fewer actors have the opportunity to press executive decision makers for explanations and justifications. Indeed, some critics of state secrecy argue that "by inhibiting input, oversight, and criticism within and outside government, secrecy and compartmentalization will often lead to lower-quality policies" and that "debate and dissent may be muted, important facts and insights may be overlooked, and preexisting biases may be amplified."[37] A 2020 report by the Center for New American Security agrees,

---

[32] Doe v. Gonzales, 449 F.3d 415, 422 (2d Cir. 2006) (Cardamone, J., concurring) ("Unending secrecy of actions taken by government officials may also serve as a cover for possible official misconduct and/or incompetence."); Thomas I. Emerson, *National Security and Civil Liberties*, in THE FIRST AMENDMENT AND NATIONAL SECURITY 83, 84–85 (1984) ("The secrecy attached to many national security issues allows the government to invoke national security claims in order to cover up embarrassment, incompetence, corruption or outright violation of law.").

[33] Helga Hernes, *Foreword*, in INTERNATIONAL INTELLIGENCE COOPERATION AND ACCOUNTABILITY xi (Hans Born, Ian Leigh & Aidan Wills eds., 2011) ("There is an obvious danger that all or part of the information shared with foreign partners could be wrong or inaccurate . . . .").

[34] Loch K. Johnson, *Governing in the Absence of Angels: On the Practice of Intelligence Accountability in the United States*, in WHO'S WATCHING THE SPIES? ESTABLISHING INTELLIGENCE SERVICE ACCOUNTABILITY 61 (Hans Born, Loch K. Johnson & Ian Leigh eds., 2005) (noting that the major problem facing U.S. intelligence in 2005 was that the CIA had "not been gathering enough quality data").

[35] Exec. Order No. 12,356 § 1.6, 3 C.F.R. 166 (1982). The Obama administration's policy on the invocation of the state secrets privilege contains comparable language. *See* Off. of Att'y Gen., *Memorandum for Heads of Executive Departments and Agencies & Memorandum for the Heads of Department Components* (Sept. 23, 2009).

[36] *See* PALLITTO & WEAVER, *supra* note 28, at 2–3; FREDERICK A.O. SCHWARZ JR., DEMOCRACY IN THE DARK: THE SEDUCTION OF GOVERNMENT SECRECY 2 (2015) ("[T]oo much is kept secret not to *protect America* but to keep embarrassing or illegal conduct *from Americans*.").

[37] David E. Pozen, *Deep Secrecy*, 62 STAN. L. REV. 257, 278 (2010).

noting, "Public debate and political checks reduce error as well as excess, and they promote legitimacy—but they cannot function effectively when operations are characterized by stealth."[38] Consider, for example, the fact that the U.S. national security establishment seemed to have developed a secret war plan for responding to a Soviet first strike that involved launched missiles at China, potentially killing 175 million people.[39] Had that policy been debated publicly, it seems unlikely that it would have remained in place.

Eliding accountability for errors. Secrecy also renders it harder to hold a decision maker accountable for the mistakes he has made. Consider, for example, President George W. Bush's decision to block employees from the Office of Professional Responsibility in the Department of Justice from obtaining the necessary clearances to investigate government lawyers' roles in approving the NSA's warrantless wiretapping program.[40] Similarly, the Bush White House prevented the General Counsel of the NSA himself from reading a Justice Department legal opinion about that wiretapping program, even though NSA itself was responsible for executing it.[41] By withholding classified information from overseers or expert government lawyers, the Executive used secrecy to elide assessments of whether certain national security decision makers had made legally supportable decisions or flawed ones.

Avoiding the need to justify decisions. There is a fourth reason that the Executive benefits from—and at time abuses—government secrecy. When the Executive can make and execute policies in secret, executive officials need not fight for and defend those programs in the public political process.[42] Particularly where Congress and the President represent different parties or otherwise have an adversarial relationship, the President faces far fewer obstacles if he can authorize his desired programs and policies in secret and avoid having to defend those choices to Congress or the public. The Obama administration's decision to secretly obtain the phone records of an Associated Press journalist might serve as an example, as might the secret

---

[38] Richard Fontaine, Lauren DeJonge Schulman & Stephen Tankel, *War Powers: What Are They Good For?*, Ctr. for New Am. Security (Dec. 9, 2020).

[39] James Baker, The Centaur's Dilemma: National Security Law for the Coming AI Revolution 184 (2020).

[40] Neil A. Lewis, *Bush Blocked Ethics Inquiry, Gonzales Says*, N.Y. Times (July 19, 2006).

[41] Timothy B. Lee, *Lawyers Said Bush Couldn't Spy on Americans. He Did It Anyway*, Wash. Post (June 27, 2013) (noting that the White House also initially did not share the legal opinion with the Foreign Intelligence Surveillance Court, which oversees foreign intelligence surveillance).

[42] Pallitto & Weaver, *supra* note 28, at 6 ("Where a president may do what is desired in secret, there is no reason to withstand the ordeal of a political battle to achieve the same ends."); Pozen, *supra* note 37, at 279 (discussing how secrecy provides "insulation from scrutiny").

internal government analyses about the lack of progress in the Afghanistan conflict.[43] By not revealing to congressional overseers or the public that the U.S. role in stabilizing and rebuilding Afghanistan was not going well, the Executive avoided having to justify that continued role and expenditure of funds.

One way to think about each of these four potential forms of abuse is that they constitute violations of the public law values that we expect the Executive to uphold.[44] When the Executive acts in secret, it is easier for it to treat those values with less care, and it is more difficult for the public to identify when the Executive is acting in a manner inconsistent with those values. Actions that "check" illegality or flawed execution, force the Executive to justify its decisions to another actor inside or outside the executive branch, or challenge the Executive's classification decisions as excessive therefore can promote public law values. This is particularly important when one branch of government bears a disproportionate amount of power, including the power to kill, spy, and undertake other actions overseas that could have a dramatic impact on the future of the country.

Each of these potential misuses of government secrecy—acts that are inconsistent with public law values—engenders skepticism about secret government activities, at least among some segments of the public.[45] One obvious way to mitigate that skepticism is to give other trustworthy actors access to some or all of those executive branch operations, to help minimize the pathologies endemic to government secret-keeping. Indeed, core questions that secrecy scholars must ask and answer include: Are there ways to counteract these secrecy-driven problems and to minimize the incentives that the Executive has to abuse secrecy without improperly revealing the secrets themselves? If so, what are those options?

---

[43] Craig Whitlock, *At War with the Truth*, WASH. POST (Dec. 9, 2019).

[44] *See, e.g.*, Freeman, *supra* note 27, at 818–19; Eichensehr, *supra* note 27, at 511 (treating accountability, transparency, and due process as public law values); Laura Dickinson, *Outsourcing Covert Activities*, 5 J. NAT'L SECURITY L. & POL'Y 521, 522–26 (2012) (describing transparency, some level of public participation, accountability, and respect for international law as public law values).

[45] Pozen, *supra* note 37, at 280. Significant segments of the public may be indifferent to abuses of government secrecy. *See, e.g.*, MARK FENSTER, THE TRANSPARENCY FIX 11 (2017) ("[T]oo often, the public appears incapable of acting like the democratic public that transparency assumes must exist. . . . We long for a public that can process and act on information fully and accurately, but it rarely seems to emerge.").

D. Traditional Checks: Successes and Failures

The traditional answer to these questions has been to turn to the Executive's coequal branches of government. In the wake of shocking revelations by congressional committees in the 1970s about the Executive's abuses of power and secrecy, Congress and the Executive struck what some call the "grand bargain."[46] As part of that bargain, the Executive was allowed to conduct robust intelligence operations, even domestically, but was subject to statutory restrictions on how it did so. A court comprised of federal judges, the FISC, would authorize and oversee the conduct of electronic surveillance for foreign intelligence purposes, and two newly created intelligence committees in Congress (the Senate Select Committee on Intelligence (SSCI) and the House Permanent Select Committee on Intelligence (HPSCI)) would conduct extensive oversight behind the veil of secrecy.[47] The number of committees that now oversees classified executive branch activity in their respective jurisdictions has grown to include the armed services, foreign relations, homeland security, and judiciary committees in the Senate and the House.

These congressional committees and the FISC serve today as "secrecy surrogates" for the public, in whom we place transitive trust that they will help prevent the Executive from abusing secrecy.[48] These actors can engage on at least two levels: they can make procedural judgments about whether the level of secrecy the Executive is employing is appropriate, and they can make substantive judgments about whether Executive's underlying acts are lawful and appropriate or, alternatively, abuses of power.

Congress and the courts both owe loyalty to the public and to public law values, so we might expect them to provide relatively effective checks on the Executive. Yet many believe that Congress and the courts have failed to act as potent surrogates for the U.S. public. One important reason that they have

---

[46] JACK GOLDSMITH, POWER AND CONSTRAINT: THE ACCOUNTABLE PRESIDENCY AFTER 9/11, at 87–93 (2012); Jack Goldsmith & Benjamin Wittes, *The "Grand Bargain" at Risk: What's at Stake When the President Alleges Politics in Intelligence*, LAWFARE (Apr. 4, 2017).

[47] Goldsmith & Wittes, *supra* note 46 (describing the "grand bargain").

[48] Ashley Deeks, *Secret Reason-Giving*, 129 YALE L.J. 612, 645 (2020) (articulating the concept of "transitive trust"); *see also* Michael E. DeVine, *Covert Action and Clandestine Activities of the Intelligence Community: Framework for Congressional Oversight in Brief*, CONG. RES. SERV. (2019) ("Congressional oversight of intelligence, therefore, is unlike its oversight of more transparent government activities with a broad public following. In the case of the Intelligence Community, congressional oversight is one of the few means by which the public can have confidence that intelligence activities are being conducted effectively, legally, and in line with American values.").

had difficulties is that the Executive has limited incentives to share information with Congress and the courts, which sometimes lack incentives to demand it. This section first examines Congress's achievements and challenges in serving as a secrecy surrogate, then turns to the courts, the executive branch itself, and whistleblowers, leakers, and journalists.

1. Congress as Check

a. Congress's successes

Congress possesses some compelling incentives to serve as a faithful surrogate. First, members of Congress take an oath or affirmation to support the Constitution.[49] That oath includes a commitment to the structural aspects of the Constitution, including the separation of powers and checks and balances. Although increasingly rare, some members of Congress are tangibly committed to the institution of Congress itself and work to preserve the roles and entitlements of Congress as a body. This includes a commitment to providing genuine oversight over the Executive. Second, politics can stimulate members of Congress to carefully oversee acts of a President of a different political party.[50] Third, members of Congress are susceptible to embarrassment after the fact if they ignore or overlook executive abuses that happen on their watch. Intelligence overseers were embarrassed, for instance, in the wake of the Iran-Contra affair.[51] Finally, at some level members of Congress are the best possible surrogates for the public, because they must stand for elections and are thus closely attuned to the sentiments of their constituents.[52]

Congress has three core constitutionally based powers that allow it to work as a check on government secrecy and abuses of public law values when it chooses to do so. Most obviously, it has the power to legislate. It has enacted various organic statutes that structure, empower, and regulate different national security agencies, though those statutes are written at a relatively high

---

[49] U.S. CONST. art. VI, cl. 3.

[50] Daryl J. Levinson & Richard H. Pildes, *Separation of Parties, Not Powers*, 119 HARV. L. REV. 2312, 2327 (2006).

[51] Johnson, *supra* note 34.

[52] It is unclear how much the general population cares about excessive government secrecy. Sidney A. Shapiro & Rena I. Steinzor, *The People's Agent: Executive Branch Secrecy and Accountability in an Age of Terrorism*, 69 L. & CONTEMP. PROBS. 100 (2006) ("[T]he public seems generally apathetic regarding [executive decisions to deny FOIA requests]."); Neal Kumar Katyal, *Stochastic Constraint*, 126 HARV. L. REV. 990, 1000 (2013) (describing the "popular willingness to err on the side of national security").

level of generality. Congress also has enacted procedural requirements and standards for covert action programs and foreign intelligence surveillance and, as discussed previously, has passed laws such as FOIA that empower the public to obtain certain government records. Done well, congressional oversight of the national security agencies can ensure that intelligence activities are being undertaken lawfully and that the Executive is prioritizing the right things. Asking hard questions and demanding satisfactory answers helps improve executive activities, and, when Congress is satisfied with the results, it can generate public support for military and intelligence functions.[53]

In the war powers setting, Congress has—at least in theory—an important legislative role to play in shaping and checking the Executive's use of force.[54] Recall the 2001 AUMF discussed at the chapter's start. That statute contained certain limitations on how the President used force in response to the September 11 attacks, identifying which categories of actors he could treat as potential targets. Another statute, the 1973 War Powers Resolution, looms large inside the executive branch when the President contemplates using force, because it requires the President to report to Congress within forty-eight hours of introducing U.S. forces abroad and imposes a sixty-day limit on U.S. troops engaging in hostilities without congressional authorization. In 2019, Congress passed a bill requiring the President to remove U.S. forces from hostilities in or affecting Yemen, though President Trump vetoed it.[55] By exercising both formal and informal legislative influences, "Congress can press for initiating a worthy conflict by changing public narratives and assumptions, or it can help to avoid an unwise one. Members of Congress can test prewar intelligence and political assessments and define likely costs and benefits."[56]

Second, Congress has the power of the purse; the Senate has the power to provide advice and consent to treaties and to presidential nominees; and, in the most serious cases of abuse, the House can issue articles of impeachment. Since as far back as 1796, Congress periodically has threatened to withhold funding for certain activities if the Executive fails to provide certain documents to it.[57] Similarly, the Senate also can withhold its advice and

---

[53] See Amy Zegart, Spies, Lies, and Algorithms 200 (2022).

[54] For a list of recent national security statutes, see Samuel Raschoff, *Presidential Intelligence*, 129 Harv. L. Rev. 633, 700–01 (2016).

[55] White House, Presidential Veto Message to the Senate to Accompany S.J. Res. 7 (Apr. 16, 2019).

[56] Fontaine & Schulman, *supra* note 25.

[57] See Louis Fisher, *Congressional Access to Executive Branch Information: Legislative Tools*, Cong. Res. Serv. 5–6 (May 17, 2001).

consent to a President's nominee if the President does not share a particular document. The Senate did this with David Barron's nomination to be a federal judge, refusing to provide advice and consent unless the Executive gave it an Office of Legal Counsel memo that Barron had authored about targeted killings.[58]

Third, Congress can convene hearings, demand responses by administration officials to "questions for the record," and produce committee reports, powers that are understood to be subsidiary to its power to legislate and appropriate money. In this way, Congress can build public pressure on the Executive to disclose certain information or alter a national security policy, because hearings (at least those that are public) drive news coverage.[59] Further, when Congress mandates unclassified reports, those reports give outside actors the ability to analyze and critique the Executive's activities, which can help Congress do its job.[60] This power can lead to serious friction between the branches: the Executive often feels as though Congress demands so much information—in the form of formal testimony and briefings, informal briefings, and statutorily required reports—that it barely has enough time to get its daily work done. Congress, on the other hand, complains that the Executive is hesitant at every turn to share information, especially classified information. Representative Norman Mineta, who served on the HPSCI during President Ronald Reagan's administration, famously complained that the Executive treats Congress like mushrooms: "They keep us in the dark and feed us a lot of manure."[61]

In addition to formal tools such as hearings, Congress can gather information about national security activities through informal means.[62] Legislators can convene hearings that feature outside experts and their staffs can collect open-source intelligence about a situation from journalists, think tank experts, and other nongovernmental sources.[63] Another way that members of Congress acquire information about national security or foreign policy topics is by traveling on congressional delegations abroad, which can include

---

[58] Adam Serwer, *White House Compromises on David Barron Targeted Killing Memos*, MSNBC (May 6, 2014).

[59] Fontaine & Schulman, *supra* note 25.

[60] Scott Anderson, *What a New Resource Says About the Value of War Powers Reporting*, LAWFARE (Feb. 27, 2020).

[61] Edward Luce, *The Shifts in US National Security Policy Since 9/11*, FIN. TIMES (Nov. 7, 2014) (quoting Representative Mineta); ZEGART, *supra* note 53, at 215.

[62] Fontaine & Schulman, *supra* note 25.

[63] Ashley Deeks, *Will Cyber Autonomy Undercut Democratic Accountability?*, 96 INT'L L. STUD. 464, 491 (2020).

meetings with foreign officials and citizens. This can even include witnessing in person how U.S. wars are going, as when members visit troops overseas. Senator John McCain did this in Iraq while he was helping to develop the strategy to surge thousands of troops there. This allows members to ask questions of people who are not included on the formal agenda that the executive branch has organized for them and thus acquire richer, unscripted information.[64]

Members of Congress also can be strategic about hiring staff who have deep experience within the executive agencies that their committees oversee. Sometimes staffers are former Defense Department or intelligence community officials who know about certain classified agency programs and are well positioned to monitor and adjust those programs using the levers of Congress. However, in other cases their former association with those agencies may render them unduly sympathetic to those agencies and cautious about pushing too hard for change.

It is worth remembering that, as a general matter, the Executive prefers to have smooth relationships with Congress when possible. Perhaps more than outsiders expect, the Executive asks itself how members of Congress will respond to particular policies—a "what would Congress do?" approach—because reducing friction with Congress makes the President's life easier. Framed in legal terms, the Executive prefers to act within Justice Jackson's famous "Category 1," a situation in which the President both draws from his own constitutional power and acts with the blessing of Congress in the form of statutory authorization.[65]

Congress thus can deploy a basket of tools that help check whether the Executive is complying with public law values. There are, however, a range of reasons why Congress often fails to use these tools effectively.

b. Congress's challenges
Insufficient incentives and excessive partisanship. As in all principal-agent relationships, Congress serves as an imperfect agent for the public. First, members of the intelligence committees lack strong incentives to provide effective oversight because they are poorly rewarded for doing so.[66] Amy

---

[64] Fontaine & Schulman, *supra* note 25.

[65] Youngstown Sheet & Tube Co. v. Sawyer, 343 U.S. 579 (1952) (Jackson, J., concurring).

[66] *See* Amy B. Zegart, *The Roots of Weak Congressional Intelligence Oversight* 4, HOOVER INST. (June 14, 2010) ("Congress has struggled with intelligence oversight for a long time.").

Zegart notes that intelligence committee members rarely receive credit from their constituents for the intelligence oversight they conduct.[67] Further, it is hard for those members to exercise strong control over the intelligence community via appropriations because most of the intelligence budget is buried within the Defense Department's budget, which deprives the committee authorizers of leverage.[68] Additionally, members of Congress sometimes prefer not to be fully briefed about potentially controversial secret programs to avoid being tainted electorally if the programs go badly.[69] Members of Congress sometimes become co-opted by the executive branch because they overidentify with the intelligence community[70] or choose to be unduly deferential because they believe that the intelligence community has deeper experience than they do.[71] Finally, members of Congress might choose not to challenge the Executive in certain contexts for fear of losing access to intelligence that the Executive has the discretion but not the obligation to share, or because they wish to protect the President politically. All of these incentives render congressional committees less than fully effective overseers.

Today's partisanship and gridlock in Congress makes these problems worse. The number and effectiveness of hearings is declining.[72] It is very difficult for Congress to pass national security legislation, other than the "must pass" annual National Defense Authorization Act. Even with bipartisan legislative support for repealing the 2002 AUMF and a President who agreed with the effort, Congress was unable to repeal the 2002 AUMF because five Senators sought more information about the issue.[73] Even when given the opportunity to claw back congressional power over war, Congress has been unable to act with authority.

Insufficient staffing and expertise. Second, congressional committees may lack sufficient capacity and expertise to conduct robust oversight.

[67] *Id.* at 7; Johnson, *supra* note 34, at 68–69 (discussing intelligence overseers' limited commitment to their jobs).

[68] Zegart, *supra* note 66, at 13; Michael E. DeVine, *Intelligence Community Spending: Trends and Issues* 11, CONG. RES. SERV. (2019).

[69] House Speaker Nancy Pelosi denied knowing about waterboarding, for instance. Marc A. Thiessen, *Ex-CIA Counterterror Chief Says Pelosi "Reinventing the Truth" About Waterboarding*, WASH. POST (Apr. 30, 2012).

[70] Johnson, *supra* note 34, at 72; Tim Johnson & Ben Wieder, *Intelligence Committees Lean on Ex-Spies to Oversee Spy Agencies*, MCCLATCHY (Sept. 5, 2017) (discussing "capture" of intelligence committees by intelligence agencies).

[71] Johnson, *supra* note 34, at 72.

[72] Fontaine & Schulman, *supra* note 25.

[73] Letter from Sen. Mitt Romney et al. to Senate Foreign Relations Chairman Robert Menendez (June 19, 2021).

The committees are understaffed: HPSCI has about two dozen staffers to oversee an intelligence community of 107,000 people (as of 2017).[74] The members themselves often have limited expertise in intelligence before they join the committees, and the classified nature of the work makes it more complicated and time-consuming for those members to read background documents and attend briefings. The committees' rotation rules, which were crafted to avoid co-optation, end up limiting the amount of expertise that members can develop.[75] Finally, members and staffers often lack the technological sophistication necessary to provide deep oversight over programs involving complicated electronic surveillance, cyber, or artificial intelligence technologies.[76] As one think tank notes, "Congress has simply not given itself the resources needed to efficiently and effectively absorb new information—particularly on complex [science and technology] topics."[77]

As a related matter, even if militaries share information with legislators about their technological capabilities or doctrines, legislators may have difficulty understanding those capabilities, including autonomous capabilities and the risks attendant thereto. There are many reasons to think that the average legislator is not particularly savvy about technology.[78] In one salient example, several U.S. senators proposed legislation in 2016 that would have required companies to provide the government with access to encrypted data when a court had so ordered. Critics savaged the bill, not only because they objected to the policy but also because the bill seemed to reflect a flawed understanding of encryption technology.[79] Finally, although Congress often appropriates money for specific military and intelligence programs, appropriations laws do not always articulate in detail the types and nature

---

[74] Johnson & Wieder, *supra* note 70.

[75] Zegart, *supra* note 66, at 8–10; Johnson, *supra* note 34, at 72.

[76] Jenna McLaughlin, *Congress May Lack Technical Expertise to Properly Investigate Russian Hacking*, INTERCEPT (Feb. 28, 2017) (noting that the bulk of intelligence committees' staff are "lawyers, policy wonks, and budget experts" rather than experts in "coding, information security, and attribution"); Zach Graves & Daniel Schuman, *The Decline of Congressional Expertise Explained in 10 Charts*, TECHDIRT (Oct. 18, 2018).

[77] Mike Miesen et al., *Building a 21st Century Congress: Improving Congress's Science and Technology Expertise* 9, Belfer Ctr. for Sci. & Int'l Aff. (Sept. 2019) (discussing root causes of Congress's lack of technological capacity).

[78] Karen Hao, *Congress Wants to Protect You from Biased Algorithms, Deep Fakes, and Other Bad AI*, MIT TECH. REV. (Apr. 15, 2019) (noting that "only a handful of members of Congress have a deep enough technical grasp of data and machine learning to approach regulation in an appropriately nuanced manner"); Julia Black & Andrew Murray, *Regulating AI and Machine Learning: Setting the Regulatory Agenda*, 10 EUR. J.L. & TECH. 3, § 5 (2019) ("[T]here is little evidence that regulators have the necessary capacity properly to evaluate all the actual and potential uses of AI in their regulatory domains. Asymmetries of knowledge and skills are amplified in the highly technical area of AI.").

[79] Julian Sanchez, *Feinstein-Burr: The Bill that Bans Your Browser*, JUST SECURITY (Apr. 29, 2016).

of weapons that militaries are and are not authorized to develop. Thus, the Executive retains ample discretion to choose.

Executive reluctance to share classified information. Adding to the challenges of partisanship, staffing, and inexpertise, the Executive has the power to deny Congress access to certain intelligence programs, even when Congress demands that it be kept fully informed. The fact that the Executive exclusively collects, classifies, and analyzes intelligence renders this a structural problem that is difficult for Congress to remedy.[80] The Executive by statute is required to keep Congress "fully and currently informed of the intelligence activities of the United States,"[81] including covert actions, but Congress has difficulty getting access to information about certain programs.[82] For instance, it took Congress almost a year to obtain access to the Trump administration's rules regulating offensive cyber operations.[83] The Executive also is cautious about sharing intelligence with Congress when the information comes from foreign partners because it views leaks of partner intelligence as particularly harmful.[84] More generally, the Executive seeks to preserve its institutional authorities from encroachment, even if in a particular instance it might not be costly to share information about a program or policy.[85]

Recall the 2001 AUMF issue that opened this chapter. On the heels of that September 18, 2001, statute, the Executive had to interpret the text to determine which groups it could target. Concluding that it could target al Qaeda and the Taliban was straightforward. However, as time passed and al Qaeda metastasized, harder questions arose about whether particular terrorist

---

[80] *See* Pozen, *supra* note 37, at 318–19 (noting that "some amount of publicity is a necessary precondition for information-access disputes to arise in the first place" and that "Congress and the public will always be the 'losers' of access disputes that never materialize").

[81] 50 U.S.C. §§ 3091–93 (2012).

[82] Johnson, *supra* note 34, at 70 (noting that "Congress's Joint Committee complained in 2002 about stonewalling by the second Bush Administration"); Sudha Setty, National Security Secrecy 39–41 (2017); Michael E. DeVine, *United States Foreign Intelligence Relationships: Background, Policy and Legal Authorities, Risks, Benefits* 8, Cong. Res. Serv. (2019) (noting that Congress has difficulty overseeing classified intelligence sharing agreements); Katrina Mulligan, *Oversight of the Intelligence Community*, Just Security (Oct. 16, 2020) (stating that "intelligence leaders reject Congress's reasonable requests and openly refuse to appear at public hearings that have long provided accountability about intelligence related to threats to the United States").

[83] Joseph Marks & Tonya Riley, *The Cybersecurity 202: Congress Peels Back Secrecy to Review Trump Hacking Policy*, Wash. Post (Dec. 18, 2019); Mark Pomerleau, *After Tug-of-War, White House Shows Cyber Memo to Congress*, Fifth Domain (Mar. 13, 2020) (describing a multi-month struggle to obtain access to National Security Presidential Memorandum 13).

[84] Hernes, *supra* note 33, at xi ("[N]ational oversight bodies are usually either obliged to show restraint in asking for access to such material, or they are totally cut off from it.").

[85] Pallitto & Weaver, *supra* note 28, at 3 (noting executive interest in "maintain[ing] presidential prerogative against congressional inquiries and judicial orders").

groups were covered by the 2001 AUMF, and in some cases the Executive began to target groups other than core al Qaeda. It did not, however, share that information with Congress. As Brian Finucane wrote, "The problem of waging war against unknown enemies first captured public attention during a 2013 public hearing before the Senate Armed Services Committee. Early in the hearing it became apparent that Chairman Carl Levin and likely other Senators didn't know whom the United States was using force against under the 2001 AUMF."[86] It took until 2017—and a legislative provision in an authorization act—for the Executive to inform Congress which groups the Executive was treating as "associated forces" of al Qaeda, rendering them targetable.[87] Some subset of those forces still remains classified.[88]

In sum, while the Executive provides congressional committees with a significant number of briefings and reports about its national security activities, Congress often proves both unwilling and unable to cabin those activities, including the use of wartime detentions, targeted killings, and the introduction of troops abroad.[89] Congress tends to lack knowledge about the details of such activities, including the advanced technologies that the military and intelligence agencies are using. Congress fears being blamed if, as a direct or indirect result of restrictive laws that it enacts, the country suffers an attack or crisis. Finally, when Congress is divided, it faces the ordinary partisan gridlock that occurs whenever it tries to legislate. Add to this the Executive's persistent incentives to withhold certain information from Congress and it is clear that Congress is, at best, a flawed secrecy surrogate. As we will see, though, Congress's checking role is more robust than that of the courts.

2. Federal Courts as a Check

Recall our 2001 AUMF puzzle, including the Executive's decision to interpret the statute as authorizing force against groups that did not on their face appear to be covered. An outside observer to the U.S. system might wonder why, in the face of what appears to be an executive branch violation of the

[86] Brian Finucane, *Putting AUMF Repeal into Context*, JUST SECURITY (June 24, 2021).

[87] *See* National Defense Auth. Act for Fiscal Year 2018, P.L. 115-91, § 1264. *See also* U.S. State Dep't, *Digest of United States Practice in International Law* (2017) (listing groups covered by the 2001 AUMF).

[88] Finucane, *supra* note 86 ("[T]he full span of the war on terror is unknown to the U.S. public, in part, because the complete list of groups that the United States is at war with is classified.").

[89] Ashley Deeks, *Facebook Unbound?*, 105 VA. L. REV. ONLINE 1 (2019).

Constitution and a statute, federal courts have not stepped in to correct that interpretation. One of the core tenets of U.S. national security doctrine, however, is that courts play a deeply modest role in shaping and adjudicating the Executive's national security decisions. In most of the cases in which plaintiffs have tried to persuade a court that the Executive has impermissibly extended the reach of the 2001 AUMF, the courts have rejected their arguments.[90] In 2021, for example, when a Guantanamo detainee claimed that the United States lacked authority to detain him under the 2001 AUMF because U.S. military operations in Afghanistan had ceased, a district court concluded that it was "constrained to respect the decision of Congress to grant the Executive a broad power [in the 2001 AUMF] that is not bound by geography and to defer to the Executive's representations that its conflict with al Qaeda is ongoing."[91] Because this type of judicial restraint is widespread, courts provide only a modest check on executive national security decisions.

a. Courts' successes

Like Congress, courts that encounter cases implicating secret government operations have some incentives to serve as effective surrogates for the public in checking government illegality. First, judges take an oath to uphold the law and must identify illegality in those cases over which they have jurisdiction. Second, judges seek to preserve their reputation among their peers and the public.[92] For instance, in a rendition case involving state secrets, the Ninth Circuit went to great lengths to try to persuade the public of its credibility as a secrecy surrogate by discussing the care with which it reviewed the government's (classified) claims.[93] In concluding that the state secrets doctrine required it to dismiss the case, the court noted:

> We . . . acknowledge that this case presents a painful conflict between human rights and national security. As judges, we have tried our best to evaluate the competing claims of plaintiffs and the government and resolve that conflict according to the principles governing the state secrets doctrine set forth by the United States Supreme Court.[94]

---

[90] See, e.g., Al-Alwi v. Trump, 901 F.3d 294 (D.C. Cir. 2018).
[91] Gul v. Biden, 573 F. Supp. 3d 148 (D.D.C. 2021).
[92] Deeks, supra note 48, at 622–23.
[93] Mohamed v. Jeppesen Dataplan, Inc., 614 F.3d 1070, 1092–93 (9th Cir. 2010) (en banc).
[94] Id. at 1093; see also N.Y. Times Co. v. U.S. Dep't of Just., 915 F. Supp. 2d 508, 515 (S.D.N.Y. 2013) (bemoaning the "Alice-in-Wonderland"–like quality of the case and the judge's inability to force the government to disclose a Justice Department opinion).

Third, unlike members of Congress, judges with life tenure may be less susceptible to political pressures. In short, the courts possess baseline incentives to check secret executive activities in egregious cases.

In a few contexts, Congress has given federal courts statutory authority to hear national security-related questions. Most notably, the FISC, which is comprised of Article III judges, hears the government's foreign electronic surveillance applications.[95] Article III courts also review classified information and activities in FOIA litigation and certain criminal cases, where Congress has enacted the Classified Information Procedures Act (CIPA) to guide the courts through cases in which classified evidence arises. The criminal case against Donald Trump for retaining and concealing classified documents at Mar-a-Lago offers a high-profile example of CIPA in action.

Against this backdrop of limited direct judicial involvement in its security policies, the Executive is highly attuned to potential court action. When the Executive faces a credible threat of litigation or a specific case is pending, it sometimes alters the affected national security policy in ways that render it more rights-protective. I have referred to this as the "observer effect": the effect on the Executive when it becomes aware that a court soon may review on the merits a particular executive policy.[96] For example, in 2017 the Department of Defense detained a U.S.-Saudi dual citizen in Syria on the ground that he had fought for ISIS. Doe's lawyers argued that the United States was detaining him unlawfully because the 2001 and 2002 AUMFs did not apply to ISIS fighters. When it appeared as though the D.C. Circuit might address that issue on the merits—something the United States neither expected nor wanted—the United States mooted out the case by transferring him, with his consent, to Bahrain.[97] The observer effect thus can stimulate the Executive to shift its policies in a more rights-sensitive direction to avoid adverse judicial outcomes.

---

[95] Article III judges are nominated by the President, confirmed by the Senate, and have life tenure unless convicted of high crimes and misdemeanors. Even here, the FISC has limits as a surrogate because it usually only hears the government's arguments. Under the USA FREEDOM Act, the FISC can appoint amici to help it address challenging legal questions by offering a perspective that may differ from the government's. USA FREEDOM Act of 2015, Pub. L. No. 114-23, 129 Stat. 279.

[96] Ashley Deeks, *The Observer Effect: National Security Litigation, Executive Policy Changes, and Judicial Deference*, 82 FORDHAM L. REV. 827 (2013).

[97] Robert Chesney, Doe v. Mattis *Ends with a Transfer and a Cancelled Passport: Lessons Learned*, LAWFARE (Oct. 29, 2018).

b. Courts' challenges

In most cases, courts use abstention doctrines and other tools to decline to hear national security cases on the merits—such as cases about the use of armed force, covert action, surveillance, and military detention. When courts do hear these cases, they often issue decisions that are highly deferential to executive choices. The courts' behavior in the wake of the September 11, 2001, attacks largely bears this out: courts declined to reach the merits of almost all of the cases challenging executive policies on renditions, detainee treatment and transfers, lethal targeting, and warrantless wiretapping. And even where the courts stepped in, they usually focused on the decisional processes that surround executive decision-making, rather than on the substance of those decisions themselves.

Some national security scholars support this state of affairs because they think that courts are structurally ill-equipped to assess the Executive's intelligence and security calculations, which often must be made rapidly and which carry important foreign policy implications. These scholars also believe that the Executive is more accountable to the public than courts, such that its decisions will be guided and tempered by the public will. Other scholars bemoan the absence of courts from the playing field. To them, the Executive has undue incentives to emphasize security values over liberty values, and only a vigorous judicial role can counter that. More broadly, these scholars view robust judicial deference to the Executive as weakening a critical tool by which to inhibit a single branch of government from accruing undue power.

The courts face several hurdles to serving as robust secrecy surrogates. First, they necessarily are reactive: they can only hear cases that others bring. This means that they review only a small subset of secret government activities. Other than the FISC, which engages deeply with executive requests to conduct classified foreign intelligence surveillance, federal courts only sporadically confront cases that implicate government secrecy: in the past decade they have heard several cases involving renditions and surveillance in which the government invoked the state secrets privilege;[98] about a dozen litigated uses of the Classified Information Procedures Act;[99] an occasional use of force case involving military operations;[100] some cases involving

---

[98] *See, e.g., Mohamed*, 614 F.3d 1070.

[99] *See, e.g.*, United States v. El-Mezain, 664 F.3d 467 (5th Cir. 2011).

[100] *See, e.g.*, Hedges v. Obama, 724 F.3d 170 (2d Cir. 2013).

detentions at Guantanamo; and some national security-focused FOIA litigation.[101]

Second, for separation of powers and competence reasons, courts traditionally defer to executive assertions about national security equities, classification questions, and factual issues linked to intelligence or military decisions.[102] The courts often articulate in their opinions their self-perception that they lack the technical, military, and foreign-policy experience to correctly decide these questions.[103] In cases ranging from *Haig v. Agee*[104] to *Al-Aulaqi v. Obama*,[105] courts have deferred to what they describe as the Executive's unique capacities to protect the country from national security threats.

Third, like Congress, courts perceive that national security decisions have high stakes and worry about reaching decisions that might result in national security harms.[106] Though the Supreme Court issued several high-profile detainee-related decisions in the decade after September 11, 2001, the Court and lower federal courts have avoided reaching decisions on the merits of a range of national security cases. The courts often signal that Congress, not the courts, should make the hard policy decisions embedded in these cases because Congress is politically accountable in a way that the courts are not. In a case about the review procedures to which detainees at Guantanamo were entitled, for instance, Judge Brown of the D.C. Circuit wrote in a concurrence that "the circumstances that frustrate the judicial process are the same ones that make this situation particularly ripe for Congress to intervene pursuant to its policy expertise, democratic legitimacy, and oath to uphold and defend the Constitution. These cases present hard questions and hard choices, ones best faced directly."[107] In a case challenging the Executive's alleged plan to militarily target a U.S. citizen abroad, a D.C. district court avoided deciding the case on the merits, noting that courts are ill-suited to

---

[101]   *See, e.g.*, ACLU v. U.S. Dep't of Defense, 628 F.3d 612 (D.C. Cir. 2011).

[102]   *See, e.g.*, Rahul Sagar, Secrets and Leaks 55 (2013) ("Can judges, far removed from the cut and thrust of diplomacy and international intrigue, really challenge the president's contentions as to what information should not be made public?").

[103]   Deeks, *supra* note 89.

[104]   Haig v. Agee, 453 U.S. 280 (1981) (interpreting the Passport Act of 1926 as permitting the Executive to revoke a passport when necessary for national security purposes).

[105]   Al-Aulaqi v. Obama, 727 F. Supp. 2d 1, 9 (D.D.C. 2010).

[106]   Robert Chesney, *National Security Fact Deference*, 95 Va. L. Rev. 1361, 1428 (2009) (discussing judicial concerns about institutional self-preservation in national security cases).

[107]   Al-Bihani v. Obama, 590 F.3d 866 (D.C. Cir. 2010) (Brown, J., concurring).

"make real-time assessments of the nature and severity of alleged threats to national security."[108]

Finally, as with its posture toward Congress, the Executive has traditionally proven very reluctant to make classified information available to courts (other than the FISC). The government often expresses concern about leaks[109] and argues for extensive judicial deference to its policy decisions.[110]

For all of these reasons, the courts often rely on a range of nonjusticiability doctrines, including the political question doctrine, standing, ripeness, and the state secrets privilege, to avoid wading deeply into the merits of the Executive's intelligence or military activities.[111] For instance, a court concluded that individuals were barred by the political question and standing doctrines from challenging U.S. government efforts to target an American citizen in Yemen.[112] Other courts rejected challenges by detainees who claimed to have been subject to rendition and mistreatment by the CIA, based on the state secrets privilege. Even more recently, in *United States v. Zubaydah*, the Supreme Court upheld the government's use of the state secrets privilege to refuse to confirm or deny information about an alleged secret detention facility, even when that information had entered the public domain through unofficial sources.[113]

In sum, Congress offers a modest avenue for pressing the Executive to explain controversial or misguided policy choices and programs of questionable legality, and sometimes holds executive decision makers to account. Federal courts generally face a range of challenges to serving as robust secrecy surrogates who can check executive actions that may be inconsistent with public law values, though they will sometimes step in when they perceive a manifest rights violation. These checks shed some light on the national security black box, but they are hardly comprehensive. It is therefore important to examine what other actors may drive the Executive toward legality, competence, accountability, and justification.

---

[108] *Al-Aulaqi*, 727 F. Supp. 2d at 9.

[109] *See, e.g.*, United States v. U.S. Dist. Ct. for the E. Dist. of Mich., 407 U.S. 297, 319 (1972).

[110] *See* Chesney, *supra* note 106 (noting that the executive branch often argues that judges should defer to its factual judgments in national security cases).

[111] *See, e.g.*, *Al-Aulaqi*, 727 F. Supp. 2d at 45 ("An examination of the specific areas in which courts have invoked the political question doctrine reveals that national security, military matters and foreign relations are 'quintessential sources of political questions.'" (quoting El-Shifa Pharm. Indus. Co. v. United States, 607 F.3d 836, 841 (D.C. Cir. 2010))); Laura K. Donohue, *The Shadow of State Secrets*, 159 U. PA. L. REV. 77, 85–86 (2010) (counting over four hundred state secrets cases since 1953).

[112] *Al-Aulaqi*, 727 F. Supp. 2d at 4.

[113] 595 U.S. 195 (2022).

3. Executive Self-Checks

It seems paradoxical to look to actors within the executive branch itself as potential checks on the Executive. But executive actors can and do play this role. Indeed, these actors are among the most effective ways we have to ensure compliance with public law values, though they perform that role *within* the national security black box. In *Federalist 51*, Madison gave voice to a key insight: that the ambition of one government actor can be harnessed to minimize another actor's ambitions (and ability) to accrete undue power to himself.[114] Those same ambitions are alive and well within and among the different national security agencies today, which sometimes put their agency-specific ambitions to good use in enhancing public law values inside the executive branch more broadly.

a. Interagency Frictions
Not all agencies are identically situated when it comes to developing, assessing, and executing national security operations. The Defense Department (which includes the National Security Agency) and the CIA are the two most operational agencies when it comes to on-the-ground activities overseas. For DOD, this includes warfighting, military assistance to allies and partners, detention, cyber operations, and clandestine "preparation of the environment" for future conflicts. For the CIA, this includes covert action, foreign intelligence surveillance, and human intelligence collection. Each agency controls the classification of its programs (subject to being overruled by the President), and each creates buckets of very tightly compartmented information about highly sensitive activities: "special access programs" for DOD and "controlled access programs" for the CIA.[115] This means that many actors within other agencies that work on national security,

---

[114] THE FEDERALIST NO. 51, at 322 (James Madison) (Clinton Rossiter ed., 1961) ("This policy of supplying, by opposite and rival interests, the defect of better motives, might be traced through the whole system of human affairs, private as well as public. We see it particularly displayed in all the subordinate distributions of power, where the constant aim is to divide and arrange the several offices in such a manner as that each may be a check on the other that the private interest of every individual may be a sentinel over the public rights."). For academic literature discussing the role of interagency checks and balances, see Neal K. Katyal, *Internal Separation of Powers: Checking Today's Most Dangerous Branch from Within*, 115 YALE L.J. 2314 (2006); Elizabeth Magill & Adrian Vermeule, *Allocating Power Within Agencies*, 120 YALE L.J. 1032 (2011); Gillian Metzger & Kevin Stack, *Internal Administrative Law*, 115 MICH. L. REV. 1239 (2017); and Chris Walker & Rebecca Trumbull, *Operationalizing Internal Administrative Law*, 71 HASTINGS L.J. 1227 (2020).

[115] Michael DeVine, *Controlled Access Programs of the Intelligence Community*, CONG. RES. SERV. (Apr. 20. 2022).

including the State, Justice, and Homeland Security Departments, do not have ready access to these "deep secrets."

Yet policymakers and lawyers within those other departments want to know and understand what their military and intelligence counterparts are doing, because those activities can complement—or directly interfere with—their own missions. Consider a situation in which the State Department, in consultation with the White House, has decided to make a widespread international push for censorship-defeating peer-to-peer communications technologies.[116] U.S. diplomats spend time articulating to foreign audiences the importance of creating secure, decentralized networks that allow human rights defenders to communicate with each other within autocratic states. Imagine that at the same time, unbeknownst to the State Department, the CIA is developing tools to penetrate those same types of networks because it believes that terrorists have begun to use them. If and when the CIA program comes to light, it will undercut entirely the State Department's diplomatic efforts.[117]

Because agency officials bring distinct, and sometimes competing, missions and perspectives to issues, these agencies can serve as checks on each other, using both policy and legal arguments to challenge what they see as unlawful, ineffective, or poorly conceived programs. On some occasions, an official from one agency may even leak to the press information about another agency's program, moving the debate from inside the black box to outside it and increasing the transparency of the national security policy at issue.

b. Reason-Giving Requirements

Reason-giving—the process of offering justifications for a decision—is essential to democratic governance.[118] Judge Harold Leventhal noted, "Reasoned decision promotes results in the public interest by requiring the agency to focus on the values served by its decision, and hence releasing the clutch of unconscious preference and irrelevant prejudice."[119] When issuing rules, for example, executive agencies give and publish their reasoning so that

---

[116] U.S. Dep't of State, *Internet Freedom: Advancing and Promoting Peer-to-Peer Communications* (Feb. 13, 2020).

[117] Another example is the CIA's use of a doctor to try to gain access to Osama bin Laden's compound by purporting to run a hepatitis vaccination program. When revealed, this had a significant backlash and adversely affected USAID's vaccination programs. In 2014, the CIA banned the use of vaccination programs as a way to gather intelligence. Jackie Northam, *How the CIA's Hunt for Bin Laden Impacted Public Health Campaigns in Pakistan*, NPR (Sept. 6, 2021).

[118] Deeks, *supra* note 48.

[119] Greater Boston Television Corp. v. FCC, 444 F.2d 841, 852 (D.C. Cir. 1971).

the public can see them; courts do the same when issuing opinions. Public reason-giving requirements may improve the quality of decisions, deter abuses of authority, and enhance fidelity to legal standards.[120]

As I wrote previously:

> Using reason-giving as a way to hold the decision-maker accountable requires first that the decision-maker articulate and record a reason that an audience can assess.... When the Executive makes clear why it has pursued a particular course of action, a wide range of actors gains the opportunity to evaluate those reasons. If the reasons are found wanting, some of those actors will be in a position to sanction the reason-giver, whether by overruling the decision, voting the decision-maker out of office, or, more mildly, offering public critiques of the decision or reason. Those sanctions can, in turn, force the Executive to alter the underlying policy for which its reasons proved insufficient.[121]

So what happens when the government cannot make public the reasons for its decisions, as in the national security context? It turns out that the Executive often engages in secret reason-giving, even if those reasons do not become public. The Executive sometimes provides secret reasons to Congress and the courts to justify a variety of national security programs. More surprisingly, though, the Executive also engages in secret reason-giving that remains entirely within the executive branch. Unlike public reason-giving, the primary goal of secret reason-giving is not to facilitate effective review by outsiders or to promote the transparency of government operations. Instead, secret reason-giving improves the overall quality and effectiveness of government decision-making and operations, constrains the decision maker, strengthens the decision maker's legitimacy, and fosters her accountability for the choices she made. Secret reason-giving inside the Executive therefore advances each of the public law values at issue here.

A few examples illustrate the point. In the FISA context, the Department of Justice provides secret reasons to the FISC when it seeks to obtain a court order authorizing foreign intelligence surveillance.[122] This submission allows the FISC to probe the government's classified request, facts, and

---

[120] Edward H. Stiglitz, *Bureaucratic Reasoning* 5 (unpublished manuscript) (on file with author).

[121] Deeks, *supra* note 48, at 633.

[122] For an example of a redacted and released FISA application, see Verified Application, *In re Page* (FISA Ct. Oct. 2016).

justifications to ensure that the request meets the statutory requirements. The covert action statute requires the President to notify Congress of any covert action he approves "as soon as possible after such approval."[123] If he decides to notify only certain members of Congress, the statute requires that he provide "a written statement of the reasons for limiting such access."[124] If the delay in notification exceeds 180 days and the President does not provide access to all members of the congressional intelligence committees, the President "shall ensure that . . . a statement of reasons that it is essential to continue to limit access to such finding or such notification to meet extraordinary circumstances affecting vital interests of the United States is submitted" to a select group of congressional leaders.[125]

Most surprising, but perhaps most interesting, are cases in which the Executive imposes *on itself* a requirement to provide reasons. When different agencies disagree about a particular legal interpretation, for example, each agency may present its legal views to the President and Cabinet (frequently in the form of a White House–drafted decision memorandum articulating those competing legal views).[126] A prominent case of classified legal reasongiving occurred in the debate over the use of force in Libya in 2011. The legal question was whether the War Powers Resolution required the President to cease employing U.S. military force in Libya after sixty days, absent congressional authorization. Although no written products containing secret reasongiving have been made public, news reports reflect that the Departments of Defense, State, and Justice and the White House Counsel's Office all offered the President legal reasons why the United States did or did not need to cease military force after sixty days.[127] This allowed the President to consider a full range of executive branch views before making a decision, something that presumably improved the quality of the decision. In this way, legal reasongiving, coupled with some leaks, also created public accountability for the actors who took particular legal positions.

---

[123] 50 U.S.C. § 3093(c)(1).

[124] 50 U.S.C. § 3093(c)(5)(A).

[125] 50 U.S.C. § 3093(c)(5)(B).

[126] Memorandum Opinion, Protect Democracy Project v. Dep't of Def., Case No. 17-cv-00842 (CRC), 10-13 (D.D.C. Aug. 21, 2018) (describing the process within the National Security Council and the White House for presenting the President with legal advice); Michael P. Scharf, *International Law in Crisis: A Qualitative Empirical Contribution to the Compliance Debate*, 31 CARDOZO L. REV. 45, 71 (2009) (quoting former State Department legal advisers describing how the National Security Council would present divergent agency legal opinions to the President).

[127] Daphna Renan, *The Law Presidents Make*, 103 VA. L. REV. 805, 839–41 (2017).

c. Virtuous Agents

Several scholars have identified that certain offices within executive agencies have mandates that render them "offices of goodness."[128] Using the Department of Homeland Security's (DHS's) Office for Civil Rights and Civil Liberties as an example, Margo Schlanger details how certain offices within agencies are "value infused," meaning that they are "explicitly assigned to further a particular value that is not otherwise primary for the agency in which they sit."[129] Schlanger describes how Congress, by statute, empowered the office to oversee DHS's compliance with constitutional, statutory, regulatory, and policy requirements related to the civil rights and civil liberties of people affected by DHS's programs. She illustrates how the Office, and its equivalents in other agencies, is able to use its inclusion in working groups, its ability to review draft documents and programs, its informal advice-giving, its reporting to Congress, and its authorities to investigate complaints to "increase the amount of Goodness in an agency."[130] Similarly, Shirin Sinnar argues that inspectors general play a significant role in monitoring how agencies' national security practices curtail individual rights. Here, too, internal executive officials can enhance public law values by introducing transparency into certain national security policies, identifying legal violations, and causing agencies to reconsider legally questionable practices. Both Schlanger and Sinnar acknowledge the limitations of these actors, including the possibility that they may experience agency capture and that they need to rely on political actors to implement their proposed reforms. Still, actors like these can make a modest dent in the national security black box.

Agency lawyers can help too. Take, for example, the phenomenon of secret treaties.[131] The United States has entered into a range of secret agreements with other states, many of which involve military and intelligence issues. Some of these agreements have leaked. We might expect them to be rife with violations of international law. But many of these agreements are actually consistent with international legal norms, including norms contained in the UN Charter. Why do states comply with their substantive international law obligations in documents that they intend to keep secret? Why do they not

---

[128] Margo Schlanger, *Offices of Goodness: Influence Without Authority in Federal Agencies*, 36 Cardozo L. Rev. 53 (2014); *see also* Shirin Sinnar, *Protecting Rights from Within?: Inspectors General and National Security Oversight*, 65 Stan. L. Rev. 1027 (2013).

[129] Schlanger, *supra* note 128, at 61.

[130] *Id.* at 103.

[131] Ashley Deeks, *A (Qualified) Defense of Secret Agreements*, 49 Ariz. St. L.J. 1 (2017).

take advantage of that secrecy to circumvent international legal rules that might be inconvenient or that fail to advance their short-term interests? The answer is likely based in part on the role of lawyers in the agreement-making process.

Government lawyers are habituated to law compliance as part of their training and culture. Lawyers are almost always present when states are negotiating and drafting international agreements or nonbinding arrangements. Although lawyers cannot always prevent policymakers from violating international law, it seems more likely that the default posture will be to comply with international law if a foreign ministry lawyer is in charge of crafting the text in the first instance. A 2015 meeting of international law legal advisers affirmed that the "principal role of the Legal Adviser is to ensure the government (or other body) complies with international law. The Legal Adviser is 'both counsellor and conscience.'"[132] When faced with one policy proposal that is consistent with international law and another proposal that is not, most legal advisers would recommend that a client pursue the former.

Likewise, most officials within a legal office whose job is to develop and interpret law believe in the value of that body of law, at least as a general matter. Once hired into that office, those individuals generally want to (and may feel pressure to) perform that job in a manner consistent with the office's ethos. There are a variety of circumstances in which policymakers insist on pursuing policies that do not fall squarely within the four corners of what domestic and international law permit, but even here, lawyers play a critical role in managing the size of the violation. In the United States, for example, the CIA has indicated that, "*[a]s a general matter*, and including with respect to the use of force, the United States respects international law and complies with it *to the extent possible* in the execution of covert action activities."[133] This statement deliberately avoids articulating what international rules are relevant to such activities, but it also identifies the value that the United States puts on compliance with international law.[134] It further suggests that the U.S. government—presumably with the assistance of its national security and international lawyers—attempts to minimize any violations that do

---

[132] British Institute of International and Comparative Law, Conf. Report, *The Role of Legal Advisers in International Law* 2 (Feb. 26, 2015).

[133] S. Select Comm. on Intel., Additional Prehearing Questions for Ms. Caroline D. Krass Upon Her Nomination to Be the General Counsel of the Central Intelligence Agency (emphasis added).

[134] Ashley S. Deeks, *Intelligence Communities and International Law: A Comparative Approach, in* COMPARATIVE INTERNATIONAL LAW 264–65 (Anthea Roberts et al. eds., 2018).

ultimately occur. Lawyers and their customary commitment to domestic and international law adherence clearly play a role in achieving that outcome.

d. Summary

As with the other checks already described in this chapter, reliance on intra-executive tensions and the ethos of certain clusters of executive officials is hardly enough to sufficiently enforce public law values. Sometimes an agency's program is such a deep secret that no one outside the agency—or even outside a particular office within that agency—knows about it. Sometimes executive officials develop groupthink, unable to step outside of their bubble to appreciate how problematic a proposal is. Indeed, even when they function well, intra-executive checks do little to reduce the opacity of the national security black box. However, these tensions do real work to improve the quality of executive decision-making and to reduce illegality.

4. Whistleblowers, Leakers, and Journalists as Checks

Whistleblowers, leakers, and journalists have an important role to play in shaking, if not cracking open, the national security black box. A whistleblower is someone who attempts to reveal evidence of executive waste, fraud, abuse, or illegality by following statutorily created channels, while a leaker is someone within the executive branch who discloses classified information to a journalist without authorization and with the expectation of anonymity.[135] These three sets of actors serve as bolder secrecy surrogates than courts but lack their constitutional imprimatur; they also have less regular access to classified information than Congress. Much of the scholarship on government secrecy identifies the positive potential of statutory whistleblowing regimes but views the current system as ineffectual as a practical matter.[136]

---

[135] *See, e.g.,* Whistleblower Protection Act of 1989, Pub. L. No. 101-12, 103 Stat. 16 (codified as amended in scattered sections of 5 U.S.C.); Whistleblower Protection Enhancement Act of 2012, Pub. L. No. 112-199, 126 Stat. 1465; Intelligence Community Whistleblower Protection Act of 1998, Pub. L. No. 105-272, §§ 701–02, 112 Stat. 2396, 2413–17 (codified as amended at 5 U.S.C. § 8H, 50 U.S.C. § 3033(k)(5), and 50 U.S.C. § 3517); Whistleblower Protection for Contractor and Grantee Employees, Pub. L. No. 114-261, 130 Stat. 1362 (2016).

[136] David Pozen, *The Leaky Leviathan: Why the Government Condemns and Condones Unlawful Disclosures of Information,* 127 HARV. L. REV. 512, 527 (2013).

It treats leakers as an unfortunate but critical aspect of our secrecy ecosystem.[137]

Whistleblowers in national security agencies have the potential to serve as important secrecy surrogates: they have access to classified information, can identify problematic executive activity, and can report it in a way that does not expose classified information to the public. Through whistleblower statutes, Congress has established procedures by which whistleblowers may report their concerns to their agency's inspector general, who in turn can report the information to the appropriate congressional committee if she finds it credible.[138] The statutes protect whistleblowers against retaliation if they follow this process. However, the process rarely works as intended: the statutes are not user-friendly and do not prevent agencies from revoking whistleblowers' security clearances, which provides a disincentive for whistleblowers to come forward.[139] Whistleblowers thus play only a minor surrogacy role in the national security space.

Unlike whistleblowers, national security leakers often act anonymously and disclose classified information to journalists who then publish it. Leaking classified information poses several obvious problems. First, it is usually illegal to do so.[140] Second, the information that leakers reveal can adversely impact national security or can be misleading because the leaker only reveals a small piece of the overall landscape. Third, those engaged in leaks may be motivated by self-aggrandizement or revenge; at the very least, they arrogate authority to themselves to make policy decisions that they lack the legal right to make.[141] Fourth, as Neal Katyal notes, "leaking as a check suffers from the same problem as the judicial check—it is far too haphazard a practice around which to build a constitutional system."[142]

Leaking admittedly provides some benefits in ensuring that the Executive's national security practices adhere to public law values. Scholars such as Bruce Ackerman argue that leakers are "patriotic" and that their disclosures

---

[137] See, e.g., SAGAR, supra note 102, at 204 ("That we must rely on a regulatory weapon [i.e., leaking] that has the tendency to backfire at least as often as it finds its target—*this* is the dilemma that state secrecy creates for democracy.").

[138] See, e.g., Intelligence Community Whistleblower Protection Act §§ 701–02; see also Michael E. DeVine, *Intelligence Community Whistleblower Protections* 2, CONG. RES. SERV. (2019).

[139] See Pozen, supra note 136, at 527 (noting that in the national security context whistleblowers "play a marginal role").

[140] See id. at 522–24 (listing range of criminal statutes that apply or might apply to leaking).

[141] See, e.g., Beverly Gage, *Deep Throat, Watergate, and the Bureaucratic Politics of the FBI*, 24 J. POL'Y HIST. 157, 175 (2012) (arguing that FBI official Mark Felt leaked information to *Washington Post* reporters in an effort to reassert FBI autonomy from President Nixon).

[142] Katyal, *supra* note 52, at 1003.

promote our national security by "preserving our constitutional integrity."[143] Further, the threat of leaks may have a positive impact on executive behavior ex ante if the Executive perceives that decisions it makes in secret may become public in the short term.[144] Finally, some leakers reveal very problematic executive acts that the public would want to see halted and condemned.

Even those scholars who recognize that leaks can impose serious costs often conclude that it is necessary to live with a system that periodically tolerates leaks while prosecuting some leakers.[145] David Pozen, for instance, identifies the commonly held and somewhat paradoxical view that "leaking 'is a problem of major proportions' and that 'our particular form of government wouldn't work without it.'"[146] This tolerance for some level of leaks reflects a frustration with the weaknesses of our congressional and judicial surrogates.

Journalists are an important part of the secrecy ecosystem as well: through journalists, the leaks' contents find their way into the public conversation. Like leakers, journalists lack constitutional duties to the public and have a range of incentives to reveal classified information. Journalists often see themselves as acting in the public interest and argue that revealing secret government abuses of authority advances the public's interest in an accountable government.[147] Responsible journalists try to balance U.S. national security concerns against the public interest in understanding what the government is doing,[148] though they sometimes get that balance wrong.[149] Journalists also seek to sell newspapers, however; publishing secrets is a surefire way

---

[143] Bruce Ackerman, *Protect, Don't Prosecute, Patriotic Leakers*, N.Y. TIMES (June 12, 2012).

[144] Deeks, *supra* note 48, at 649.

[145] GOLDSMITH, *supra* note 46, at 218 ("And so we have a system in which the executive branch, in the secret aspects of its wars and intelligence operations, sometimes makes mistakes that can harm national security, and in which the press and others seeking to hold the executive branch accountable sometimes publish information that can harm national security. There are costs and benefits to national security from both secrecy and disclosure.").

[146] Pozen, *supra* note 136, at 514 (citations omitted).

[147] *See* RonNell Andersen Jones, *Litigation, Legislation, and Democracy in a Post-Newspaper America*, 68 WASH. & LEE L. REV. 557, 591 (2011) (noting that the media "have routinely acted as proxy for the larger public, putting the legislative tools to use after fighting for their enactment").

[148] Bart Gellman, *Secrecy, Security and Self-Government: An Argument for Unauthorized Disclosures*, CENTURY FOUND. (Sept. 3, 2013) ("The Washington Post and its peers routinely consult responsible agencies before publishing anything classified. . . . We often ask for explanation of the stakes. . . . We can identify more and less harmful forms of secrecy, better and worse reasons to withhold information from 'we the people,' and factors that heighten and diminish the case for disclosure. . . . Sometimes strong security interests collide with weak public interests in disclosure. . . . We seldom if ever agree to withhold information that exposes a government lie, even a well-intended one.").

[149] GOLDSMITH, *supra* note 46, at 213–18 (providing examples of media disclosures of leaked information that had significant negative consequences for intelligence gathering).

to achieve that.[150] Journalists thus serve as another example of secrecy surrogates who—like leakers—reveal classified information in situations in which the public might not agree with the fact of the disclosures.

In short, while leakers and journalists can sometimes reveal inept or illegal programs that the public ultimately condemns, their actions can have a significant adverse impact on national security. It is problematic, then, that many scholars and practitioners have the intuition that a system that uses leaks as a backstop is the best we can do. In David Cole's words, "leakers are a terrible answer to the problem, but they're the only answer we have . . . ."[151] The next section challenges that conclusion, arguing that there are several other categories of secrecy surrogates whose ability to check the Executive's misuse of secrecy complements that of the surrogates discussed in this Part, and who can do so without seriously compromising national security.

E. Nontraditional Checks

As this discussion shows, the U.S. system contains a variety of legal and political structures and doctrines that perpetuate the Executive's dominance in the national security sphere relative to the other branches of government. However, there are some additional (though less predictable) actors, including *foreign allies*, *private companies*, and *states and localities*, that serve to help check a national security Executive that is only lightly accountable.[152] These tools work only in certain categories of national security activity, though, and, like the tools of traditional surrogates, cannot completely eradicate the national security black box.

Between 2001 and 2020, the national security threat landscape shifted from one of overt, kinetic state-to-state conflict to a landscape dominated by

---

[150] *See* Note, *Media Incentives and National Security Secrets*, 122 HARV. L. REV. 2228 (2009) (exploring how the media makes decisions about publishing national security secrets).

[151] Alex Abdo et al., *A New Paradigm of Leaking*, 8 J. NAT'L SECURITY L. & POL'Y 5, 31 (2015); *see also* Gellman, *supra* note 148 ("It turns out that I am making an argument for something like the status quo. In practice today, the flow of information is regulated by a process of struggle. The government tries to keep its secrets, and people like me try to find them out. Intermediaries, with a variety of motives, perform the arbitrage. No one effectively exerts coercive authority at the boundary. And that's a good thing."); SAGAR, *supra* note 102, at 203 (arguing that sporadic leaks are the best realistic option for our system).

[152] For a discussion of "giant distributed networks of lawyers, investigators, and auditors, both inside and outside the executive branch, that rendered U.S. fighting forces and intelligence services more transparent than ever, and that enforced legal and political constraints, small and large, against them," see GOLDSMITH, *supra* note 46, at xi–xii.

nonstate actors and clandestine, hostile operations by foreign governments using new technologies. (Since 2020, the major threats have shifted again to include near-peer China and Russia.) These new threats manifested themselves in the form of hostile cyber operations, including ransomware and clandestine access into U.S. infrastructure such as telecommunications networks, ports, and computer applications; election interference; disinformation; and terrorist acts. As a result, the Executive has had to engage with a new set of actors that are in close proximity to, and sometimes direct victims of, these threats. Three groups have assumed critical—though underappreciated—roles in the U.S. national security ecosystem. Why do these actors have access to national security secrets? Because the Executive has, by necessity, begun to expand and diversify the number and type of secret keepers in areas that reach far beyond the executive branch or Congress. In so doing, the government is both decreasing the depth of its secrets (because more people know the secret) and positioning these actors to check some of the persistent problems of government secrecy: the concealment of incompetent execution or illegality and the ability of the Executive to avoid justifying its decisions to outsiders.

These three groups have several important advantages over our traditional secrecy surrogates. First, they possess specific expertise about the new threats and new targets that Congress, the courts, and leakers might not have. Certain technology companies and allies are highly specialized in intelligence-gathering and analysis, and so are particularly well-suited to detect problematic executive performance in the secrecy space. Second, each of the three groups brings to the table access to information and infrastructure that the Executive needs to perform its job. For technology companies, it is the ability to observe and defend the front lines of critical infrastructure systems, attribute the sources of cyberattacks, and operate the very systems that are subject to foreign manipulation.[153] For states and localities, it is control over and knowledge about election operations and machinery and other critical infrastructure at the subfederal level, as well as ground-level intelligence about terrorist activities inside the United States. For foreign allies, it is intelligence and expertise that the United States may not possess about shared threats. The Executive has persistent incentives to share intelligence with these actors to allow them to take necessary steps to help enhance

---

[153] *See, e.g.,* SCOTT SHAPIRO, FANCY BEAR GOES PHISHING: THE DARK HISTORY OF THE INFORMATION AGE, IN FIVE EXTRAORDINARY HACKS (2023); CrowdStrike, *CrowdStrike's Work with the Democratic National Committee: Setting the Record Straight* (June 5, 2020).

U.S. national security. This, in turn, renders them an audience that the Executive must persuade of the soundness of its intelligence and proposed operations. Third, unlike leakers, these three groups are positioned to challenge secret government operations without revealing those operations.

U.S. technology companies, states and localities, and foreign allies possess the capacities and incentives to check problematic uses of government secrecy. For example, technology companies exchange threat information and operational details of cyberattacks with government officials, comparing intelligence and sometimes litigating to contest government decisions to keep programs secret. Foreign allies sometimes disagree with the U.S. intelligence community's substantive intelligence judgments, challenging the United States to produce more or better intelligence. Although there are limited public examples of states and localities challenging secret executive activities directly in the election and cyber arenas, these subfederal officials have the potential to do so because they possess fine-grained information about the election systems and critical infrastructure that are the targets of hostile cyber operations. Further, they historically have challenged certain federal counterterrorism programs, which suggests that they could start to push back in the election and cyber settings as they gain expertise about the threat landscape.

Corporations will not always help us with our black box problem. Sometimes corporations actually exacerbate the problem. For example, as Jon Michaels has shown, the use of national security contractors can worsen the black box, allowing government actors to duck accountability more easily than they can when they are acting directly.[154] Private security companies are often exempt from the laws and regulations to which federal employees must adhere, and statutes such as FOIA do not apply to their work.[155] On the other hand, we recently have seen companies decline to work with the federal government where doing so would enhance the government's ability to conduct targeting in war or to use facial recognition software for surveillance and border control purposes.[156] Kristen Eichensehr has captured this duality well in the cyber ecosystem, where cyber companies sometimes push back against government requests and sometimes facilitate them.[157] She surmises

---

[154] *See* Jon Michaels, *All the President's Spies: Private-Public Intelligence Partnerships in the War on Terror*, 96 CAL. L. REV. 901, 904 (2008).

[155] Gillian Metzger, *The Constitutional Duty to Supervise*, 124 YALE L.J. 1836 (2015).

[156] DARRELL WEST & JOHN ALLEN, TURNING POINT: POLICYMAKING IN THE ERA OF ARTIFICIAL INTELLIGENCE 178 (2020).

[157] Kristen Eichensehr, *Digital Switzerlands*, 167 U. PA. L. REV. 665, 713–14 (2019).

that "companies will fight against or resist governments when the companies
. . . can credibly argue that they are protecting the interests of users against
governments" but are likely to cooperate with the government when, based
on the companies' assessment, "there is an alliance between users and
governments," which generally occurs when the government is complying
with or enforcing democratically enacted laws.[158] Chapter 5 explores in
more detail what role companies—or their employees—may play in penetrating the double black box.

These, then, are our nontraditional secrecy surrogates: actors who are
given access to secret information that average U.S. citizens are not and who
can improve secret executive operations and help mitigate abuses. These
surrogates are positioned to enhance the Executive's adherence to public
law values by (1) stimulating the Executive to improve the accuracy of its intelligence; (2) diminishing the Executive's opportunity to undertake illegal
actions; and (3) increasing the Executive's accountability for its classified
choices. It is difficult to obtain empirical, unclassified information about the
full range of effects of these secrecy surrogates. However, based on available
analyses of the ways that technology companies, foreign allies, and states
and localities have behaved to date in the surveillance, cybersecurity, and
counterterrorism settings, it is clear that these actors can help ensure that
U.S. intelligence operations are attentive to legal, procedural, and accuracy
concerns.[159]

For many of the same reasons that our traditional secrecy surrogates do
not act as fully faithful agents for the public, these secrecy surrogates offer
at best partial fixes to our secrecy challenges, even if they are independently
powerful actors. They have their own pathologies and policy preferences,
have incomplete access to classified information, and could serve as a
new source of leaks. These actors will not supplant the existing messiness
of the interplay among the Executive, Congress, the courts, and leakers.
Rather, they will supplement the reach of existing surrogates, expanding
what Jack Goldsmith has framed, in the wider national security setting, as a
"synopticon"—a distributed network of actors that surveils the Executive.[160]

---

[158] *Id.* at 704–06.
[159] Deeks, *supra* note 27, at 1398–1404.
[160] GOLDSMITH, *supra* note 46, at 205–07.

Adding knowledgeable players to the "secrecy synopticon" who can provide increased checks and monitoring without sacrificing much secrecy is a development worth sustaining.[161] And as Chapter 5 argues, these nontraditional surrogates will have an important role to play in narrowing the size of the double black box.

[161] Deeks, *supra* note 27, at 1405.

2

The Algorithmic Black Box

A. Introduction

This chapter turns to the "black box" nature of advanced algorithms. It starts by providing a basic description of artificial intelligence, machine learning systems, and deep neural networks, and it explains why governments such as the United States and China are starting to deploy these tools to advance their national security goals. The chapter then identifies the most common critiques of machine learning: the concern that its developers often use biased data; the uncertainty about who to hold accountable for flawed algorithms; the fact that users may place unwarranted trust in AI predictions; the general perception that AI dehumanizes social and law-based interactions; and—importantly for this book's arguments—a lack of transparency about how the systems produce their results and evolve over time.

It is because of this lack of transparency that AI/ML is often referred to as a black box: it is often difficult for a user of a machine learning system or someone affected by the system to understand the basis on which the system makes its predictions. As algorithms become more sophisticated, this problem may worsen. As a result, officials may not be able to meaningfully explain the basis for their decisions to the individuals adversely affected by them—or even understand the basis for the results themselves. Addressing this lack of transparency can help mitigate the other concerns that surround AI; indeed, some recent developments in "explainable AI" (xAI) provide partial responses to the "black box" problem. But xAI has not been perfected, and many argue either that true xAI is impossible to create or that building xAI requirements into AI/ML tools will diminish their accuracy and therefore meet resistance.

To provide greater texture to the claims that democracies will increasingly confront algorithmic black boxes as they perform their homeland security and national security operations, the chapter briefly describes what we know about the current state of AI/ML tools at work within these government agencies. The chapter then shows why algorithmic black boxes, which are opaque both to the democratic public and to their governmental users, complicate our pursuit of the public law values of legality, competency, accountability, and justification.

B. Artificial Intelligence and Machine Learning: The Basics

A dictionary definition of artificial intelligence is "the ability of a digital computer or computer-controlled robot to perform tasks commonly associated with intelligent beings."[1] The term often refers to "the ability of machines to perform tasks that typically require human intelligence, for example, recognizing patterns, learning from experience, drawing conclusions, making predictions, or taking action."[2] References to "AI" include various fields of study, including computer vision, speech recognition, natural language processing, language translation, logical reasoning, game-playing, making predictions, and continuous learning.[3] AI and autonomy are not synonyms, but AI can facilitate increased autonomy in a range of systems.

Experts distinguish between artificial general intelligence—a system that can understand and learn in the same way and to the same level that a human can—and narrow or "weak" AI, which focuses on solving a discrete problem. Most experts predict that artificial general intelligence is many years away, if it ever happens at all. Narrow AI, on the other hand, has arrived. As a result, this book focuses on narrow AI tools that are or will be used to accomplish specific national security activities.[4]

---

[1] B.J. Copeland, *Artificial Intelligence*, BRITANNICA (describing "systems endowed with the intellectual processes characteristic of humans, such as the ability to reason, discover meaning, generalize, or learn from past experience"); David Engstrom et al., *Government by Algorithm: Artificial Intelligence in Federal Administrative Agencies* 12, Admin. Conf. of the United States (Feb. 2020) (defining AI as "feats of recognition that, if undertaken by humans, would be generally understood to require intelligence").

[2] U.S. Dep't of Defense, *Summary of the 2018 Department of Defense Artificial Intelligence Strategy* 5. The National Artificial Intelligence Act of 2020 defines it as "a machine-based system that can, for a given set of human-defined objectives, make predictions, recommendations or decisions influencing real or virtual environments." 15 U.S.C. § 9401(3).

[3] Rob Toews, *What Does "Artificial Intelligence" Really Mean?*, FORBES (Feb. 17, 2020); STUART RUSSELL & PETER NORVIG, ARTIFICIAL INTELLIGENCE: A MODERN APPROACH (3d ed. 2014) (citing machine learning, natural language processing, knowledge representation, automated reasoning to answer questions, computer vision, and robotics).

[4] The following section is drawn from Ashley Deeks, *Predicting Enemies*, 104 VA. L. REV. 1529 (2018).

1. AI and Machine Learning

Many computer algorithms are based on traditional forms of data analysis, which use statistical tools to find relationships between variables and then predict outcomes based on those relationships.[5] A particular category of algorithms employs machine learning (ML), which is considered a subfield of AI. ML algorithms generate predictions by allowing data itself—rather than human programmers—to dictate how information contained in the inputs is assembled to forecast the value of an output.[6] ML systems improve their own quality and accuracy by testing their propositions against ever more data. The improvement process is called training: training algorithms on examples (in the form of data) generates a model (a piece of code) that can accomplish the task that it has been trained for.[7]

A concrete example will help. Computer scientists have created machine learning algorithms that recognize and classify handwritten numbers. A computer scientist trains the algorithms on large sets of handwritten samples, then shows new samples to the algorithm and "rewards" or "punishes" it, depending on its error rate. (You may have contributed data to this set of samples when you completed a "reCAPTCHA" test to prove that you are not a robot![8]) The system self-corrects by reweighting variables, sometimes in ways that humans cannot understand. This ultimately results in an algorithm that produces low error rates when it confronts and interprets new handwriting samples that it has never evaluated before.[9]

One type of ML is especially opaque in how it makes its predictions. "Deep learning" uses neural networks, which are loosely inspired by the way neurons in the human brain signal to each other, to develop outputs. Those networks, which consist of input layers, output layers, and multiple hidden layers of nodes in between, connect to each other. Each node has an associated weight and threshold and passes along data to the next node when it is activated by certain values.[10] These tools allow users to "classify and cluster

---

[5] Thomas Cormen et al., Introduction to Algorithms 5 (3d ed. 2009).

[6] Cary Coglianese & David Lehr, *Regulating by Robot: Administrative Decision Making in the Machine-Learning Era*, 105 Geo. L.J. 1147, 1156–57 (2017).

[7] Tim Hwang, *Shaping the Terrain of AI Competition* 1, Ctr. for Security & Emerging Tech. (June 2020).

[8] Google, reCAPTCHA (describing how Google uses reCAPTCHA results to "digitize text, annotate images, and build machine learning datasets").

[9] Coglianese & Lehr, *supra* note 6, at 1157–58 (using handwriting example).

[10] Larry Hardesty, *Explained: Neural Networks*, MIT News (Apr. 14, 2017).

data at a high velocity"[11] and generally do not require humans to label the data in order to make sense of it. However, because these systems rely on hidden layers, they are particularly opaque—a challenge discussed in the following sections.

Actors in government, science, medicine, and business rely more than ever on algorithmic decision-making, applying machine learning tools to a wide range of problems, including diagnosing lung cancers and predicting heart attacks,[12] recommending movies to watch,[13] and mastering Go, the complex Chinese board game.[14] ML is excellent at helping users detect anomalies in data, make connections between things that humans might otherwise miss, and classify images.[15] GPT-4 now can generate sonnets, draft movie scripts, design video games, debug code, and design proteins exceedingly fast.[16] In many—though not all—cases, these tools can make more accurate predictions and judgments than humans can.

2. Why Is AI/ML an Important National Security Tool?

The promise of accurate predictions built upon large amounts of data has attracted users in the fields of law enforcement, criminal justice, homeland security, intelligence, and defense. Indeed, the leaders of the United States, Russia, and China have all identified AI as key to their national security and international competitiveness.[17] Some U.S. states have already employed criminal justice algorithms, and there is reason to believe that all three of these countries are embedding ML tools in their defense and intelligence systems.

The nature of AI/ML illustrates several reasons why states want to develop these tools to help them surmount national security challenges. First is the need for speed. In national security settings, "autonomous systems powered

---

[11] IBM, *What Is a Neural Network?*

[12] Economist, *Of Prediction and Policy* (Aug. 20, 2016).

[13] Tom Vanderbilt, *The Science Behind the Netflix Algorithms That Decide What You'll Watch Next*, Wired (Aug. 7, 2013).

[14] Economist, *The Latest AI Can Work Things Out Without Being Taught* (Oct. 21, 2017).

[15] Damien Van Puyvelde, Stephen Coulthart & M. Shahriar Hossain, *Beyond the Buzzword: Big Data and National Security Decisionmaking*, 93 Int'l Aff. 1397, 1405–06 (2017).

[16] Noelia Ferruz, Steffer Schmidt & Birte Hocker, *ProtGPT2 Is a Deep Unsupervised Language Model for Protein Design*, 13 Nature Comms. 4348 (2022).

[17] Eric Schmidt, *AI, Great Power Competition & National Security*, 151(2) Dedalus 288 (Spring 2022).

by machine learning will have a speed-based edge in decision-making and re-action times" compared to humans.[18] ML systems can process much greater amounts of data in a much shorter amount of time, whether they are trying to detect a needle in a haystack of electronic surveillance data or assessing whether a fighter jet should swerve left or right to avoid an incoming missile. Militaries will seek to outpace their enemies' operations using AI/ML to gain both strategic and tactical advantages.

Second, national security has become a big-data business. Consider the Utah Data Center, a million-square-foot data storage facility that the U.S. Intelligence Community built to store the exabytes of data that the National Security Agency and other intelligence agencies have collected.[19] (The global internet traffic that crosses the wires in a month is estimated to amount to one exabyte.) In the words of James Bamford, who has studied the NSA exten-sively, the Center functions as "NSA's external hard drive."[20] To perform their predictive activities, intelligence and homeland security agencies collect and must process vast amounts of data from the internet, telephony, satellites, weather stations, seismographs, ports of entry, commercial reporting, and virtually everything else that can be collected or measured. In Amy Zegart's words, "government spy agencies are drowning in data."[21] AI/ML tools help these agencies put this data to effective use.

Third, detecting anomalies—something ML is very good at—is an im-portant part of intelligence, counterintelligence, military, and homeland security activities. For instance, a soldier on patrol in occupied territory needs to be able to spot abnormal activity that may signal an imminent attack. ML is also good at classifying images, which militaries and intelli-gence agencies must do to understand threats—the location and number of weapons, the launching of ballistic missiles, or troop movements. Fourth,

---

[18] Michael Horowitz, *When Speed Kills: Lethal Autonomous Weapons Systems, Deterrence and Stability*, 42 J. STRATEGIC STUD. 764, 769 (2019). *See also* Kenneth Anderson & Matthew Waxman, *Law and Ethics for Autonomous Weapons Systems* 20–22, HOOVER INST. (2013) (noting that the push toward autonomy will be driven by factors "such as reaction speeds and the tempo of particular kinds of operations"); Frank Sauer, *Stepping Back From the Brink: Why Multilateral Regulation of Autonomy in Weapons Systems Is Difficult, Yet Imperative and Feasible*, 913 INT'L REV. RED CROSS 235, 243 (Mar. 2021) (noting that "the promise of gaining the upper hand by allowing for the com-pletion of the targeting cycle at machine speed is arguably the main motivation behind increasing weapon autonomy"); Darrell West & John Allen, *How AI Is Transforming the World*, BROOKINGS INST. (Apr. 24, 2018) (envisioning "hyperwar," where militaries use autonomous systems capable of lethal outcomes at automatic speeds).

[19] Ingrid Burrington, *A Visit to the NSA's Data Center in Utah*, ATLANTIC (Nov. 19, 2015).

[20] Howard Berkes, *Booting Up: New NSA Data Farm Takes Root in Utah*, NPR (Sept. 23, 2013).

[21] AMY ZEGART, SPIES, LIES, AND ALGORITHMS 6 (2022).

AI/ML offers the prospect of increased accuracy compared to human judgment. As Michael Horowitz notes, "[A]utonomous systems could be more accurate than humans in following their programming, helping overcome parts of the way fatigue, confusion and the limitations of the human mind can lead to mistakes on the battlefield."[22] Finally, because AI/ML enables autonomy in systems, governments in the wartime and intelligence collection settings will be able to send autonomous systems rather than humans into dangerous or denied areas, enhancing the governments' ability to operate there.[23] Their goal is not (or at least not yet) to conduct war entirely without soldiers[24]—but their goal may be for *their side* to conduct war largely without having their soldiers exposed on the ground, against human soldiers on the other side.

C. Critiques of AI/ML

The basic concerns that surround the use of AI—wherever deployed—will be familiar to anyone who has read news or journal articles about AI tools. I discuss them briefly here because some of these concerns illuminate why we must ensure that the U.S. executive branch (and governments in other democracies) is developing, adopting, and deploying AI systems responsibly.

1. Biased or Inaccurate Algorithms

One of the most significant critiques of predictive algorithms stems from the fact that it is easy to inadvertently use biased data used to train them. Computer scientists might train an algorithm on data that contains gender, racial, or economic biases, which the algorithm will then replicate in its outputs. Assume that a company builds a bail algorithm that incorporates data about past arrests when predicting how likely it is that a person will reoffend if released on bail. If the police arrest Black men at a disproportionately higher rate than other racial groups engaged in the same activities, the algorithm will predict that Black men will be more likely to reoffend when out

---

[22] Horowitz, *supra* note 18, at 770.
[23] Anderson & Waxman, *supra* note 18, at 6–7.
[24] Roberto González, War Virtually: The Quest to Automate Conflict 1 (2022).

on bail, even if that is not statistically true. In this example, police bias skews the data used to build the algorithm. Algorithmic biases arise in a variety of contexts but are particularly troubling where the algorithmic prediction affects a person's life or liberty.

In the criminal justice context, critiques of algorithms generally revolve around racial biases. In military algorithms, other types of biases could find their way into the data. For example, a computer scientist building an algorithm to predict the level of risk posed by a Yemeni detainee must be aware that possessing a weapon may not have much significance for the level of risk that a person poses, given how common it is for men to carry weapons in Yemen. Computer scientists might inadvertently build a wide range of biases into algorithms unless they are keenly aware of the cultural meaning of actions in the individual's country of origin and the area of conflict, where an action's meaning might be radically different from the meaning of the same action in the United States. Algorithms built with inadvertent biases would very likely provide predictions that would undercut the military's compliance with international law and make its missions less effective.

A related concern is the use of low-quality or insufficient data. If the algorithm is trained on outdated data, or if the data is entered incorrectly or is simply factually incorrect, the algorithm will fail to make accurate predictions about a new input. Likewise, an attempt to use an algorithm for a task when the algorithm was developed for a different purpose is likely to lead to flawed outcomes, even if the original quality of the data was high. For example, the U.S. military developed an anti-ballistic missile (ABM) computer program to operate in the upper atmosphere against Patriot anti-aircraft missiles. The military developed the ABM program to fire on any target in that area because all targets in the upper atmosphere were reasonably deemed hostile. However, the military later employed that same ABM program, which remained biased toward firing on all targets, in a different, lower-atmosphere context in which not all targets were necessarily hostile. As a result, the Defense Department shot down two friendly aircraft.[25]

The quantity of data can also be an issue. In general, training AI/ML systems on large quantities of data produces more accurate systems than those trained on smaller quantities of data. In some fields, there is a vast quantity of data—social media posts, for example. In the national security

---

[25] This section is drawn from Deeks, *supra* note 4, at 1564–65.

space, however, there may be limited examples of certain kinds of events.[26] The United States may only have access to satellite imagery of thirty cases in which another state constructed a missile manufacturing facility, for instance. That data would likely be insufficient to allow the system to reliably predict when particular activity reflects construction of a new missile facility, however tempting it may be to try.

In the military context, the quality of data also may be a significant issue. One problem is that the individuals responsible for collecting the data that computer scientists will use to develop algorithms may lack adequate incentives to do so carefully. For instance, a team in Iraq that was dedicated to removing improvised explosive devices (IEDs) tried to use big data and algorithms to help stop such attacks.[27] However, the military forces that gathered the data placed a low priority on data collection, because they were understandably focused on avoiding the IED attacks rather than gathering data about when, where, and what type of IED they encountered. Another problem might be that the military collects some types of data and not others. IEDs that exploded produced less information than IEDs that failed to explode, leading to the irony that the U.S. government possessed better information about less effective weapons. Decision makers often possess only selective pieces of information, because either they have not collected or are unable to obtain a full set of facts. Nevertheless, in the algorithmic context, this poses a particular problem when people treat recommendations from computer algorithms as more accurate than they really are.

2. Automation Bias

Some studies show that individuals experience "automation bias," meaning that they are unduly willing to accept a machine's recommendation or they fail to act because a machine did not prompt them to do so.[28] This bias arises because they believe that the machines have greater analytic capabilities than they themselves do.[29] Professor Frank Pasquale worries about the use of criminal justice algorithms because he views judges, like most people, as

[26] Lindsey Sheppard, *Artificial Intelligence and National Security* 8, CTR. FOR STRATEGIC & INT'L STUD. (Nov. 2018).

[27] Deeks, *supra* note 4, at 1565.

[28] Mary Cummings, *Automation Bias in Intelligent Time Critical Decision Support Systems*, AIAA 1ST INTELLIGENT SYSTEMS TECH. CONF. (2004).

[29] SIMON CHESTERMAN, WE, THE ROBOTS? 9 (2021).

susceptible to automation bias. He argues, "Judges are all too likely to assume that quantitative methods are superior to ordinary verbal reasoning, and to reduce the task at hand (sentencing) to an application of the quantitative data available about recidivism risk."[30] This type of bias seems just as likely to appear in the military context. Workload, task complexity, and time constraints increase the amount of automation bias a person suffers, because these factors place pressure on a person's cognitive resources.[31] Military operations typically occur under great time pressure. Depending on the type of operation, military operators might be asked to undertake several complex tasks at once. Further, the average military operator is presumably more familiar and comfortable with technology than the average judge. From this we might infer that the military operator willingly would place even more confidence in a computer recommendation than a judge would.

At the same time, some AI/ML users are likely to suffer from a "reverse automation bias." That is, when presented with a prediction from an AI/ML black box system, some will (not unreasonably) distrust the system unless and until it develops a proven track record.[32] Indeed, as discussed later, the "opacity of AI reasoning may cause [military] operators to have either too much or too little confidence in the system."[33] Militaries will not thrive in combat if they are given systems that they do not trust.

3. Oversight and Accountability

It can be challenging to determine whether actors are using algorithms appropriately and, in the face of errors or misuse, whom to hold accountable. This type of accountability question arises in a range of contexts. Consider a case in which a judge relies on an algorithmic recommendation to sentence a defendant to a longer sentence than she otherwise might have, even though the algorithm was flawed. Who do we blame: The computer scientist who wrote the algorithm? The company for which the computer scientist works? The judge? Or the legislators or court administrators who authorized the judge to use the algorithmic tool?

---

[30] Deeks, *supra* note 4, at 1575.
[31] *Id.* at 1576.
[32] Horowitz, *supra* note 18, at 774.
[33] Kelley Sayler, *Artificial Intelligence and National Security* 32, CONG. RES. SERV. (Aug. 26, 2020).

People have focused intently on this accountability debate in the context of lethal autonomous weapons systems (LAWS), generally defined as weapons that can select their targets and use kinetic force without further human intervention. Nongovernmental organizations such as Human Rights Watch have argued that states should ban LAWS because (among other reasons) it is unclear who to hold responsible for mistaken LAWS attacks.[34] If someone is killed based on a flawed targeting algorithm, do we hold to account the engineer who developed the program? The members of the armed forces who compiled the data that the engineer used to train the algorithm? Higher-level officials in the Defense Department who authorized their officers to use the algorithm? Or the personnel who deployed the system on the battlefield? Even if there will be few opportunities to impose accountability for flawed military operations driven by an algorithm, the military will need to determine the source of the error to improve the algorithm's reliability.

A second, related concern is whether affected individuals can challenge the use of algorithms in specific cases, such as where a person reasonably believes that the government acted on a flawed algorithmic recommendation. In the criminal justice context, various defendants have challenged their sentences or parole denials on the grounds that the decision makers relied on a flawed algorithm, invoking their constitutional rights under the Fourth and Fourteenth Amendments and trying to use the exclusionary rule. Even here, though, courts have declined to scrutinize carefully the state's and judges' use of algorithms. Most prominently, the U.S. Supreme Court denied certiorari in *Wisconsin v. Loomis*,[35] a Wisconsin state case in which the defendant argued that the judge had violated the defendant's due process rights by relying on a sentencing algorithm that Wisconsin bought from a company.[36] The court upheld the company's proprietary rights to the software, making it impossible for the defendant to obtain access to and challenge the accuracy and scientific validity of the algorithm's assessment.[37]

During armed conflicts, where detention and targeting play out in foreign countries and are usually directed against foreign nationals, there

[34] Human Rights Watch, *Losing Humanity: The Case Against Killer Robots* 4, 42–45 (2012) (discussing possibility of holding responsible the manufacturer, military commander, programmer, and the robot itself).

[35] Wisconsin v. Loomis, 371 Wis.2d 235 (Wisc. 2016).

[36] U.S. Supreme Court, Order List, 582 U.S., 16-6387 (cert. denied).

[37] Brief for the United States as Amicus Curiae, Loomis v. Wisconsin, No. 16-6387 (May 2017). The United States conceded that a sentencing court's use of actuarial risk assessments raises novel constitutional questions and that the lack of transparency about the algorithm could raise serious issues. *Id.* at 12.

are far fewer legal protections for the affected individuals and very few opportunities for U.S. courts to oversee the military's exercise of power. As a result, the costs of getting it wrong are lower for the military, though they are high for the affected individuals. Long-running debates about how the Defense Department should handle cases in which the U.S. military inadvertently kills civilians using regular, non-AI/ML-driven kinetic tools illustrate this challenge. It already is difficult for the families of the deceased to get information about the strike and, ideally, obtain ex gratia payments from the United States. It will be even more difficult for families (and for congressional overseers) to obtain satisfactory information about the use of detention and targeting algorithms. Further, even if detainees or families of victims were able to obtain such information, they most likely would lack the knowledge and resources to evaluate it.[38]

4. Dehumanization

Another challenge that the use of predictive ML algorithms must overcome, at least at this stage of their development, is skepticism among some actors about their use. This reaction may stem from a perception that using predictive algorithms to make decisions that affect people's bodily integrity is dehumanizing. In the criminal justice context, for instance, algorithmic models lack access to the softer types of data that humans have access to—such as a judge's perception about a defendant's sense of remorse (or lack thereof) at a sentencing hearing. Other sources of distrust may flow from public reports about the use of biased algorithms and high-profile stories about egregious algorithmic mistakes, such as when Amazon's ML algorithm recommended bomb-making products to be sold together. In the military context, some argue that only humans, exercising human capabilities, should be responsible for restraining another person's liberty or taking another person's life. Those who hold this view will be skeptical about accepting recommendations from machines about whether and when to conduct these acts.[39]

---

[38] *See* Brent Daniel Mittelstadt et al., *The Ethics of Algorithms: Mapping the Debate* 6, BIG DATA & SOC'Y (July–Dec. 2016).

[39] Deeks, *supra* note 4, at 1563–77.

5. Opacity

A final critique of AL/ML algorithms—and especially of systems that use neural nets—is a critical one for this book: their opacity. This critique forms the heart of the "algorithmic black box" problem. It is often difficult for the algorithm's human user to understand precisely why the program makes a particular prediction or decision. As a Defense Department study group put it, "[T]he sheer magnitude, millions or billions of parameters . . . which are learned as part of the training of the net . . . makes it impossible to really understand how the network does what it does."[40] Consider, for example, the algorithm called AlphaGo Zero, which computer scientists trained to play the game of Go. Using neural nets, AlphaGo Zero discovered and preferred specialized sequences of moves that it invented, resulting in a style of play that humans found baffling and "distinctly non-human,"[41] but that was able to beat human Go masters.[42] The opacity exists in government uses of algorithms too: Danielle Citron reports that the administrators of "no-fly list" algorithms that prevent certain people from boarding airplanes "are unable to understand the logical and factual bases for the inferences made by the program."[43]

It is worth teasing apart several different types of AI/ML opacity and why this opacity is a problem. Shedding light on how an algorithm produces its recommendations can help address the other critiques just discussed, by allowing observers to identify biases and errors in the algorithm.[44]

Different types of opacity. Most people describe AI/ML tools as being "black boxes" without being specific about what they mean. But different layers of nontransparency may surround AI/ML tools: the inability to know that an actor is employing an algorithm in the first place (which this book treats as part of the "national security black box" problem discussed in the previous chapter); the inability to obtain information about the type of data on which a programmer trained an algorithm; the inability to know the

---

[40] JASON, *Perspectives on Research in Artificial Intelligence and Artificial General Intelligence Relevant to DoD* 27 (Jan. 2017). *See also id.* at 27 (noting that "it is not clear that the existing AI paradigm is immediately amenable to any sort of software engineering validation and verification").

[41] *The Latest AI Can Work Things Out Without Being Taught,* THE ECONOMIST (Oct. 21, 2017).

[42] Google DeepMind, *AlphaGo Zero: Starting from Scratch* (Oct. 18, 2017).

[43] Danielle Keats Citron, *Technological Due Process,* 85 WASH. U. L. REV. 1249, 1277 (2008).

[44] Finale Doshi-Velez & Been Kim, *Towards a Rigorous Science of Interpretable Machine Learning* 1, 3 (2017) ("[I]f the system can *explain* its reasoning, we then can verify whether that reasoning is sound with respect to . . . other desiderata—such as fairness, privacy, reliability, robustness, causality, usability and trust . . . .").

algorithm's code; the inability to learn how the algorithm weighed values to reach an outcome, due to the highly complex nature of neural networks; the inability to understand how the algorithm learns and evolves; and the inability to know how accurate the algorithm's recommendations are.

There is a further opacity surrounding the crafting and training of algorithms: whether and how the coders attempted to translate a desired policy or legal constraint into computer code. In this case, the code itself may be discoverable, but it may be very hard for all but the most expert coders to understand what types of legal, interpretive, or value judgments the programmer (who rarely will be a lawyer or policymaker) had to make during the process of translating policy into code. And the algorithm itself may be built on flawed assumptions about human behavior.[45]

Different actors in the national security ecosystem will care more or less about these different types of AI/ML opacity. Congressional overseers may care most about knowing *when* executive officials are using AI/ML tools and about how accurate those tools are. Executive officials using those tools may care more about the quality of the data and the legal and policy choices reflected in the algorithm. The "targets" of the tools—foreign governments, foreign soldiers, immigrants at the border, and possibly American citizens— may care most about the fact that the government is using them and about what types of data the government used to train them.

To some extent, these types of opacity are not unique to military tools that employ AI/ML. Most U.S. citizens have no idea how a range of military equipment works, including Osprey helicopters, Predator drones, or Patriot missile batteries. However, these systems have been around for decades and their operations and effects are widely known and reasonably predictable. Further, a range of specialized open-source intelligence companies such as Janes provide detailed descriptions and explanations of how these weapons and weapon systems operate and which states use them. The most important difference between these types of military systems and AI/ML systems is that the former generally behave the same way each time they are used and rely on fixed algorithms to control their operation. Militaries and intelligence agencies can test and verify these tools and, once verified, can reasonably anticipate how they will perform. In contrast, AI/ML tools evolve over time in ways that are difficult to track, even as that evolution alters

---

[45] González, *supra* note 24, at 135–36 (describing PredPol's flawed analogy between criminals and hunter-gatherers).

their performance. They therefore contain an additional layer of opacity compared to other high-tech military tools.

Opacity's effect on users. As noted, the opaque nature of AI/ML tools can cause users to "overtrust" or "undertrust" the systems.[46] Some users will adopt the recommendations of AI/ML tools instinctively (due to the algorithmic bias discussed previously), even when the recommendations do not comport with common sense. For others, however, the opacity will reduce their overall comfort level with using the algorithm—at least initially. A U.S. official using an algorithm that produces recommendations generally should want to understand the bases on which the algorithm makes those recommendations. That official should also want to be able to test or audit whether the system is meeting the standards that the government established.[47] Absent what is called "explainable artificial intelligence" (which is discussed later in section E), officials may not trust, and therefore decide not to use, the algorithm at all.[48] To address this, U.S. intelligence and military officials might choose to emphasize in official instructions that it is acceptable to ignore or give little weight to an algorithmic prediction where the officials do not believe that they can articulate the basis for the prediction itself. In the words of a U.S. military official, "Only 'prudent trust' will confer a competitive advantage for military organizations."[49] Absent some reduction in opacity, we should want our officials to be cautious about trusting AI/ML systems.

[46] Sayler, *supra* note 33, at 32 (noting that the "opacity of AI reasoning may cause operators to have either too much or too little confidence in the system"). To some extent, this challenge arises in any system that uses standard operating procedures, where we might worry that some actors insist on following the procedures even in situations in which they are obviously unsuitable.

[47] *Id.* at 33 ("Due to their current lack of an explainable output, AI systems do not have an audit trail for the military test community to certify that a system is meeting performance standards."); Michele Flournoy, Avril Haines & Gabrielle Chefitz, *Building Trust Through Testing* 5, WestExec Advisors (Oct. 2020).

[48] DARRELL WEST & JOHN ALLEN, TURNING POINT: POLICYMAKING IN THE ERA OF ARTIFICIAL INTELLIGENCE 207 (2020).

[49] Sayler, *supra* note 33, at 32 (quoting Eric Van Den Bosch, *Human Machine Decision Making and Trust, in* CLOSER THAN YOU THINK: THE IMPLICATIONS OF THE THIRD OFFSET STRATEGY FOR THE US ARMY 111 (2017)).

D. The Current State of AI in Homeland Security and National Security

There is some uncertainty about the current state of AI within governments, including inside the U.S. government. It is clear that democracies such as the United States, the United Kingdom, Israel, France, and South Korea are pursuing the use of AI/ML across a range of areas. It is also clear that Russia and China are firmly committed to investing heavily in—and ultimately deploying—AI to advance their security goals. However, we do not know much about which tools these governments are developing or using because the programs are often classified.[50] This section provides an overview of what we know about the state of play on AI within the U.S. homeland security and national security agencies and provides a few examples of AI/ML tools that have come to light. These examples highlight why we will want responsible individuals outside the government to understand and oversee officials' use of these tools.

1. AI in Law Enforcement and Homeland Security

Because most homeland security and law enforcement activities take place within the United States or at its borders, the circumstances surrounding the use of AI/ML tools for these activities look different from those surrounding military or intelligence tools. Most importantly, the U.S. Constitution applies to protect those in the United States who are the objects or targets of AI/ML systems. Very often the objects or targets are U.S. persons, which means that the public, members of Congress, and civil liberties organizations are focused with greater intensity on these types of operations (compared to operations that target foreigners overseas). Additionally, it is often easier for journalists to observe or gain access to information about these tools because they are used within the United States, sometimes overtly. Notwithstanding these factors, we still lack full visibility into which AL/ML tools agencies such as DHS and the FBI are using; how the tools function; and how well the tools are working.

---

[50] Sheppard, *supra* note 26, at 3–4 ("While AI is something of a buzzword that promoters of all kinds like to advertise as something they are not only pursuing but implementing, it can be surprisingly hard to get agreement among a group of experts on just how much 'real' AI has actually been adopted in both the commercial and public sectors.").

Let's start with law enforcement. The U.S. criminal justice system already uses predictive algorithms, mostly at the state and local levels. First, courts commonly employ risk assessment algorithms to assess whether someone who has been arrested is suitable for release on bail or to help determine whether someone who has been convicted of a crime should receive a prison sentence rather than a punishment that does not require her to be confined.[51] Second, police employ computer algorithms to guide their decisions about where to deploy their limited resources, based in large part on algorithmic predictions about where particular types of crimes are most likely to occur and who is likely to be involved (either as a victim or perpetrator) in those crimes. This helps them determine where and when to patrol.

Police departments have started to use facial recognition software (which is driven by AI) to identify criminal suspects, as happened in a 2018 mass shooting at a Baltimore newspaper office.[52] They use video analysis tools to detect crime-relevant footage amid many hours of video.[53] A local police department in California has started using drones that it can instruct to follow particular individuals around.[54] It is not hard to imagine other, future uses for AI/ML predictions in law enforcement: identifying confluences of events that indicate terrorist plotting, using those predictions as probable cause for arresting criminal suspects, and attempting to introduce AI predictions as evidence at trials.[55]

In the homeland security setting, U.S. Customs and Border Protection (CBP) within DHS has turned to AI tools to assess people and objects entering at land borders, airports, and maritime ports, and to patrol for people who may have entered the United States illegally.[56] Like police departments, CBP is using drones with cameras that can spot movement and track individuals.[57] Indeed, in some cases, CBP appears to lend its drones to

---

[51] Rebecca Wexler, *When a Computer Program Keeps You in Jail*, N.Y. TIMES (June 13, 2017) (describing use of algorithms in policing, bail, evidence, sentencing, and parole contexts).

[52] Electronic Frontier Found., *Atlas of Surveillance* (mapping which jurisdictions use various tools such as facial recognition software, gunshot detection, and predictive policing and showing over 10,000 data points).

[53] Herbert Dixon, *Artificial Intelligence: Benefits and Unknown Risks*, AM. BAR ASS'N (Jan. 15, 2021).

[54] Cade Metz, *Police Drones Are Starting to Think for Themselves*, N.Y. TIMES (Dec. 5, 2020).

[55] Surveillance states such as China and Iran already use facial recognition software (FRS) at will. There have been many reports about Chinese authorities' use of FRS in Xinjiang, and Iran reportedly uses FRS to target women who are not complying with strict hijab laws. Khari Johnson, *Iran Says Face Recognition Will ID Women Breaking Hijab Laws*, WIRED (Jan. 10, 2023).

[56] Engstrom et al., *supra* note 1, at 31 (noting that CBP "has invested significant resources in artificial intelligence").

[57] John David, *Small But Mighty*, U.S. Customs & Border Protection (Nov. 9, 2020).

local law enforcement.[58] CBP seems to use these systems (some of which are military-type Predator drones and some of which may include AI/ML technology[59]) not only near the border but well inside the U.S. border too, causing skeptics—including some members of Congress—to worry about ubiquitous monitoring and the lack of transparent rules for the government's domestic use of drones.[60] CBP also uses predictive algorithms to assemble its "no-fly" lists.

To help detect threats posed by people and cargo attempting to enter the United States, in 2014 DHS began using what it calls the Risk Prediction Program (RPP), which employs ML. The RPP builds on a long-standing program at DHS called the "Automated Targeting System" (ATS) program, which helped to identify individuals who required enhanced screening before boarding flights.[61] Although the government made public certain information about ATS in 2006, it no longer does so.[62] According to DHS, CBP now deploys a "family" of automated targeting systems. One of these, the RPP, "incorporates innovative applications of behavioral and machine-learning sciences to develop software" to further CBP's targeting and screening mission.[63] One type of RPP uses ML to identify possible threats before they enter the United States, based on complex and evolving threat patterns.[64] A second type of RPP helps analysts adjudicate the ATS's risk recommendations. It identifies key aspects of an air passenger's or sea cargo's travel characteristics to determine that entity's risk. According to DHS, RPP improved target

---

[58] Somini Sengupta, *U.S. Border Agency Allows Others to Use Its Drones*, N.Y. TIMES (July 3, 2013) (noting that in 2010, CBP reported to Congress that it might eventually equip its drones with "nonlethal weapons" to immobilize people, though in 2013 it disavowed that goal); Tim Cushing, *CBP "Discovers" an Additional 200 Drone Flights It Didn't Include in Its FOIA Response*, TECHDIRT (Jan. 15, 2014).

[59] Micah Hanks, *Drones: Flight of the Force Multipliers*, THE DEBRIEF (Mar. 2, 2021) (discussing CBP's use of Skydio drones, which reportedly use deep learning algorithms to analyze imagery and "predict into the future").

[60] Sengupta, *supra* note 58.

[61] Tal Zarsky, *Transparent Predictions*, 2013 U. ILL. L. REV. 1503, 1515 (describing ATS-P program and noting that "[v]arious governmental databases ... are analyzed to generate predictions regarding the risks associated with those striving to cross borders").

[62] Engstrom et al., *supra* note 1, at 33.

[63] DHS Science & Tech. Directorate, *Risk Prediction Program*.

[64] *Id*. Unisys, which received a 5.5-year contract in 2018 to support the RPP, stated that its software "uses advanced data analytics and machine learning to help border agents more accurately assess risk associated with travelers or cargo shipments before admitting them into a country." More specifically, it helps CBP officers and agents "automatically identify which shipments or travelers present a low risk appropriate for 'low touch' automated clearance and those that present a higher risk requiring additional investigation or inspection." Unisys, *U.S. Customs and Border Protection Awards Contract to Unisys to Help Agency Assess Potential Threats from Travelers and Cargo Crossing into U.S.* (May 9, 2018).

accuracy by 300%, but the DHS information does not include a denominator for the number of travelers and cargo loads assessed.

Although it is publicly known that DHS is using this system (and so its use does not fall squarely within the national security black box), little is known about the algorithms within the RPP, the specific sources and quality of data that the RPP uses, what factors the algorithms weigh in determining riskiness, and what their error rates are. That is, the RPP is an algorithmic black box. In terms of sources of data, one study reports that the RPP "uses information from a wide variety of government and non-government data sources," including not only DHS, FBI, and Justice Department databases but also airlines carriers and "seizure data."[65] That study also notes, "As in the facial recognition context, CBP has not publicly released the specific technologies its Risk Prediction Program uses to process this data. CBP has both a security and liability incentive to keep its technologies opaque: Doing so wards off adversarial learning while insulating the agency from legal challenges."[66] Although it is not clear which other actors have access to CBP's risk scores, CBP appears to share its information with other government entities. DHS itself reported that CBP's cargo screening ML algorithms can help identify individuals and entities of interest to domestic and foreign law enforcement and intelligence agencies.[67] Finally, it is unclear whether CBP has the internal capacity to assess the quality and accuracy of RPP; in an internal CBP report about a different tool (iris scanning), CBP admitted "that it was unable to explain the failure rates" because it was using proprietary technology to which it lacked access.[68] And RPP is not the only set of ML tools that CBP is pursuing to assess risks.[69]

Among the concerns that the RPP black box creates are concerns that the ML systems are using inaccurate or corrupted data from third parties; that the RPP is using AI/ML algorithms that create too many false positives or false negatives (or both) and so are detaining the wrong travelers (such as *New York Times* journalists) or letting suspicious cargo in; or that malicious actors have accessed and gamed or corrupted the RPP, unbeknownst to CBP. It is hardly ideal to use systems that produce false positives, though it

---

[65] Engstrom et al., *supra* note 1, at 33; U.S. Dep't of Homeland Security, *2020 and 2021 Data Mining Report* 36 (Aug. 2023) (listing data sources).

[66] Engstrom et al., *supra* note 1, at 33.

[67] Data Mining Report, *supra* note 65, at 23–24.

[68] U.S. Dep't of Homeland Security, *Southern Border Pedestrian Field Test* 7 (Dec. 2016).

[69] U.S. Customs & Border Protection, *Artificial Intelligence to Harness Key Insights at CBP* (Mar. 24, 2023).

generally just means that false-positive travelers are slowed down in the airport by having to go to secondary questioning.[70] But if the data in the system
about the traveler is wrong, it could lead to more significant problems for the
traveler, including detention and referral for criminal investigation.[71]

Two *New York Times* journalists encountered the opacity of the RPP black
box directly. Christopher Chivers and Mac William Bishop were unable to
extract more information about the RPP, even after filing a FOIA request
to obtain records related to their questioning at John F. Kennedy Airport as
they were about to board a flight to Turkey and, for Chivers, after he returned
to the United States from Turkey. In 2014, the journalists requested all information and records about them that DHS possessed.[72] DHS initially asserted
that it could not locate any responsive documents, but, after being pressed by
plaintiffs, identified some responsive documents that came from DHS's ATS
database or a specific computer system that conducts analysis, screening,
and information sharing to identify high-risk passengers.[73] Although it
does not appear to use complex algorithms, the system weights different
factors to identify suspicious passengers and cargo. The plaintiffs received
several redacted documents and litigated those redactions. DHS defended
its redactions under a FOIA exemption that protects records and information compiled for law enforcement purposes, "but only to the extent that the
production of such records . . . would disclose techniques and procedures
. . . or guidelines for law enforcement investigations."[74] DHS asserted that
disclosing the redacted information would reveal critical law enforcement
techniques, which would allow individuals to effectuate countermeasures
and compromise the integrity of the investigatory process. The court agreed,
concluding that DHS properly withheld the information because revealing it
"would implicitly suggest that such factors played a role in CBP's analysis."[75]

The RPP does not lie inside the double black box because, unlike for many
national security programs, we know that the system exists. But we can't
see inside it. We can't even see what kinds of factors it takes into account.

---

[70] Zarsky, *supra* note 61, at 1517 ("A variety of harms, however, might be at play—such as harms to
autonomy, lack of due process, and even 'mere' annoyance and inconvenience.").

[71] Because this concern arises in the non-AI/ML context as well, DHS instituted a "Traveler
Redress Inquiry Program" to help those improperly put on "no-fly lists" to correct the record. *See*
Transp. Security Admin, Travel Redress Program.

[72] Mac William Bishop & Christopher Chivers v. U.S. Dep't of Homeland Security, 45 F. Supp.3d
380, 383 (S.D.N.Y. 2014).

[73]   *Id.* at 384.

[74]   5 U.S.C. § 552(b)(7)(E).

[75]   45 F.Supp.3d at 394.

And RPP reportedly does not even rely on advanced machine learning algorithms—algorithms that, in the "no-fly list" setting, DHS admits that it does not fully understand.[76] There may be good reasons why DHS redacted the information in the documents it gave to Chivers. But the fact that a *New York Times* journalist got pulled aside twice for secondary screening raises questions about how accurate the RPP system is. And what happens when DHS begins to use more advanced systems that are trained on vast amounts of data, the source, integrity, and reliability of which is at best questionable and at worst unknown to the government users? What will FOIA responses look like then?

DHS previously pursued several ML initiatives that came under such intense criticism that it abandoned them. In particular, DHS developed plans for an Immigration and Customs Enforcement Visa Lifecycle Vetting Initiative (which, in a questionable marketing approach, it called the "Extreme Vetting Initiative"). The initiative sought to use ML tools to "automatically mine Facebook, Twitter and the broader Internet to determine whether a visitor might commit criminal or terrorist acts or was a 'positively contributing member of society.'"[77] The ten thousand or so individuals who the system deemed to pose the greatest potential risk to national security would then be subject to deportation investigations or visa denials. Criticism abounded. A group of ML experts argued to DHS that "no computational methods can provide reliable or objective assessments of the traits that ICE seeks to measure. In all likelihood, the proposed system would be inaccurate and biased."[78] Others explicitly framed the project as a "digital Muslim ban," noting that this use of predictive algorithms would "inevitably resort to using proxies that reflect the biases of programmers, with minority communities left most impacted."[79] Some congressional Democrats joined in, arguing to DHS that the program would be "ineffective, inaccurate . . . and ripe for profiling and discrimination."[80] DHS dropped the ML element of the program, but it framed the changes as driven by cost and convenience rather than by ethics or law. This suggests that the concept may have legs in the future.

---

[76] *See supra* note 68.

[77] Drew Harwell & Nick Miroff, *ICE Just Abandoned Its Dream of "Extreme Vetting" Software That Could Predict Whether a Foreign Visitor Would Become a Terrorist*, WASH. POST (May 17, 2018).

[78] Hal Abelson et al., Letter to Homeland Security Secretary Duke (Nov. 16, 2017).

[79] Faiza Patel & Harsha Panduranga, *DHS' Constant Vetting Initiative: A Muslim-Ban by Algorithm*, JUST SECURITY (Mar. 12, 2018). *See also* Brennan Center for Justice, *ICE Extreme Vetting Initiative: A Resource Page* (last updated May 24, 2018).

[80] Harwell & Miroff, *supra* note 77.

Another ML-driven system that DHS has explored is called AVATAR: Automated Virtual Agent for Truth Assessments in Real Time. The idea is to use AI to create an automated lie detector at the border, which would ask travelers questions, film their responses, and look for deception signals.[81] It would then categorize the traveler based on risk level; those deemed high risk would face questions by a human official.[82] Advocates claim an 80% accuracy rate. Critics challenge the system's efficacy. It is unclear what state of deployment AVATAR is in, though the European Union's AI Act categorizes "emotion recognition" tools as "high risk."[83] Some European states, including France and Italy, have announced that they are using AI within their borders to assist with policing.[84] In the lead-up to the 2024 Olympics, France deployed "sweeping algorithmic video surveillance . . . , including technology that can detect sudden crowd movements, abandoned objects and someone lying on the ground."[85]

Chapter 3 will further consider the questionable quality and effectiveness of these programs. For now, it is clear that, even when the Executive knows that its use of these AI/ML tools will become public, it has used these tools in ways that seem premature and incompletely understood at best, and legally questionable or ethically irresponsible at worst.[86] Some of the tools also seem inaccurate, testing our public law values of efficiency and competence.

2. AI in Intelligence Operations

Intelligence communities are increasingly drawn to AI/ML as well, although secrecy makes it harder to know what tools they have adopted. It is likely that the U.S. IC is using—or considering how to use—AI/ML tools to engage in

---

[81] Jeff Daniels, *Lie-Detecting Computer Kiosks Equipped with Artificial Intelligence Look Like the Future of Border Security*, CNBC (May 15, 2018).

[82] Katherine Hignett, *AI Lie Detector Set to Quiz Travelers at Border Control*, NEWSWEEK (Nov. 1, 2018).

[83] Euro. Comm'n, *Commission Welcomes Political Agreement on Artificial Intelligence Act* (Dec. 9, 2023).

[84] Anthony Faiola, *AI Is Powering a Revolution in Policing, at the Olympics and Beyond*, WASH. POST (Dec. 18, 2023).

[85] *Id.*

[86] *See, e.g.*, Sen. Jeff Merkley (D-OR), *Merkley, Markey, Booker, Warren, Sanders, Call for Immediate Halt of TSA's Facial Recognition Technology and Practices at Airports* (Feb. 9, 2023) ("Increasing biometric surveillance of Americans by the government represents a risk to civil liberties and privacy rights . . . We urge the Agency to immediately halt its deployment of facial recognition technology.").

all three of its core missions: intelligence collection and analysis, counterintelligence, and covert action.

Collection and analysis. For actors whose goal is to collect and analyze data about past events in order to predict future events, systems that help make sense of huge volumes of data and detect anomalies and trends are a natural fit. These predictions may range from the likelihood of a conflict breaking out in a particular location, to the probability that a particular group of nonstate actors intends to bomb a government building, to the likelihood that a particular facility is being used to develop nuclear weapons.[87] The CIA's Director for Digital Innovation reported that, with the help of AI/ML tools, the CIA is now able to "anticipate the development of social unrest and societal instability to within three to five days out."[88] Another CIA official described 137 pilot projects related to AI, including those that would allow the CIA "to be more predictive with what's about to go down, like the North Koreans are about to launch this or about to do this."[89] For a relatively simple example, consider an AI/ML model intended to predict an attack on a military base. Computer scientists could train an AI/ML model on millions of emails, including emails recovered from those who undertook actual prior attacks. The algorithm would discern what types of words or phrases could predict that users are planning an attack and flag new emails containing such examples, which would help military bases defend themselves in the future.[90]

A different actor in the U.S. intelligence community, the National Reconnaissance Organization (NRO), uses a system called Sentient, which has been described as "classified artificial brain."[91] An NRO document more blandly—though probably more accurately—describes it as a system that will "automatically fuse multi-[intelligence] 'big data' in context to understand current activity, predict new activity, and discovery unknown activity."[92] (The NRO operates U.S. reconnaissance satellites and provides satellite and signals intelligence to other U.S. intelligence agencies.) Sentient appears to be an all-source system that integrates signals, human, and image intelligence with other types of data such as financial data, weather data,

---

[87] *See, e.g.,* Alexa O'Brien, *The Power and Pitfalls of AI for US Intelligence,* WIRED (June 21, 2022) (discussing the IC's use of AI to find an unidentified weapons of mass destruction research and development facility by tracking bus routes).

[88] Van Puyvelde, Coulthart & Hossain, *supra* note 15, at 1411–12.

[89] Patrick Tucker, *What the CIA's Tech Director Wants from AI,* DEFENSE ONE (Sept. 6, 2017).

[90] Marcus Roth, *Artificial Intelligence at the CIA—Current Applications,* EMERJ (Nov. 22, 2019) (discussing this example).

[91] Sarah Scoles, *It's Sentient,* THE VERGE (July 31, 2019).

[92] Nat'l Reconnaissance Org., Sentient Program.

shipping statistics, Google searches, and drug purchases.[93] The United States is not alone in these efforts: the United Kingdom, for example, is using AI to process "enormous biometric data sets" to identify patterns of behavior among terrorists and criminal suspects.[94] Israel has announced that its spy service, Shin Bet, has created its own generative AI platform akin to ChatGPT and, using that platform, has "spotted a non-inconsequential number of threats."[95] And China reportedly has developed a "geopolitical environment and prediction platform" that recommends various courses of action to support Chinese foreign policies.[96] There is debate about how successful these uses of AI have been to date, but it is clear that ICs are increasingly incorporating these tools into their work.

Counterintelligence. Spy agencies do more than just spy; they also try to detect when people are spying on their country and stop them. AI/ML tools turn out to be useful for this job as well. States such as Singapore are using AI/ML tools to monitor foreign agents who are suspected of spying, which requires less manpower than they would need to physically tail suspected spies.[97] The CIA also reportedly has counter-counterintelligence AI/ML projects underway to keep agents informed if they are being followed, and to help them avoid a foreign government's monitoring cameras.[98] As I wrote previously, "If the Chinese government can recognize every person on the street and easily track a person's comings and goings, this will make it even harder for foreign intelligence agencies to operate inside the country. Not only will U.S. and other Western intelligence agents be even easier to follow (electronically), but the Chinese government will also be able to identify Chinese nationals who might be working with Western intelligence services—perhaps using machine learning and pattern detection to extract patterns of life. China's facial recognition efforts thus facilitate its counterintelligence capacities."[99] Amy Zegart and Michael Morell highlight this

---

[93] *Id.*

[94] David Bond, *Inside GCHQ: The Art of Spying in the Digital Age*, FIN. TIMES (May 22, 2019).

[95] REUTERS, *Israel's Shin Bet Spy Service Uses Generative AI to Thwart Threats* (June 27, 2023). *See also* Marissa Newman, *Israel Quietly Embeds AI Systems in Deadly Military Operations*, BLOOMBERG (July 16, 2023).

[96] Heather Roff, *Uncomfortable Ground Truths: Predictive Analytics and National Security* 1, BROOKINGS INST. (Nov. 2020).

[97] Jenna McLaughlin, *CIA Agents in "About 30 Countries" Being Tracked by Technology, Top Official Says*, CNN (Apr. 22, 2018).

[98] *Id.*

[99] Ashley Deeks, *China's Total Information Awareness: Second Order Challenges*, LAWFARE (Jan. 16, 2018). *See also* Sayler, *supra* note 33 ("Artificial intelligence could also be used to create full 'digital patterns-of-life,' in which an individual's digital 'footprint' is 'merged and matched with purchase histories, credit reports, professional resumes, and subscriptions' to create a comprehensive

double-edged nature of AI, where the tools enhance an agency's ability to improve its own collection and analysis but also "make traditional clandestine operations difficult."[100]

One potential counterintelligence use of AI/ML systems is particularly relevant to U.S. persons (and therefore U.S. values): using AI/ML to identify suspected "agents of foreign powers" (i.e., spies) inside the United States.[101] The Foreign Intelligence Surveillance Act allows the FISC to authorize the U.S. government to spy on individuals—including U.S. persons—where there is probable cause that they are agents of foreign powers. This means that the IC's AI/ML systems may directly impact U.S. civil liberties.

Covert action. In the United States, covert action is defined as an activity "to influence political, economic, or military conditions abroad, where it is intended that the role of the United States Government will not be apparent or acknowledged."[102] Just as the military is beginning to use AI/ML to enhance its threat assessment and targeting decisions, the CIA will likely use similar technology when undertaking covert actions that involve targeted killings. Indeed, Israel's foreign intelligence agency reportedly used an "A.I.-assisted, remote-control killing machine" to assassinate an Iranian nuclear scientist inside Iran.[103] But covert action extends far beyond targeted killings to include propaganda, influence operations, sabotage, economic manipulation, and the provision of support to rebel groups. Tools such as deepfakes are—if undetected for a period of time—an easy way to wreak political havoc inside another state, undercutting the stability of a foreign government. And states that do not view assassinations of foreign leaders as unlawful may be drawn to AI/ML-facilitated microdrones equipped with facial recognition software that can enter a leader's home or office and explode in his face. We also need to worry about another state or nonstate actor gaining possession

---

behavioral profile of servicemembers, suspected intelligence officers, government officials, or private citizens. As in the case of deep fakes, this information could, in turn, be used for targeted influence operations or blackmail.").

[100] Amy Zegart & Michael Morell, *Spies, Lies, and Algorithms*, FOREIGN AFF. (May/June 2019).
[101] *See generally* Christopher Moran, Joe Burton & George Christou, *The US Intelligence Community, Global Security, and AI: From Secret Intelligence to Smart Spying*, 8 J. GLOBAL SECURITY STUD. (June 2023) (arguing that the IC has "broadened its focus to consider how AI can improve all stages of the intelligence cycle").
[102] 50 U.S.C. § 3093(e).
[103] Ronen Bergman & Farnaz Fassihi, *The Scientist and the A.I.-Assisted, Remote-Control Killing Machine*, N.Y. TIMES (Oct. 26, 2021).

of an advanced tool developed by the U.S. intelligence community and deploying the tool against U.S. citizens.

Unlike in the military setting (discussed later), intelligence communities in democratic states seem less likely to deploy autonomous tools that take actions without human intervention. Rather, the outputs of these AI/ML tools are more likely to serve as key inputs into intelligence analysis and criminal espionage investigations. Nevertheless, because intelligence reports build on themselves and because policymakers do not generally have the time to unpack the citations in each report, it will be critical for analysts preparing those reports to understand which of their puzzle pieces derive from AI/ML tools, what data those tools are built around, and how reliable the tools are. Some observers (and perhaps some IC officials too) are skeptical about the accuracy and capacity of these tools today, even as they worry that adopters may not be sufficiently skeptical.[104]

3. AI in Cyber Operations

Offensive and defensive cyber operations may be the area in which the U.S. government is deploying the most developed AI/ML-driven tools. DHS uses AI-driven or AI-enabled technologies to undertake "predictive analysis for malware evolution; [to enable] defensive techniques to be established ahead of a future malware variant; [to detect] anomalous network traffic and behaviors to inform cyber defensive decision making; and [to help] identify, categorize and score various adversarial Telephony Denial of Service (TDoS) techniques."[105] Some DHS programs use machine learning to block robocalls and potentially fraudulent calls as well as to build more robust defenses against Distributed Denial of Service (DDoS) attacks. DHS also has awarded a range of grants to private companies that are pursuing AI-related projects that could help DHS operations.

Another major player in cyberspace is U.S. Cyber Command (CYBERCOM). A former commander of CYBERCOM testified before Congress in 2016 that "relying on human intelligence alone in cyberspace is 'a losing strategy.' "[106] In his book *Army of None*, Paul Scharre predicts that

---

[104] *See, e.g.,* Roff, *supra* note 96; Van Puyvelde, Coulthart & Hossain, *supra* note 15, at 1399.

[105] U.S. Dep't of Homeland Security, Written Testimony of Douglas Maughan, *Game Changers: Artificial Intelligence Part II; Artificial Intelligence and the Federal Government,* House Comm. on Oversight and Gov't Reform (Mar. 7, 2018).

[106] Sayler, *supra* note 33, at 11.

the trend toward increased autonomy in weapons systems will also manifest itself in cyberweapons.[107] Another scholar argues that states already are widely deploying autonomous cyberweapons.[108] Stuxnet is an example of a cyber operation that entailed considerable autonomy: the cyber worm was "an autonomous goal-oriented intelligent piece of software capable of spreading, communicating, targeting and self-updating."[109] Although directed at a narrow target, the worm (or an earlier iteration of the worm) ended up spreading throughout Iran and into Indonesia, China, Germany, and the United States.[110]

There are at least two reasons why states increasingly will rely on autonomy in their cyber operations.[111] First, the speed of adversaries' offensive cyber operations requires states to *defend* their systems at the same battle speed—which may be faster than a human can react.[112] A 2016 Defense Science Board (DSB) report described existing U.S. autonomous systems that "carry out real-time cyber defense" while "also extract[ing] useful information about the attacks and generat[ing] signatures that help predict and defeat future attacks across the entire network."[113] It also cited a tool called Tutelage, which autonomously inspects and analyzes three million packets per second on an unclassified Defense Department computer system to prevent attacks.[114] The DSB report further imagined the existence of autonomous systems "to control rapid-fire exchanges of cyber weapons and defenses."[115] The U.S. government seems to have pursued those systems. In 2017, the Defense Innovation Unit Experimental contracted for the Voltron project, which uses artificial intelligence to "automatically detect, patch and

---

[107] Paul Scharre, Army of None: Autonomous Weapons and the Future of War 222 (2018).

[108] Rebecca Crootof, *Autonomous Weapons and the Limits of Analogy*, 9 Harv. Nat'l Security J. 51, 81 (2018); *see also* Rain Liivoja et al., *Autonomous Cyber Capabilities Under International Law* 11–12, NATO Cooperative Cyber Defence Centre of Excellence (2019) (discussing existing defensive and offensive cyber capabilities).

[109] Stamatis Karnouskos, *Stuxnet Worm Impact on Industrial Cyber-Physical System Security*, 37th Annual Conference of the IEEE Industrial Electronics Society (2011).

[110] Peter Beaumont, *Iran Nuclear Experts Race to Stop Spread of Stuxnet Computer Worm*, Guardian (Sept. 25, 2010); Gregg Keizer, *Why Did Stuxnet Worm Spread*, Computer World (Oct. 1, 2010).

[111] Much of the following discussion comes from Ashley Deeks, *Will Cyber Autonomy Undercut Democratic Accountability?*, 96 Int'l L. Stud. 464 (2020).

[112] Crootof, *supra* note 108, at 81 (noting that "the speed of cyber will nearly always require that countermeasures be automated or autonomous to be effective").

[113] U.S. Dep't of Defense, Defense Science Board, *Summer Study on Autonomy* 92 (June 2016).

[114] *Id.* at 58.

[115] *Id.* at 4.

exploit existing software vulnerabilities."[116] Although the contract outlined defensive use cases, the system also "has the potential to be used for offensive hacking purposes."[117]

Second, deploying *offensive* cyber systems that take advantage of machine learning tools will make it easier for states to identify and exploit adversaries' cyber vulnerabilities.[118] These tools can identify patterns or abnormalities among vast quantities of data, which is helpful when trying to detect flaws in and infiltrate adversaries' cyber defenses. As James Johnson and Eleanor Krabill note, "The machine speed of AI-augmented cyber tools could enable even a low-skilled attacker to penetrate an adversary's cyber defenses. It could also use advanced persistent threat tools to find new vulnerabilities."[119]

Scharre contemplates a world in which offensive cyber operations go a step further. Instead of simply developing tools that actively manage implants or seek out enemy vulnerabilities, states might develop cyber tools that, once deployed, can fix themselves in the field and resist attack. He notes, "Adaptive malware that could rewrite itself to hide and avoid scrutiny at superhuman speeds could be incredibly virulent."[120] In the Defense Advanced Research Projects Agency's 2016 Grand Cyber Challenge, ForAllSecure's system was "capable of automatically healing a friendly system while simultaneously scanning and attacking vulnerabilities in adversary systems."[121] The U.S. National Security Agency reportedly sought to develop a system that would employ algorithms that constantly analyze metadata to detect malicious patterns, stop those attacks, and autonomously initiate retaliatory counterattacks.[122] Others envision decentralized swarms of autonomous cyber agents that could attack systems without the need for centralized command and control.[123]

---

[116] Chris Bing, *The Tech Behind the DARPA Grand Challenge Winner Will Now Be Used by the Pentagon*, CYBERSCOOP (Aug. 11, 2017).
[117] *Id.*
[118] United Nations Institute for Disarmament Research, *The Weaponization of Increasingly Autonomous Technologies: Autonomous Weapons and Cyber Operations* 4 (2017); Eric Messinger, *Is It Possible to Ban Autonomous Weapons in Cyberwar?*, JUST SECURITY (Jan. 15, 2015).
[119] James Johnson & Eleanor Krabill, *AI, Cyberspace, and Nuclear Weapons*, WAR ON THE ROCKS (Jan. 31, 2020).
[120] SCHARRE, *supra* note 107, at 226; *see also* Alessandro Guarino, *Autonomous Intelligent Agents in Cyber Offense*, 2013 5th International Conference on Cyber Conflict (envisioning autonomous agents that can identify "possible threats from defenders" and "prevent and react to countermeasures").
[121] Bing, *supra* note 116.
[122] Nicholas Sambaluk ed., *Conflict in the 21st Century: The Impact of Cyber Warfare, Social Media, and Technology* 55 (ABC-CLIO 2019).
[123] Guarino, *supra* note 120.

The United States is hardly the only state interested in bolstering the autonomy of its cyber operations. The United Kingdom has expressed an interest in pursuing autonomous cyberweapons as well.[124] Russian officials view artificial intelligence as "a key to dominating cyberspace and information operations," which suggests they intend to rely on certain levels of autonomy to achieve that goal.[125] China also appears committed to developing autonomous cyber capabilities.[126] Although fully autonomous offensive cyber systems may remain speculative today, they lie within the realm of possibility. It is therefore worth considering how these tools—or even systems with moderate levels of autonomy—might escalate low-level cyber exchanges into uses of force that implicate international and domestic laws, or leave states poised on the brink of armed conflict.

As the next chapter discusses, increased cyber autonomy has the potential to lead to increased and possibly unintentional hostilities among states. Even if an initial offensive cyber operation does not rise to the level of a use of force, some scholars believe that escalation is likely in the cyber domain.[127] And existing constraints on escalation may weaken when a state employs highly autonomous cyber systems. Those systems might by their nature be able to penetrate adversary systems more quickly and deftly than human-in-the-loop systems. Further, if clear signaling is a good way to avoid unintended escalation, it may be harder for a government's cyber operators to signal their intent to adversaries in advance of or during an autonomous cyber operation when those operations may happen without human preplanning and possibly without knowledge of the opponent's identity. Third, highly autonomous cyber tools may act less predictably than human-in-the-loop systems, especially when confronting other autonomous systems.

---

[124] United Kingdom, National Cyber Strategy 2022, ¶ 40.

[125] Peter Apps, *Are China, Russia Winning the AI Arms Race?*, REUTERS (Jan. 15, 2019).

[126] Bill Gertz, *US and China Racing to Weaponize AI*, ASIA TIMES (Nov. 7, 2019) (stating that "Chinese multi-domain AI warfare will expand the battlespace from traditional air, sea, and land, to ... cyberspace" and discussing military operations to include "cybertakeover").

[127] *See, e.g.*, Herbert Lin, *Escalation Dynamics and Conflict Termination in Cyberspace*, 6 STRATEGIC STUD. Q. 46 (2012); Flournoy, Haines & Chefitz, *supra* note 47, at 8 ("The potential for unintended engagement or escalation is even greater when U.S. and/or adversary systems have the sorts of advanced autonomy features that deep learning can enable, and their interaction cannot be studied or fully tested in advance of deployment.").

4. AI in Military Operations

AI/ML is poised to become an integral part of military operations. Machine learning algorithms hold significant promise in finding patterns or detecting anomalies in large quantities of data—something modern militaries have in spades. It is easy to envision how these tools will be useful when trying to predict what enemy forces plan to do next or how a particular person will behave, in light of millions of past examples of human behavior.[128] Every day, especially on the urban battlefield, militaries need to understand what they are seeing: Is that person holding a video camera or a rocket launcher?[129] Why is there very little pedestrian traffic in the market today? Is the person my team just detained likely to endanger our forces if released? Will a strike on that warehouse using a joint direct attack munition produce excessive collateral damage?[130] Each of these questions requires decision-making in the face of uncertainty.

We know that DOD already uses AI-powered computer vision tools to identify threatening activities—and potential targets—among thousands of hours of drone footage.[131] Militaries will also use AI/ML to enable pilotless underwater submarine hunter vessels; enable cooperative behavior among its systems (such as air and underwater drone swarms); and detect missile launches, among many other things.[132] At the 2022 Aspen Security Conference, the U.S. general in charge of the U.S. Air Force's Northern Command stated that the United States and Canada were investing in artificial intelligence systems to help identify possible intrusions into U.S. airspace.[133] In fall 2023, DOD announced its "Replicator" initiative, which is intended to "produce an array of thousands of air-, land- and sea-based

---

[128] Military technology has been transported into policing in the past. *See, e.g.*, Adam Goldman, *Trump Reverses Restrictions on Military Hardware for Police*, N.Y. TIMES (Aug. 28, 2017); Timothy Williams, *Facial Recognition Software Moves from Overseas Wars to Local Police*, N.Y. TIMES (Aug. 12, 2015).

[129] *See* Ashley Deeks, *Coding the Law of Armed Conflict: First Steps, in* THE FUTURE LAW OF ARMED CONFLICT (M. Waxman & T. Oakley eds., 2022).

[130] *See, e.g.*, Margarita Konaev, *With AI, We'll See Faster Fights, But Longer Wars*, WAR ON THE ROCKS (Oct. 29, 2019) (noting that "AI can help refine collateral damage assessments and enable commanders to make better and faster decisions about target selection and engagement"). In the United States, the level of expected civilian losses informs not only the underlying proportionality analysis but also how senior the decision maker must be.

[131] Daisuke Wakabayashi & Scott Shane, *Google Will Not Renew Pentagon Contract That Upset Employees*, N.Y. TIMES (June 1, 2018); Sayler, *supra* note 33, at 10.

[132] For missile launch, see Horowitz, *supra* note 18. For drone swarms, see Sayler, *supra* note 33, at 12.

[133] Julian Barnes, Helene Cooper & Edward Wong, *What's Going on Up There? Theories But No Answers in Shootdowns of Mystery Craft*, N.Y. TIMES (Feb. 12, 2023).

artificial-intelligence systems that are intended to be 'small, smart, cheap'"
and to have those systems produced and delivered by August 2025.[134] DOD
also is considering "space-based autonomous systems that would be so numerous they would be difficult for an adversary to destroy and autonomous
systems that could defend against incoming missiles."[135] The U.S. government may already be using autonomous weapons (which would rely on
these types of algorithms) in contexts in which action is purely defensive and
civilians are not at risk.[136]

AI/ML is likely also to play a prominent role in DOD's command and con-
trol processes. DOD has announced that it is pursuing a "Joint All-Doman
Command and Control" (JADC2) Strategy. According to DOD's summary,
"JADC2 developed capabilities will leverage Artificial Intelligence and Machine
Learning to help accelerate the commander's decision cycle. Automatic
machine-to-machine transactions will extract, consolidate and process massive
amounts of data and information directly from the sensing infrastructure."[137]
DOD also strives to "better integrate conventional and nuclear C2 processes
and procedures."[138]

More controversially, DOD might begin to deploy deepfakes as part of its
"military information support operations," which it defines as "planned operations to convey selected information and indicators to foreign audiences
to influence their emotions, motives, objective reasoning, and ultimately the
behavior of foreign governments, organizations, groups, and individuals in a
manner favorable to the originator's objectives."[139] One news report indicates
that U.S. Special Operations Command is "gearing up to conduct internet
propaganda and deception campaigns online using deepfake videos."[140]
Critics note that, "by casting doubt on the credibility of all content and information," such operations "ultimately erode the foundation or democracy
itself" and argue that if the military plans to use them, "their use needs to be

---

[134] Nancy Yousef & Michael Gordon, *Pentagon Plans Vast AI Fleet to Counter China Threat*, WALL
St. J. (Sept. 6, 2023); Connor O'Brien, *Pentagon Bets on Quick Production of Autonomous Systems to
Counter China*, POLITICO (Aug. 28, 2023).

[135] Yousef & Gordon, *supra* note 134.

[136] Anderson & Waxman, *supra* note 18, at 388 (stating that such weapons are generally "limited to
use in defensive contexts against other machines and are deployed in environments such as the air or
sea in which civilian risk is very small").

[137] U.S. Dep't of Defense, *Summary of the Joint All-Domain Command and Control Strategy* 5
(Mar. 2022).

[138] U.S. Dep't of Defense, *DoD Announces Release of JADC2 Implementation Plan* (Mar. 17, 2022).

[139] U.S. Dep't of Defense, Joint Pub. 3-13.2. *See also* Sayler, *supra* note 33, at 12.

[140] San Biddle, *U.S. Special Forces Want to Use Deepfakes for Psy-Ops*, INTERCEPT (Mar. 6, 2023).

subject to review and oversight."[141] This criticism is salient, particularly because it came to light in 2022 that Special Operations Command had been using fake Twitter/X and Facebook accounts to spread phony news items, including a claim that Iran was stealing organs of dead Afghan refugees.[142] That revelation prompted an internal DOD review that led to a new requirement that senior DOD, CIA, and State Department officials sign off on these types of clandestine online operations.[143] Those operations were not ML-driven; one might worry that ML-driven versions of such operations might be even more pernicious.

To date, DOD has put ethics at the forefront of its AI policies, emphasizing that the United States should not lose sight of our ethical values just to maintain a technological edge. When the Deputy Secretary of Defense signed out DOD's Responsible Artificial Intelligence Strategy and Implementation Pathway, she wrote, "To ensure that our citizens, warfighters, and leaders can trust the outputs of DoD AI capabilities, DoD must demonstrate that our military's steadfast commitment to lawful and ethical behavior apply when designing, developing, testing, procuring, deploying, and using AI."[144] However, that policy may be hard to sustain, "particularly if an enemy's automated systems are making such judgments at much faster than human speed."[145] Richard Danzig argues, "You can claim the 'human in the loop' still has the final say, but if the machine is providing them all the data for their decision, they're not really an independent check on its operations."[146] As a result, today's bright-line rules for AI during combat will increasingly come under pressure.

Most of these examples are of tools that militaries would use during an armed conflict. More speculatively, states may also use AI to help anticipate attacks by other states, including incoming missile or even nuclear attacks. The UN Charter recognizes that states may lawfully use force in self-defense if they suffer an armed attack, and many think that a state may use force to defeat an imminent armed attack too. A state that fears that it may be the

[141] *Id.*

[142] Ellen Nakashima, *Pentagon Opens Sweeping Review of Clandestine Psychological Operations*, WASH. POST (Sept. 19, 2022).

[143] Ellen Nakashima, *Clandestine Online Operations Now Require Sign-Offs by Senior Officials*, WASH. POST (Dec. 5, 2023).

[144] U.S. Dep't of Defense, *Responsible Artificial Intelligence Strategy and Implementation Pathway* (June 2022).

[145] Apps, *supra* note 125.

[146] Sydney Freedberg Jr., *Why a "Human in the Loop" Can't Control AI: Richard Danzig*, BREAKING DEF. (June 1, 2018).

subject of an armed attack will want to understand the probability that a threatened attack will manifest in actual violence. That state will also want to understand which actor attacked it, whether it needs to use force in response to that attack, and whether its response would be proportional to the attack. In situations such as these, it appears increasingly likely that states will seek to use machine learning technology to strengthen their decision-making processes, to react to attacks, predict those attacks, and develop suitable responses.[147]

The United States has plenty of company in developing and using AI/ML in its systems and even deploying autonomous military tools. According to the Israeli Defense Forces, Israel uses AI to "assist its offensive decision-making, for example to determine if a target is a military or a civilian one."[148] News reports describe an AI-driven Israeli targeting system called the Gospel, a "target-creation platform" that Israel is using to identify targets in its conflict in Gaza.[149] South Korea has long had an AI-guided system to guard the demilitarized zone,[150] and it appears to have developed an air-to-ground missile system that can identify and target fixed objects without an operator's intervention.[151] Russia possesses autonomous underwater vehicles as well as drone swarms.[152] And China's People's Liberation Army is pursuing unmanned autonomous weapons; processing large quantities of information through machine learning (based on information from, among other sources, undersea sensors); using AI to accelerate military decision-making; and using AI for "cognitive warfare."[153] In sum, there is a huge amount of AI/ML-related military activity happening behind the veil of secrecy, with only small parts of the iceberg revealed.

---

[147] *See* Ashley Deeks, Noam Lubell & Daragh Murray, *Machine Learning, Artificial Intelligence, and the Use of Force by States*, 10 J. NAT'L SECURITY L. & POL'Y 1, 4 (2019).

[148] Tal Mimran & Lior Weinstein, *The IDF Introduces Artificial Intelligence to the Battlefield—A New Frontier?*, ARTICLES OF WAR (Mar. 1, 2023); Marissa Newman, *Israel Quietly Embeds AI Systems in Deadly Military Operations*, BLOOMBERG (July 16, 2023).

[149] Harry Davies, Bethan McKernan & Dan Sabbagh, *"The Gospel": How Israel Uses AI to Select Bombing Targets in Gaza*, GUARDIAN (Dec. 1, 2023).

[150] Inder Singh Bisht, *South Korea to Deploy Rail-Mounted Robot and AI Surveillance on Border*, DEFENSE POST (June 17, 2021).

[151] Rahul Udoshi, *South Korea Completes Development of Cheongeom ATGM*, JANES (Dec. 21, 2022).

[152] Mark Episkopos, *Unmanned Underwater Vehicles Could Augment the Russian Navy's Fleet*, NAT'L INTEREST (Jan. 9, 2022).

[153] Koichiro Takagi, *Can China Build a World-Class Military Using Artificial Intelligence?*, REAL CLEAR DEFENSE (Feb. 7, 2023).

E. The Algorithmic Black Box

This large and diverse set of algorithms renders AI/ML-enabled national security operations a black box to several different audiences. Where the public learns about them (as with some DHS efforts discussed previously), the operations themselves are not inside the national security black box, but algorithms behind those operations are a black box to the general public and, more specifically, to those directly affected by them, such as those who have been placed on an algorithmically created no-fly list. They will be an algorithmic black box to many of the government's senior policymakers, who will be asked to decide which types of AI are acceptable for the government to develop and to make decisions based on AI-driven recommendations. The systems will be a black box to many government lawyers whose clients ask them whether it is lawful to make a decision based on a series of AI/ML recommendations or to use an autonomous system for a particular task. They will be a black box to the U.S. government's foreign allies, with which the United States undertakes joint military operations or shares threat intelligence, such as suspicions about who is a terrorist or a spy. And they will even be a black box to many of the military and intelligence employees who use these tools in their daily work.

Recall the opening hypothetical scenario of this book. It should cause us to ask a range of questions to plumb the nature of the algorithmic black box: Did the algorithms weigh lawful factors in concluding that the DOD target was the number three operative in al Qaeda? How reliable are the facial recognition systems that DOD has embedded in the drone swarms? How confident is the military or the intelligence community about the quality of the data on which the algorithms were trained? Is it lawful (under both domestic law and international law) to rely on an autonomous drone swarm to execute the operation? These are some examples of the algorithmic black box challenges associated with the AI tools that our national security agencies will deploy.

1. Challenges to Public Law Values

As we saw in Chapter 1, when we worry about secret national security operations, what we are really concerned about is that their secret nature makes it easier for the government to establish programs that are unlawful or that

reflect bad policy choices; that it is difficult to hold the decision makers behind those programs accountable; and that secrecy helps the government
avoid explaining and defending its choices, even to an appropriate group of
overseers. The algorithmic black box raises similar concerns for each of these
public law values: it is possible that the U.S. government will—intentionally
or inadvertently—allow the development and use of AI tools that are unlawful or incompetent or that advance bad policy, and do so in a way that
makes it difficult to assess who to hold accountable or to force the U.S. government to defend its use. This is not to argue that the U.S. government
makes flawless decisions without algorithms (it does not) or that historians
are always able to unpack the precise reasons why decision makers made
the choices they did using non-algorithmic tools (they are not). Nor is it to
argue that the use of AI/ML tools will necessarily make government officials'
decisions worse. Indeed, the hope is that the use of these tools will generally
make their decisions better. But it is to argue that adding AI/ML into the
decision-making process will make it even harder to assess the government's
compliance with public law values.

Legality. The use of algorithmic black boxes in national security operations makes it harder for the public and government officials themselves to
assess the operations' domestic and international legality. Consider the ways
in which the government may use national security algorithms to identify
individuals for prosecution or detention—and thus engage in deprivations
of liberty. DHS may engage in deportations based on AI/ML algorithms.
The Department of Defense may use predictive algorithms to identify
individuals as posing an "imperative threat to security," which is grounds for
detention during an armed conflict.[154] The CIA very likely will use AI/ML
algorithms to track individuals' patterns of life as a way to identify members
of terrorist groups and thus render them targets for airstrikes. The standard
of confidence that the CIA must meet is presumably identified in a classified executive branch document, but how will the government translate
an English-language standard into a qualitative confidence level? Courts
usually provide some checks on executive branch action in the criminal
prosecution and deportation contexts, and so they will have to put the government through its paces on its algorithmic prosecution and deportation

---

[154] *See generally* Deeks, *supra* note 4.

decisions.[155] But for decisions about detention and targeting overseas, especially during wartime, the courts play little role, as Chapter 1 noted.

Another area in which black box algorithms may complicate legal questions is with regard to privacy harms. The United States today obtains permission from the Foreign Intelligence Surveillance Court to conduct electronic surveillance inside the United States on an individual where there is probable cause that the person is an "agent of a foreign power." If the United States uses unreliable algorithms that erroneously identify someone as a foreign agent based on "pattern of life" data collected from a range of sensors, the government nevertheless may request and the FISC may authorize that surveillance if they fail to realize that the algorithms are flawed. Or perhaps those algorithms took into account impermissible facts (such as the person's race) in developing predictions. Identifying that legal violation will be hard.[156]

The use of black box algorithms raises systemic legal questions as well, such as problems related to congressional control of war-initiation decisions. A use of autonomous cyber algorithms may mean that the United States enters (or initiates) an armed conflict without the proper constitutional actors (i.e., the President and Congress) affirmatively knowing or choosing to do so.[157] Section B in Chapter 3 takes this up in more detail.

On the international law front, the UN Charter sets out rules for the use of force against (or in) other states. If an AI/ML algorithm seems trustworthy but is flawed, the United States might erroneously resort to force in a situation in which it was not necessary to do so (or was impermissible to do so as a matter of international law). As Michael Horwitz notes, "the desire to fight at machine speed with autonomous systems, while making a military more effective in a conflict, could increase crisis instability. As countries fear losing conflicts faster, it could generate escalation pressure, including an increased incentive for first strikes."[158] U.S. adversaries that are less worried about ex ante legal compliance and ex post condemnation for errors may be more

---

[155] For a discussion of challenges in the criminal justice system, even when the prosecutions are public, see Brandon Garrett & Cynthia Rudin, *The Right to a Glass Box: Rethinking the Use of Artificial Intelligence in Criminal Justice*, 109 CORNELL L. REV. 561 (2024) (arguing that allowing AI secrecy in the criminal system is a poor policy choice).

[156] CHESTERMAN, *supra* note 29, at 164.

[157] *See* Deeks, *supra* note 111.

[158] Horowitz, *supra* note 18, at 766. *See also* SCHARRE, *supra* note 107, at 317 ("[T]here are scenarios in which the introduction of autonomous strike systems could result in temporary loss of high-level control over operations, and unwanted escalation.").

even inclined to use such algorithms, notwithstanding uncertainty about their quality.

Competence. The use of algorithmic black boxes, whether inside or outside the national security black box, will complicate the government's own ability to pursue competent policies, as well as its ability to understand after the fact how well it performed. Relatedly, it will complicate the public's ability to perceive how competently the government is acting.

One issue is the decision to use an AI/ML system in the first place. Let's assume that senior government officials will ask basic questions about the results of the testing, evaluation, verification, and validation of the system— including "How accurate are the system's results today?" and "Is the system sufficient for its intended use?" But the complex nature of AI/ML and neural nets will render it difficult for those leaders to probe beneath the surface to understand the open questions and real risks that may accompany the system's use. The leaders might therefore agree to authorize a system prematurely or without full appreciation of potential costs.

Another issue involves the accuracy of the system. Where the system's predictions or decisions are immediately testable, government users will be able to evaluate its accuracy quite easily. An ML-driven search for the leader of ISIS either helps the government find him or it does not. But many national security questions are almost impossible to answer empirically, so it will be hard to know (at least in the short term) whether the system is right or wrong. As a European think tank wrote, "[I]t is considerably harder for humans to anticipate or detect mistakes made by AI systems—including ones caused by adversarial action such as sabotage – than those made by traditional computers."[159] A related challenge is the "value alignment problem": it is important but difficult to ensure that AI systems do not act in ways that are inimical to the values that humans intend them to follow.[160]

The AI black box will also complicate ex post assessments of government action, which can be very helpful in improving government processes and future decision-making. Today, where the government has made a strategic error (such as a seriously flawed prediction about what another state will do or a mistaken shoot-down of a civilian aircraft) and wants to understand why that error occurred, it often undertakes an after-action review. The black box

---

[159] Ulrike Franke & Paola Sartori, *Machine Politics: Europe and the AI Revolution* 14, Euro. Council on Foreign Rel. (July 11, 2019).
[160] *The Value Alignment Problem*, Leverhulme Ctr. for the Future of Intel.

nature of AI/ML systems will make this kind of review harder. Assume, for example, that the military kills someone based on an AI/ML recommendation and then decides to open an investigation of the killing. Not only would it require on-the-ground research of the type that the Center for Civilians in Conflict and the military itself conducts to assess that the person was not a permissible target,[161] but determining how the error occurred would also require unpacking the algorithmic black box to see which step in the process (algorithmic weight, flawed data, hacking[162]) caused the error. The same is true for AI/ML recommendations that prompt the government to track John Smith as a spy when he is not one, or otherwise lead the government to take action based on a false positive prediction that it fails to detect is wrong. It will be difficult for the algorithms' users—as well as those affected by the algorithms' recommendations—to check for mistakes or challenge errors in the data inputs or in the algorithms' calculations, and thus to assess the government's competence as expressed through the algorithm.

Finally, the costs of incompetent government actions in the AI/ML space could be high. The government might lose physical control of the technology, including on the battlefield, and risk having an advanced system being turned against U.S. actors.[163] It might use military algorithms that undercut its ability to terminate an armed conflict, even if the government sought to do so.[164] Or the government might feel pressured (by Congress or by the capabilities of adversaries) to adopt AI/ML-driven systems too quickly, even if it is uncertain about the systems' reliability, which will be especially dangerous if those systems are armed.[165]

Some of these potential competency problems will produce wrong outcomes without harmful effect: using ML to process a fire hose of data on

---

[161] *See* U.S. Dep't of Defense, *Civilian Harm Mitigation and Response Action Plan Fact Sheet* (Aug. 25, 2022) (describing how DOD will mitigate civilian harm during military operations and improve its ability to assess civilian harm resulting from those operations).

[162] Horowitz, *supra* note 18, at 771 ("Even if commanders understand how the systems are supposed to work, and deploy them appropriately, the complexity of the programming raises the prospect of unintended behavior and accidents.").

[163] Richard Danzig, *Technology Roulette: Managing Loss of Control as Many Militaries Pursue Technological Superiority* 6, CTR. FOR NEW AM. SECURITY (June 2018).

[164] SCHARRE, *supra* note 107, at 299 ("If policymakers do not have very high control over their forces, because attack orders cannot be recalled or communication links are severed . . . , policymakers may not be able to de-escalate a conflict even if they wanted to.").

[165] Sheppard, *supra* note 26, at 4. *See also* Horowitz, *supra* note 18, at 766; Paul Lushenko, *AI and the Future of Warfare*, BULL. OF ATOMIC SCI. (Nov. 29, 2023) (surveying U.S. military officers, finding that officers support AI-enhanced military technologies more than they trust them, and concluding that "US officers may feel obliged to embrace projected forms of warfare that go against their own preferences and attitudes").

Twitter/X to identify ISIS sympathizers and direct anti-ISIS propaganda at them is unlikely to produce tangible physical harm, and probably little intangible harm either. Using Defense Department databases and an algorithm to predict which of its forces are at highest risk for suicide and targeting them for treatment has few downsides. In these types of cases, the computer system might be right or wrong, but will generally not produce actual, irreversible harms in the real world. But flawed algorithms that lead to detention, no-fly listings, surveillance, kinetic targeting, or uses of interstate force will not self-correct.

Accountability. National security algorithms also will foster confusion about who to hold responsible for an algorithm's mistake. Because the systems are complex and opaque, they provide "cover" for human decision makers, who can point to the systems as the cause of flawed outcomes.[166] This has been a persistent critique of black box algorithms, with only limited progress made on how to ensure appropriate accountability for their use. One approach, which Volvo has taken, is for the algorithm's manufacturer to accept full responsibility for any accidents flowing from a system's algorithm.[167] Another approach is to segregate out the different steps in algorithmic decision-making (providing data, building the algorithm, training the algorithm, testing, use) and assign an actor responsibility for each step.[168] But the systems may not be amenable to such clear-cut segregation. A third approach would be for the government to establish clear principles of command responsibility for uses of AI-driven systems. Yet another approach is to render the black box itself less opaque, which the next subsection discusses.

Justification for decisions. For many of the same reasons that it is hard to hold government decision makers accountable for the use of and reliance on algorithms, it is hard for government officials to produce transparent, explainable decisions to their political leadership, Congress, the courts, and the public—even when they want to. (The Chivers FOIA case discussed previously illustrates a case in which the government didn't want to!) Assume that in a typical interaction between Congress and the executive branch, a U.S. Treasury official testifying before Congress could explain to the members on the committee precisely what factors her agency took into account and

---

[166] *See* CHESTERMAN, *supra* note 29, at 10.
[167] Jim Gorzelany, *Volvo Will Accept Liability for Its Self-Driving Cars*, FORBES (Oct. 9, 2015) (quoting Volvo's president as stating that the company would "accept full liability whenever one of its cars is in autonomous mode").
[168] *See* Lorna McGregor, Daragh Murray & Vivian Ng, *International Human Rights Law as a Framework for Algorithmic Accountability*, 68 INT'L & COMP. L.Q. 309 (2019).

what legal parameters it worked within when it was formulating sanctions against a Russian oligarch. In contrast, in a case in which Treasury used an AI/ML algorithm to identify a set of sanctions targets based on predicted behavior and associations with others, it would be considerably more complicated for the official to explain to Congress which factors the algorithm took into account in identifying a target; what data the system was trained on; what confidence level the algorithm achieves; and how, if at all, the recommendations incorporate the legal standards that Treasury must apply when imposing sanctions. And while in this example the Treasury official is willing to provide information to Congress, "[a]t its most venal, opaqueness provides cover for the intentional manipulation of outcomes or to thwart investigation."[169]

2. Could "Explainable AI" Solve the Problem?

A core theme of this chapter is the opacity of many AI/ML algorithms—the very characteristic that creates the "algorithmic black box." One obvious way to reduce this problem is to open up the workings of these algorithms for people to see, making the algorithms' operations explainable or at least observable. Explainable AI (xAI) encompasses a range of efforts to explain—or help humans interpret—how a particular machine learning model reaches its conclusion. The concept of an algorithmic explanation "has come to refer to providing insight into the internal state of an algorithm, or to human-understandable approximations of the algorithm."[170] xAI provides a variety of benefits: it can foster trust between humans and the system, identify cases in which the system is producing results that are biased or unfair, and bolster our own knowledge of how the world works. xAI is not without costs, however. Most significantly, making an algorithm explainable may decrease its accuracy. xAI may also stifle innovation, force developers to reveal trade secrets, and impose monetary costs because it can be expensive to build.[171]

xAI can take a variety of forms, and computer scientists continue to devote much time to developing new and better forms of it.[172] Some machine

---

[169] CHESTERMAN, *supra* note 29, at 9.
[170] Sandra Wachter, Brent Mittelstadt & Chris Russell, *Counterfactual Explanations Without Opening the Black Box: Automated Decisions and the GDPR*, 31 HARV. J.L. & TECH. 841, 845 (2018).
[171] Ashley Deeks, *The Judicial Demand for Explainable AI*, 119 COLUM. L. REV. 1829 (2019).
[172] This discussion is drawn from Deeks, *id.*

learning models are built to be intrinsically explainable, but these models, which tend to take the form of decision trees or linear models rather than deep neural nets, tend to make less accurate predictions as a result. Another set of models does not attempt to actually explain the inner workings of (that is, the reasoning of) the machine learning algorithm, but tries to provide relevant information to the algorithm's user about how the model works. One such approach is to describe the model from the outside, explaining the creator's intentions behind the modeling process, the family of model the system uses, the parameters the creators specified before training the system, qualitative descriptions of the input data the creator used to train the model, how the model performed on new data, and how the creators tested the data for undesirable properties. This version of xAI basically constitutes a thick description of the parts of the model that are knowable.

Yet another approach tries to empower the individual who is the subject of the algorithmic decision—a "subject-centric" approach. This could involve, for example, providing information about the characteristics of individuals who received similar decisions or using counterfactuals. People who want to understand which factors may have been most salient in leading the algorithm to make a particular recommendation or prediction about them may, using that same algorithm, tweak the input factors to test how much a given factor mattered in the original recommendation. For example, an algorithm that deems someone who was convicted of an offense to be at high risk of reoffending could be tested with counterfactuals to see whether the recommendation would have been different if the person were ten years older or had one fewer arrest. None of these approaches requires "the data subject to understand any of the internal logic of a model in order to make use of it."[173] These approaches can be particularly useful for individuals who want to understand how they might achieve a different outcome or which factors the model weighed most heavily.

An alternative to these "external" approaches to xAI is a form of xAI that attempts to explain the model's internal reasoning. The most obvious way to do so is to reveal the source code for the machine learning model, but that approach will often prove unsatisfactory, both because of the way machine learning works and because most people will not be able to understand the code. More nuanced alternatives exist, however. One approach is to create a second system alongside the original "black box" model, sometimes called a

---

[173] Wachter, Mittelstadt & Russell, *supra* note 170, at 851.

"surrogate model." A surrogate model works by analyzing featured input and output pairs but does not have access to the internal weights of the model itself. For instance, scholars constructed a decision tree that effectively mirrored the computations of a black box model that predicted patients' risk for diabetes. The decision tree allowed computer scientists to track which factors (such as cholesterol level or nicotine dependence) the black box model weighed in making its risk assessments. These systems closely approximate the predictions made by an underlying model, while being interpretable.

Explanations are not one-size-fits-all. A military computer operator may require a different type of explanation than a military commander would, and a senior executive branch official might want yet a third type of explanation. As the United Kingdom's Royal Society wrote, "[S]ystem developers might require technical details about how an AI system functions, while regulators might require assurance about how data is processed, and those subject to a decision might want to understand which factors led to an output that affected them. A single decision or recommendation might therefore need to be explained in multiple ways, reflecting the needs of different audiences and the issues at play in different situations."[174] Any pursuit of xAI must be sensitive to the audience seeking the explanation.

xAI could help address some of the uncertainties about whether a given use of national security AI tool complies with public law values. Further, reducing the opacity of AI/ML tools is an important way to resolve many of the other concerns about the operations of AI tools themselves. That is, if an AI/ML tool is explainable or interpretable, we can explore its accuracy and biases and have a better sense of whether its predictions and recommendations fall within the legal framework within which its developer situated it. If an algorithm seems to be skewing in an inaccurate direction, xAI could help the government correct the algorithm rather than jettison it entirely, as it might have to do under an approach that simply assesses the output. Testing and verification of algorithms and their outputs is critical and will help assess the algorithms' quality, but it will not solve the black box problem entirely.

Some experts are skeptical about the possibility of obtaining useful explanations for deep learning models. As former U.S. Defense Secretary Ash Carter notes, "These computational methods make literal transparency, normally the starting point for ethical accountability, completely impractical. It is usually impossible to 'deconvolve' the series of steps leading to the

---

[174] Royal Society, *Explainable AI: The Basics* 19 (2019).

inferences made by AI."[175] Other skeptics of xAI argue that we should simply measure the reliability of the output rather than worry about what happens inside the black box. This school of thought would favor simply auditing the outcomes of the machine learning system, parsing the system's decisions or recommendations for appearances of bias or error. One problem with basing one's confidence in the algorithm on the accuracy of its output, though, is that in a range of cases there will be no one "right" answer. If an IC algorithm predicts that Country X is going to attack the United States in the next two weeks and that attack does not come to pass, the IC will now have a data point that will contribute to its judgment about the algorithm's accuracy. But a prediction that person Y is likely to commit a hostile act in the next day and that he should therefore be detained is harder to test. In particular, if the government detains him on the basis of the algorithm, it cannot test the counterfactual of whether he would have committed such an act if the government had not detained him.

Finally, even where certain systems today contain xAI tools, individuals are often not using those tools to obtain explanations.[176] At best, xAI is a work in progress.[177] As Part II of this book discusses, the government—and the companies building algorithms for the government—should continue to pursue advances in xAI and promote its use, but xAI alone will not resolve our public law values concerns.

---

[175] Ash Carter, *The Moral Dimension of AI-Assisted Decision-Making*, 151 Daedalus 299 (Spring 2022).

[176] *See* Tobias Clement et al., *XAIR: A Systematic Metareview of Explainable AI (XAI) Aligned to the Software Development Process*, 5(1) Machine Learning & Knowledge Extraction 78, 97–98 (2023) ("To explore how organizations deploy explainability methods, Bhatt et al conducted fifty interviews with different stakeholders, e.g., data scientists, managers, and domain experts. They found that the majority of deployments are not for end users affected by the model but rather for data scientists, who use explainability to debug the model itself. Accordingly, there is a large gap between explainability in practice and the goal of transparency, since explanations primarily serve internal stakeholders rather than external ones.").

[177] For a summary of DARPA's work on xAI, see David Gunning et al., *DARPA's Explainable AI (XAI) Program: A Retrospective*, Applied AI Letters (Dec. 4, 2021) ("Today, we have a more nuanced, less dramatic, and, perhaps, more accurate understanding of AI than we had in 2015. . . . There is certainly more work to be done, especially as new AI techniques are developed that will continue to need explanation.").

3

The Double Black Box

A. Introduction

This chapter pulls together the concerns raised in Chapters 1 and 2 to illustrate how national security AI (NSAI) doubles down on the oversight challenges that already attach independently to national security decisions and to the use of AI tools. The difficulties in identifying unlawful executive branch activities will be amplified by the challenges of understanding whether the use of a particular AI tool complies with the law. The difficulty in obtaining enough information to evaluate whether particular national security policy choices are optimal will be compounded by the difficulty in understanding the quality of AI recommendations and predictions that inform those choices. The difficulty in deciding who is responsible for particular illegal or ill-advised policy choices will be amplified by the challenge of determining who is responsible for significant algorithmic errors. And the ease with which the Executive can avoid defending its national security decisions due to classification will be amplified by the nontransparency and inexplicability of AI algorithms.

All of this means that the checks and balances on the Executive's national security activities will become even more tenuous when it comes to NSAI. Congress and the courts, which already struggle to oversee national security policies and operations, will now have to struggle to understand advanced technologies as well.[1] It also will be harder for extraconstitutional actors to serve as supplemental checks: leaks of algorithmic code will mean less to the public than leaks of shoddy or misguided written policies.[2] Government

---

[1] *See* Cecilia Kang & Adam Satariano, *As A.I. Booms, Lawmakers Struggle to Understand the Technology*, N.Y. TIMES (Mar. 3, 2023) ("[E]ven as lawmakers put a spotlight on the technology, few are taking action on it. No bill has been proposed to protect individuals or thwart the development of A.I.'s potentially dangerous aspects. And legislation introduced in recent years to curb A.I. applications like facial recognition have withered in Congress. The problem is that most lawmakers do not even know what A.I. is . . . ."). However, the emergence of large-language models and deepfakes have given Congress increased motivation to understand the technology.

[2] Contrast the PowerPoint slides that Edward Snowden leaked; putting aside the virtues or vices of the leak, the material that he leaked was at least digestible to journalists and ultimately the public. *See* Barton Gellman & Laura Poitras, *U.S., British Intelligence Mining Data from Nine U.S. Internet Companies in Broad Secret Program*, WASH. POST (June 7, 2013).

lawyers may find it harder to give clear legal guidance as agencies' computer scientists try to translate legal constraints into code. In short, we are doubling down on existing oversight challenges as the use of AI tools grows. This poses real difficulties for democracies that seek to further their officials' legal compliance, conduct robust oversight of executive actors, and hold the government accountable for its mistakes. Indeed, without checks, the double black box might further empower the government to make costly mistakes that do not come to light until serious damage has been done.

Not every player in the national security ecosystem will experience the double black box in the same way. It is more accurate to think of the double black box as existing on a sliding scale, with the opacity of the box most intense for actors who lack access to classified programs and have little expertise with the technology behind AI systems—that is, the general public. For the public, for many in Congress, and for most judges, the system will be a nearly complete black box: those actors will not know what AI tools the military and intelligence community are using, where, in what quantity, for what purposes, at what level of confidence, and with what level of explainability.

Then there will actors with security clearances that give them access to a wide range of classified programs, but who have only limited time and expertise to understand how AI systems operate. These include high-level executive branch policymakers—such as cabinet secretaries and the National Security Advisor—and members of Congress who sit on the armed services and intelligence committees. For them, the national security black box is less opaque but the AI black box is still powerful. Then there will be another set of executive branch actors—the lawyers and inspectors general—who may be aware of the basic parameters of the government's AI systems but who may not have clearances that entitle them to know details about particular systems and who would have difficulty understanding those systems even if they had access. They face a relatively opaque double black box, with some of the contents' contours vaguely visible.

There also may be whistleblowers or leakers who learn about AI programs or AI-driven outcomes that they perceive to be problematic, though they may not understand the systems that produced those effects. For them, the double black box is a gauzy veil. Finally, there will be military and intelligence community officials (and some government contractors) who know precisely what AI/ML systems the government possesses and generally understand how those systems work. It is for them that the double black box is least opaque, though, as discussed in Chapter 2, even they will not necessarily understand the basis of the systems' specific decisions or recommendations. These differently situated actors will face different advantages and disadvantages as we think about how their actions contribute to or help un-pack the double black box.

This chapter frames the double black box problem by considering the four key public law values discussed thus far and explaining how the intersection of national security and AI complicates the ability of both our traditional and nontraditional checks to assess whether the government is complying with these values. It then uses autonomous cyber operations as a case study to illustrate how the double black box will operate in practice, particularly in relation to the Executive's primary check: Congress.

B. Losing the Thread on Public Law Values

National security AI further complicates the roles of our secrecy surrogates. It doubles down on the same things that we already find problematic in national security generally: the lack of transparency; the difficulty that courts and Congress have in providing effective oversight; the breadth of delegations from Congress to the Executive and the Executive's broad flexibility in implementing those delegations; and limited requirements for the government to give reasons for its decisions.[3] When national security agencies are using AI tools, legal compliance becomes harder because AI tools shift power away from agency lawyers to engineers. Accountability becomes harder because AI systems create significant ambiguity about who is responsible for algorithmic errors.[4] And it is harder to force the Executive to justify its decisions and give reasons for its choices when the systems it is using do not easily reveal their decisional pathways. Further, at least at first blush, characteristics of AI reduce the potency of some of the checks on the national security Executive, including leaks and interagency tensions.

---

[3] *See* Ashley Deeks, *Secret Reason-Giving*, 129 YALE L.J. 612 (2020) (describing situations in which the government is required to give reasons).

[4] *See, e.g.,* Danielle Citron, *Technological Due Process*, 85 WASH. U. L. REV. 1249, 1253 (2008) (noting that some of the government's automated systems "adjudicate in secret, while others lack recordkeeping audit trails, making review of the laws and facts supporting a system's decisions impossible").

1. Legality

One of the most salient aspects of a democracy is that government officials, like the citizens they serve, must comply with the law. Executive branch lawyers play a key role in ensuring that this tenet is embedded in government policy and practice. Agency clients—at least those who understand the value of legal advice—consult with their general counsel's offices. Agencies and the White House seek the views of the Justice Department's Office of Legal Counsel to obtain definitive interpretations of the U.S. Constitution and statutes. Congress may call agency general counsels to testify about legal policy decisions made by those agencies. And nongovernmental actors often sue the government to enforce its obligation to comply with the law. Executive lawyering plays a particularly important role when it comes to national security operations, where courts and outside litigation play less of a role in shaping government compliance with the law.[5]

As Chapter 1 discussed, secrecy can compromise a government's rigorous commitment to acting lawfully. When only a small group of government officials is aware of a national security operation, that necessarily means that an even smaller group of lawyers will be aware of it. In the operation to capture or kill Osama bin Laden—an activity that was extremely sensitive and the outcome of which would be very high-profile—only four lawyers in the whole government advised on the legality of the plan.[6] The *New York Times* reported:

> Stretching sparse precedents, the lawyers worked in intense secrecy. Fearing leaks, the White House would not let them consult aides or even the administration's top lawyer, Attorney General Eric H. Holder Jr. They did their own research, wrote memos on highly secure laptops and traded drafts hand-delivered by trusted couriers.[7]

The smaller the circle of lawyers, the more limited the number of perspectives and the ability to test and "red team" legal arguments.[8] As a result, it is easier to get the law wrong or to embrace strained legal arguments. OLC's notorious

---

[5] Oona Hathaway, *National Security Lawyering in the Post-War Era: Can Law Constrain Power?*, 68 UCLA L. REV. 2, 7 (2021).

[6] Charlie Savage, *How 4 Federal Lawyers Paved the Way to Kill Osama bin Laden*, N.Y. TIMES (Oct. 28, 2015).

[7] *Id.*

[8] *See* David Pozen, *Deep Secrecy*, 62 STAN. L. REV. 257, 334–35 (2009).

torture memos suffered from this problem; the memos invoked areas of law that were inapplicable to the question at hand, failed to properly consider separation of powers issues,[9] and generally would have contained more persuasive analysis had they not been drafted in such deep secrecy. When those memos became more widely accessible to other government officials (including lawyers from other agencies), the Justice Department withdrew them.[10]

Executive lawyers are hardly the only actors whose behavior matters here. The secrecy of national security operations means that many members of Congress do not know about those operations and therefore cannot challenge their legality. And actors outside the government—individuals, companies, nongovernmental organizations—are even less likely to know about them and therefore cannot sue to challenge the government's legal compliance in court.[11]

Adding AI to the mix may further weaken the public's confidence that the Executive is acting consistent with the Constitution and statutes, as well as international law. From an executive branch lawyer's perspective, it will be hard to trace what data the government's computer scientists are training national security algorithms on, and even harder to trace what data a defense contractor used to train algorithms it sold to the government. This means it will be difficult to assess whether any of that data was wrongfully obtained (because, for example, the government collected it without a warrant though a warrant was required) or contains information that the government undertook not to collect as a policy matter.[12] Compared to a lawyer's engagement with a human policymaker, it is harder for the lawyers to know what factors an algorithm is weighing as it formulates predictions, or whether the system has learned to make predictions based on hidden hallucinations. Imagine if the lawyers assessing the legality of the bin Laden raid also had to take into account the fact that DOD and the CIA had used AI tools to detect and target him. A difficult job becomes even harder.

---

[9] Edward Swaine, *The Political Economy of* Youngstown, 83 S. CAL. L. REV. 263, 267 (2010).

[10] Memorandum for James B. Comey, Deputy Attorney General, from Daniel Levin, Acting Assistant Attorney General, *Legal Standards Applicable Under 18 U.S.C. §§ 2340–2340A* (Dec. 30, 2004).

[11] Even when leaks do reveal the existence of a program, lack of knowledge about the details can make it hard for the case to proceed. *See, e.g.,* Clapper v. ACLU, 568 U.S. 398 (2013) (holding that plaintiffs lacked standing to sue about an alleged government surveillance program).

[12] *See, e.g.,* White House, Presidential Policy Directive 28, Signals Intelligence Activities (Jan. 17, 2014).

In addition, it may be hard for a lawyer to know whether it is even permissible for the government to use an AI/ML system in a given setting, as where a treaty or statute is written in a way that envisions a human making a particular judgment. The breadth of many national security laws (for example, Congress's delegation to the President to use "necessary and appropriate force" in its recent authorizations for use of military force) will make it challenging to build algorithms whose recommendations accurately capture congressional and presidential intent.[13] And making representations to actors in the other branches of government about whether an operation complies with international and domestic law will be thorny. In a non-AI/ML case, the Office of the Director of National Intelligence misunderstood how National Security Agency surveillance tools operated and misrepresented the process to the Foreign Intelligence Surveillance Court.[14] Add neural nets to the mix and it is easy to see how that kind of legal error will become common.

Finally, as AI/ML becomes pervasive in the mine run of U.S. national security operations, the power to shape the operations will shift toward computer scientists and engineers and away from lawyers and policymakers, even if those engineers are not trained in law or policy. It is the engineers who—expressly or implicitly—embed values into the algorithm in deciding what initial weights to use and what outcomes to prioritize. The relative lack of sophistication about technology among certain U.S. government agencies and officials (including lawyers), as well as foreign officials, will decrease their ability to test the values, including legal rules, that undergird these AI/ML applications. As Chapter 4 argues, military and intelligence operators, ethicists, and lawyers should demand to work closely with the engineers who are crafting and testing these systems.

2. Competence

In addition to ensuring that U.S. national security operations—military targeting, electronic and human surveillance, counterintelligence, covert action—comply with the relevant legal frameworks, we want those operations to be developed and executed competently and efficiently. We do not

---

[13] *See, e.g.,* S.J. Res. 23—Authorization for Use of Force, 107th Cong., Sept. 18, 2001.
[14] Jake Tapper, *NSA Violated Phone Rules, Misinformed Secret Court, Documents Show*, CNN (Sept. 11, 2013).

want our officials to misuse the public fisc, behave self-servingly or recklessly, or double down on fruitless tools or policies. Because secrecy reduces the number of people involved in developing a policy, it can decrease the quality of the policy ex ante and help officials conceal missteps ex post. To pick just one example, if a broader set of interagency policymakers and members of Congress had known the truth about the Gulf of Tonkin incident (in which the White House falsely claimed that North Vietnam had attacked two U.S. destroyers), Congress likely would not have given President Johnson such a capacious and open-ended authorization to use force in Vietnam.

Introducing AI into this secrecy ecosystem has the potential to further compromise competent and efficient execution of U.S. national security policies. As I wrote previously about the use of AI by the Defense Department:

> The military use of predictive algorithms and machine learning tools seems certain to replicate and even exacerbate, at least for the casual observer, many of the critiques that the military has faced over the past fifteen years: a lack of transparency, a willingness to adopt aggressive interpretations of the law, a concern that the military makes detention and targeting decisions based on flawed data, and a perceived dehumanization of lethal action (in the form of drone strikes and increasingly automated decision-making).[15]

One of the most important roles for Congress—the most traditional overseer—is to help ensure that the Executive is performing competently and efficiently. And yet, at least before mid-2023, Congress as a body was woefully undereducated about AI.[16] Chapter 1 discussed why Congress often has difficulty gaining access to secret programs. Even when the relevant congressional committees do gain access to highly classified programs, Congress has had persistent challenges in understanding technologically complex programs and overseeing the Executive's use of them. This leaves the Executive undersupervised regarding the quality and efficacy of its NSAI tools.

First, AI is, in most contexts, invisible. Members of Congress and their constituents can see when the U.S. military's Bell Boeing V-22 Osprey

---

[15] Ashley Deeks, *Predicting Enemies*, 104 VA. L. REV. 1529, 1537 (2018).

[16] OpenAI's release of ChatGPT led to a spate of hearings and educational panels in Congress. Cecelia Kang, *OpenAI's Sam Altman Urges A.I. Regulation in Senate Hearing*, N.Y. TIMES (May 16, 2023).

helicopters crash.[17] In contrast, they often will have no idea in the first instance whether a particular military helicopter employed AI systems, or whether an unmanned aerial vehicle was acting in autonomous mode, or whether intelligence officials produced a key intelligence report using AI tools. This means that it will be harder for Congress to know—via the "fire alarm" of an accident or news headline[18]—that there is something that it should investigate. When DHS's machine-learning programs have become visible, the public has pushed back—on its use of AVATAR and Extreme Vetting, for example. This suggests that, in some cases that have emerged publicly from within the double black box, DHS has shown questionable judgment in its efforts to use AI. These examples should give us some reason to wonder about the quality of other programs that have yet to come to light.

Second, as Chapter 2 explained, it can be hard to understand how AI systems work, especially for the many members of Congress (and senior executive policymakers) who lack technical backgrounds. Amitai Etzioni, who was a member of the Biden administration's National AI Research Resource Task Force, reported that policymakers often struggle to grasp the issues. "I can tell you from my conversations with some of them, they're well-intentioned and ask good questions, but they're not super well-informed," he said.[19] Amy Zegart argues that "emerging technologies are likely to strain congressional oversight in new ways."[20] She notes, "[G]ood intelligence oversight requires much more technical knowledge than it used to—and Congress doesn't have it."[21] The release in spring 2023 of ChatGPT and similar generative AI tools stimulated members of Congress to convene panels on AI, attend informational briefings, and even take AI-related classes.[22] But Congress remains well behind the curve in understanding how different types of NSAI work and will affect U.S. operations. That means it will be hard for Congress to assess how well the Executive is using AI in those operations.

---

[17] Stephen Fehr & Bill Miller, *Osprey Crash Probe Awaits Salvage*, WASH. POST (July 21, 1992).

[18] Mathew D. McCubbins & Thomas Schwartz, *Congressional Oversight Overlooked: Police Patrols versus Fire Alarms*, 28 AM. J. POL. SCI. 165 (1984). This suggests the importance of enhancing the "police patrol" model of congressional oversight on AI, though that approach will require Congress to become much more sophisticated about AI tools.

[19] Karen Hao & Miles Kruppa, *Tech Giants Pour Billions into AI, But Hype Doesn't Always Match Reality*, WALL ST. J. (July 5, 2022). *See also* Tony Mills & Robert Cook-Deegan, *Where's Congress? Don't Just Blame Trump for the Coronavirus Catastrophe*, R ST. (Apr. 16, 2020) (describing Congress's lack of requisite technical expertise).

[20] AMY ZEGART, SPIES, LIES, AND ALGORITHMS 198 (2022).

[21] *Id.* at 223.

[22] Emily Wilkins, *In Congress and in Class: Rep. Don Beyer Works Toward Master's Degree in AI*, CNBC (Dec. 2, 2023).

Third, the United States has entered an economic and technological cold war with China, and there is resounding bipartisan and bicameral consensus that the United States should do more, faster when it comes to winning that cold war. Indeed, Congress sometimes appears more worried about the United States losing the AI race to China than about the Executive adopting AI that does not work or that fails to reflect U.S. values.[23] As a result, Congress may push the Executive to rush to deploy incompletely tested AI, rather than serve as a check on the systems' effectiveness and efficiency. Further, just as algorithms may ultimately distance executive policymakers from the recommendations that emerge from algorithmic systems, so too may they distance legislators from policy outcomes. Some legislators may seek active involvement in NSAI, but others may prefer being able to disassociate themselves from the systems—perhaps claiming that they are too complicated to understand—and then point fingers when an operation goes bad.

Like members of Congress, executive officials themselves may have a harder time understanding when a given NSAI tool is fit for purpose. Consider the traditional national security activities that officials may generally encounter, such as covert action, foreign electronic surveillance, and military operations. Depending on their specific portfolios, a wide range of officials at different levels of seniority are likely to have encountered those operations repeatedly and will readily understand how they are developed, approved, and executed. Now consider national security operations involving AI tools. The staff of the National Security Commission on AI, a congressionally created group of experts that produced several reports, "interviewed numerous government officials from different departments and at different levels of seniority who will freely admit they do not understand basic AI concepts."[24] The Commission continued, "[F]or the government to successfully adopt AI, many if not most end users will need to gain a baseline understanding of AI's limitations, data management requirements, and ethical use."[25] Absent that understanding, officials may not understand the strategic risks of using certain AI/ML tools, even as they face pressure to approve them to win the AI race.

---

[23] *See* Mohar Chatterfee, *The Pentagon's Endless Struggle with AI*, POLITICO (June 27, 2023) (quoting members of Congress as expressing concerns that the "military has fallen 'way behind' on AI").

[24] National Security Commission on AI, First Quarter Recommendations 37 (Mar. 2020).

[25] *Id.* at 28.

This means that it may be harder for senior national security officials to lead, rather than follow, the technology. Richard Danzig notes that "senior officials are called to make decisions about, and on the basis of, technologies that did not exist at the time of their education and earlier experience. . . . Very few have the time, talent and taste to update their understandings, [and as a result] most do not."[26] This means we may face a bottom-up approach to adopting these tools, with the attendant risks that the more junior officials and computer scientists developing them and proposing their use lack a full perspective on foreign policy risks. Further, the fact that an even smaller group of national security officials than usual is capable of assessing the quality of the AI systems could lead to "groupthink" about the wisdom of deploying the tools.[27] Insiders may misjudge public sentiment as they weigh what policies the public will support. Finally, government officials may only understand the system's flaws after the fact because of how complicated the systems are.

3. Accountability

Because we have not yet determined how to assign responsibility for errors made by AI systems, we will soon face a "double unaccountability" problem in the national security realm. We already have limited access to information about executive acts, which makes it difficult to trace when errors have happened and which person, office, or agency is responsible for that error. (Take a U.S. drone strike that produces civilian deaths: high levels of classification make it hard for observers to know whether the Defense Department or the CIA conducted a particular strike.)[28] Court cases arise so infrequently

---

.[26] Richard Danzig, *Technology Roulette: Managing Loss of Control as Many Militaries Pursue Technological Superiority* 11, CTR. FOR NEW AM. SECURITY (June 2018). Danzig quotes former CIA Director Michael Hayden describing a situation in which "no two seniors at the final approval session had left the Situation Room thinking they had approved the same [cyber] operation" because they did not understand the technology well. *Id.* at 11 (quoting MICHAEL HAYDEN, PLAYING TO THE EDGE: AMERICAN INTELLIGENCE IN THE AGE OF TERROR 147 (2016)).

[27] *See* Ashley Deeks & Kristen Eichensehr, *Frictionless Government and Foreign Relations*, 110 VA. L. REV. __ (forthcoming 2024) (discussing groupthink in foreign policy settings). *See also* JAMES BAKER, THE CENTAUR'S DILEMMA: NATIONAL SECURITY LAW FOR THE COMING AI REVOLUTION 203 (2021) (noting that the most likely outcome is a stovepipe approach to AI, with results ranging from a series of special access programs that will minimize oversight and appraisal, to open labs and dialogues, which will enhance creative energy but open the door to security and safety risks).

[28] Bryan Bender, *"I Don't Think the CIA Should Be in the Business of Carrying Out Wars,"* POLITICO (Apr. 24, 2015) (noting that "the CIA and Pentagon split responsibility for conducting drone surveillance and attacks by region").

in this setting that judges are rarely positioned to make definitive judgments that assign accountability. And even when they are in that position, their lack of familiarity with technology and their deference to the Executive means they rarely will.[29] The difficulty of detecting who is responsible for significant algorithmic errors doubles down on this challenge. The chain of AI development, training, and learning creates a range of possible actors to hold responsible. The approach that Volvo has adopted for its self-driving cars is to accept responsibility up front for any accidents that result from the use of those cars—but that company is one of only a few actors taking that approach, at least to date.[30] There is significant disagreement in the literature about how to manage the AI accountability dilemma.

Further complicating how we think about accountability is the fact that the private sector will be responsible for some AI development. Although not a problem unique to AI, the use of private companies and contractors adds another layer of actors to the product development chain. There have been reports that some of the Defense Department's contractors, which have worked on AI/ML programs such as Project Maven, are building technology that is not "revolutionary or innovative" but have successfully put their technology "in the language of military-speak" to persuade the Pentagon to buy it.[31] One article notes, "[E]ven the seemingly underdeveloped products pose ethical concerns and could lead to unproven technologies in the hands of government officials with major potential for misuse."[32] Many officials in those companies are less attuned to compliance with the laws of armed conflict than the U.S. military is.[33] Further, various U.S. laws such as FOIA do

---

[29] The Chivers FOIA case discussed in Chapter 2 serves as an example. Even with a domestic law in place to facilitate access to Department of Homeland Security documents, court involvement, American citizen targets, and nongovernmental organizations on the lookout, it has been difficult to learn about DHS's use of machine learning tools. *See* Drew Harwell, *Customs Officials Have Copied Americans' Phone Data at Massive Scale*, WASH. POST (Sept. 15, 2022) (discussing congressional concerns about various DHS data-collection programs and noting that "DHS investigators have increasingly used analytical and machine-learning tools to map out relationships and behaviors from vast reserves of phone data").

[30] Clifford Atiyeh, *Volvo Accepting "Full Liability" in Autonomous-car Crashes*, THE DRIVE (June 21, 2019) (reporting that Mercedes-Benz and Google took similar responsibility for their self-driving cars).

[31] Jonathan Guyer, *Inside the Chaos at Washington's Most Connected Military Tech Startup*, VOX (Dec. 14, 2022); Melissa Heikkila, *Why Business Is Booming for Military AI Startups*, MIT TECH. REV. (July 7, 2022) ("Companies that sell military AI make expansive claims for what their technology can do. . . . There are countless examples of AI companies' tendency to make grand promises about technologies that turn out not to work as advertised, and combat zones are perhaps among the most technically challenging areas in which to deploy AI because there is little relevant training data.").

[32] Guyer, *supra* note 31.

[33] Laura Dickinson, *Military Lawyers, Private Contractors, and the Problem of International Law Compliance*, 42 N.Y.U. J. INT'L L. & POL. 355 (2010).

not apply to contractors.[34] Nor does a range of treaties.[35] And the public generally lacks information about the contents of the government's contracts.[36] All of this makes it harder for the public—and perhaps even the military—to identify and hold responsible those who produce poor products.

Attributing responsibility after an AI-driven accident will also be more complicated than doing so after a more public, lower-technology event. First, it may be hard for overseers and the public to assess whether a given tool was or was not operating autonomously in the first place, if they are aware of the operation at all.[37] And the government may decline to specify when, where, and how it is deploying AI. As Danzig writes, "The natural tendency within the national security establishment is to minimize the visibility [of the risks of new technologies] and to avoid engagement with potentially disruptive outside actors. But this leaves technology initiatives with such a narrow [] base of support that they are vulnerable to overreaction when accidents or revelations occur. The intelligence agencies should have learned this lesson when they had only weak public support in the face of backlash when their cyber documents and tools were hacked."[38] The debate about whether to reauthorize section 702 of the FISA Amendments Act is another example of this phenomenon: although this statute serves as the basis for critical intelligence collection, its secret, technical nature and FBI errors in searching the resulting database have left the statute on shaky ground politically.[39]

Second, in the military setting, there often are only a limited number of actors who will be able to evaluate an accident. The military sometimes circles the wagons during investigations of civilian casualties, for example, especially where the underlying operation was classified, whereas in commercial aviation there is a "rich mix of interested formal organizations checking upon each other."[40] When the accident involves not just a classified operation

---

[34] Laura Dickinson, *Public Law Values in a Privatized World*, 31 YALE J. INT'L L. 383, 402 (2006).

[35] Laura Dickinson, *Regulating the Privatized Security Industry*, 63 EMORY L.J. 417, 417 (2013) (noting that when U.S. contractors committed abuses in Afghanistan and Iraq, "there were few workable accountability mechanisms on the back end").

[36] Jennifer Elsea et al., *Private Security Contractors in Iraq: Background, Legal Status, and Other Issues*, CONG. RES. SERV. (Aug. 25, 2008).

[37] *See, e.g.*, Joe Hernandez, *A Military Drone with a Mind of Its Own Was Used in Combat, U.N. Says*, NPR (June 1, 2021) (reflecting uncertainty about whether drone was in autonomous mode when it hit a target).

[38] Danzig, *supra* note 26, at 18.

[39] *See* Ryan Tarinelli & Michael Macagnone, *Congress Pits Privacy Against Intelligence as It Ponders Surveillance Renewal*, ROLL CALL (Jan. 23, 2024).

[40] Danzig, *supra* note 26, at 19 (quoting Charles Perrow). *See also* David Ignatius, *The U.S. Military's Overdue Reckoning with Civilian Casualties*, WASH. POST (Aug. 28, 2022) ("For too long, the Pentagon rejected reports of civilian deaths in Iraq, Afghanistan and Syria as false claims or enemy propaganda.").

but also a complicated machine learning system, there will be a very small number of people who are qualified and cleared to assess what happened and who was responsible. In the setting of the Israel-Gaza conflict, the director of Human Rights Watch argued, "Nobody has any insight including . . . U.S. policymakers on how Israel is conducting this war. . . . We see the outcome in the civilian casualties and the destroyed buildings, but in terms of the technology and the proportionality calculus we just have no idea. It's like a black box."[41] It is likely that a comparable use of AI by the United States for targeting recommendations today would evince a similar reaction.

4. Justification-giving

Giving reasons or justifications for choices is an important part of a democracy, where, by definition, the government answers to the people. As I have written elsewhere, "Reason-giving—the process of offering justifications for a decision—is essential to our system of governance" because it "may improve the quality of decisions, deter abuses of authority, and enhance fidelity to legal standards."[42] When operations are secret, the need to justify them publicly is nonexistent unless and until they leak. There are situations in which the Executive gives reasons in secret, including to the Foreign Intelligence Surveillance Court, to members and staff of the Senate and House intelligence, armed services, and foreign relations committees, and to itself.[43] But in general, secrecy provides the Executive with greater opportunities to avoid having to justify the choices it makes.

The nontransparency of code will amplify the lack of transparency of national security decisions, as well as the difficulty of justifying those decisions. In a range of cases, the Executive will simply be unable to articulate—to itself or to outside actors—why a particular national security algorithm produced the result or recommendation that it did. Those outside actors can still ask the Executive to justify why it decided to use an algorithm in the first place, of course, and xAI may eventually mitigate the opacity of machine learning. But a justification that simply invokes a reliance on an algorithmic recommendation will be deeply unsatisfying. The use of FOIA to obtain information

---

[41] Joseph Gedeon & Maggie Miller, *Israel Under Pressure to Justify Its Use of AI in Gaza*, POLITICO (Mar. 3, 2024).

[42] Deeks, *supra* note 3, at 615.

[43] *See id.*

about how a given AI-stimulated accident happened is more likely to reveal the "what" than the "why." There is reason to think that the military will insist on some level of explicability for its algorithms, based on the direction that its research and policies seem headed.[44] That means there might also be reason to expect that those affected by the algorithmic recommendations (such as detainees held during armed conflicts as security threats) could glean some limited information about why the algorithm operated the way it did. Extensive transparency seems highly unlikely, however, particularly where it might pose a security risk to reveal the data that went into creating a given algorithm.

5. Summary

When we introduce AI tools into our military and intelligence systems, it will be more difficult for our traditional checks to work and, as a result, even more difficult to assess whether the government's activities are aligned with our public law values. Congress, executive officials, and lawyers may not know or understand the programs and tools at play and will find themselves largely unable to see into the double black box. It will be harder for our non-traditional checks to function as well: allies may not know what tools our military and intelligence officials are using and, as a result, may be unable or unwilling to fully participate in joint operations.[45] Leaks of risky AI code, even if interpretable by some members of the public, will fail to capture the imagination in the way that plane crashes or civilian deaths do. In short, we are arriving at a destination in which many important national security activities will take place inside a double black box.

C. Cyber Autonomy: A Case Study

Chapter 2 described the U.S. government's current interest in using autonomous cyber tools as a way to defend government and private computer

---

[44] David Gunning et al., *DARPA's Explainable AI (XAI) Program: A Retrospective*, APPLIED AI LETTERS (Dec. 4, 2021).

[45] NATO already faces some interoperability challenges based in law and policy, such as where some alliance members use a particular munition and others cannot do so. *See* James Derleth, *Enhancing Interoperability: The Foundation for Effective NATO Operations*, NATO REV. (June 16, 2015).

systems—and perhaps also to engage in offensive cyber operations. This section uses the push for cyber autonomy as a case study for the double black box, illustrating how Congress, in particular, will have difficulty overseeing executive actions in this space.[46] Congress already has a hard time regulating, overseeing, and terminating U.S. uses of force abroad; looming cyber autonomy will double down on the challenges of ensuring that the Executive is acting legally and competently. Although this section focuses on the United States, other democratic legislatures will confront similar problems.

1. Background

In recent years, democratic legislatures have struggled to maintain a role for themselves in government decisions to conduct overseas military operations. Congress offers a prime example of this phenomenon, but other legislatures such as the British Parliament and the French National Assembly face similar challenges.[47] Some of these challenges are due to constitutional rules, institutional structures, and historical practice. In the United States, where the Constitution gives Congress the power to declare war, the Framers envisioned that the President would have the power to repel sudden attacks without legislative authorization—a category of activities that has expanded significantly since the 1790s. Further, executives are necessarily better structured than legislatures to collect classified information, respond quickly to urgent security threats, and direct military operations.

Not all legislative limitations are linked to constitutional rules or structures, however. Congress also struggles to preserve its role because of the changing nature of conflict, which now includes the pervasive use of unmanned aerial vehicles and operations in cyberspace that are harder to detect publicly and do not require the type of robust legislative support that large-scale conflicts do.[48] This leaves Congress struggling to learn the facts

[46] This section is drawn from Ashley Deeks, *Will Cyber Autonomy Undercut Democratic Accountability?*, 96 INT'L L. STUD. 464 (2020).

[47] *See, e.g.*, United Kingdom, Public Administration and Constitutional Affairs Committee, *The Role of Parliament in the UK Constitution: Authorizing the Use of Military Force* (Aug. 6, 2019); Delphine Deschaux-Dutard, *Parliamentary Scrutiny of Military Operations in France and Germany*, Euro. Consortium for Political Research.

[48] Jack Goldsmith & Matthew Waxman, *The Legal Legacy of Light-Footprint Warfare*, 37 WASH. Q. 7, 10 (2016) (noting that cyberattacks are low-visibility and "attract[] less public, congressional, and diplomatic scrutiny than the operations [they] replaced").

and to engage in ex post efforts to hold the Executive accountable for offensive cyber operations that could lead to international armed conflict.

The introduction of increased autonomy into this setting may further alter the existing relationships between the Executive and Congress on use-of-force decisions. Because the use of autonomous cyber tools may lead the United States into serious tensions with another state without advance notice, these capabilities pose particular hurdles for a legislature that already struggles to stay relevant on use of force and cyber issues. Additionally, the U.S. use of autonomous cyber tools may alter the dynamics among different actors *within* the executive branch itself—by, for instance, diverting deliberative input and oversight abilities away from the State and Justice Departments and the intelligence community, and toward the Defense Department in the lead-up to a conflict. Unless Congress takes steps to preserve a role for itself, and unless the executive branch ensures that an appropriate diversity of officials remains involved in use of force decisions, key vestiges of democratic accountability for those decisions may further weaken.

2. The Nature of Cyber Autonomy

The United States is increasingly likely to deploy cyber tools that use heightened levels of autonomy, a function driven by AI. This section describes the nature of and prospects for burgeoning cyber autonomy within U.S. military and intelligence systems and then details how cyber autonomy may lead to serious interstate tensions or even armed conflict.

Autonomy exists on a continuum: systems may be more or less autonomous.[49] "[A] self-governing system is more likely to be described as 'autonomous' where human observers lack the ability to precisely foresee the exact sequence of steps that the system must take in order to complete its assigned task (or, equivalently, cannot foresee all events that will transpire when the system is activated)."[50] The more self-adaptive a cyber system is, the better it will operate in uncertain environments.[51] It is possible to design systems that do not need "detailed foreknowledge of all combinations of circumstances

---

[49] Defense Science Board, U.S. Department of Defense, *The Role of Autonomy in DoD Systems* 4 (2012).
[50] Tim McFarland, *The Concept of Autonomy* 5, Law and the Future of War Research Paper, U. Queensland L. Sch. (July 2020).
[51] *Id.* at 11.

which the software entity may encounter once it is in operation."[52] Other systems may learn in the field once deployed.[53] Such systems fall on the higher end of autonomy.

Cyber operations can cause physical damage and, potentially, human harm. To date, very few of the known cyber operations have caused levels of damage that constitute uses of force or armed attacks under the UN Charter.[54] But states contemplate that cyber operations could produce such a result. A former U.S. State Department Legal Adviser envisioned cyber operations that trigger a nuclear plant meltdown, open a dam above a populated area, or disable air traffic control, resulting in airplane crashes.[55] These types of operations are well within the realm of the possible using cyberattacks with either low or high levels of autonomy.

Because it is harder to predict the impact of a given cyber operation than to predict the impact of a missile, there is greater room for miscalculation. As Paul Scharre notes, "You can have an accident that spirals out of control very badly that has a widespread effect in ways that are not possible with people" because humans cannot make the same number of errors as quickly.[56] Even if there are political or strategic constraints on deploying certain cyber tools today, autonomy may weaken those constraints. It can be hard for states to signal their intentions in cyberspace, which is an important way to avoid inadvertent escalation.[57] This is particularly true before or during an autonomous cyber operation, which may happen without human preplanning and possibly without knowledge of the opponent's identity. Further, highly autonomous cyber tools may act less predictably than human-in-the-loop systems, especially when confronting other autonomous systems. Even if a state itself takes steps to avoid a "flash conflict" between its own cyber algorithm and another actor's algorithm, a third state could deliberately design a cyber operation to trigger this type of event between two of its adversaries.[58]

---

[52] *Id.* at 12.

[53] *Id.*

[54] Gary Corn & Eric Jensen, *The Use of Force and Cyber Countermeasures*, 32 TEMPLE INT'L & COMP. L.J. 127 (2018).

[55] Harold Hongju Koh, Legal Adviser, U.S. Department of State, *Remarks at the USCYBERCOM Inter-Agency Legal Conference: International Law in Cyberspace* (Sept. 18, 2012).

[56] Johanna Costigan, *Four Specialists Describe Their Diverse Approaches to China's AI Development*, NEW AM. (Jan. 30, 2020).

[57] Brandon Valeriano, *Managing Escalation Under Layered Cyber Deterrence*, LAWFARE (Apr. 1, 2020).

[58] United Nations Institute for Disarmament Research, *The Weaponization of Increasingly Autonomous Technologies: Autonomous Weapons and Cyber Operations* 10 (2017).

This is not to argue that the developers of highly autonomous systems lack control over the parameters of their systems; after all, the "behavior of an autonomous software entity is ultimately dependent upon actions of people in relevant positions, notably its designer and operator, due to the nature of computers and software."[59] But it does suggest that a highly autonomous AI/ML system may not act entirely predictably on its own and may act especially unpredictably when it confronts another actor's autonomous system. This situation—when the system deviates in problematic ways from human decision-making—gives rise to new types of democratic and strategic concerns.

3. Congress's Role in the Use of Force

The United States and its adversaries are likely to pursue high levels of cyber autonomy to protect their military systems. Such autonomy, if not carefully managed, raises the possibility of deliberate or unplanned escalation into hostilities. In light of this, how can Congress ensure that the Executive deploys cyber autonomy in a manner consistent with the Constitution and laws, as well as our other public law values?[60] In particular, how should Congress regulate autonomous cyber tools to ensure that the executive branch remains faithful to domestic and international law regulating the resort to interstate force or other military operations?[61] This section considers the several roles that Congress plays today in authorizing or overseeing military operations, to set the stage for an analysis of how cyber autonomy may alter those dynamics.

---

[59] McFarland, *supra* note 50, at 8; *see also* Defense Science Board, *supra* note 49, at 1–2 ("[A]ll autonomous systems are supervised by human operators at some level, and autonomous systems' software embodies the designed limits on the actions and decisions delegated to the computer.").

[60] The UK House of Lords made a similar point in its 2023 study of autonomous weapons systems, noting, "Parliament is at the centre of decision-making on the development and use of AWS. Parliament's capacity for oversight depends on the availability of information . . . and on its ability to hold ministers to account. The Government must allow sufficient space in the Parliamentary timetable and provide enough information for Parliament, including its select committees, to scrutinise its policy on AI effectively. We naturally understand that elements of policy development may be highly sensitive, but . . . [a]rguments of secrecy must not be used to sidestep accountability." UK House of Lords, *Proceed with Caution: Artificial Intelligence in Weapon Systems* 3 (2023).

[61] Some scholars argue that remote warfare technologies are *intended* to subvert democratic control of war. *See, e.g.,* Peter Singer, *Do Drones Undermine Democracy?*, BROOKINGS INST. (Jan. 22, 2012) (arguing that "new technology is short-circuiting the decision-making process for what used to be the most important choice a democracy could make"). This book assumes that the United States wishes to retain democratic accountability for its use of autonomous military systems.

Legislatures that play a role in a state's decision to use interstate force provide democratic accountability for those choices. One reason why this matters is that mature democracies usually do not go to war with each other. They also are more likely to win the wars that they fight against autocratic states.[62] Thus, there are virtues to retaining a healthy role for democratic legislatures in war-making decisions because they may help their states avoid "bad" wars and fight only "good" wars.

Some constitutional systems establish a role for legislatures in authorizing force ex ante. The U.S. Constitution, for instance, assigns to Congress the power to declare war. However, the Executive currently interprets the Constitution to allow it to use force abroad without advance congressional authorization as long as the action is in the U.S. national interest and the number of troops and the circumstances in which they would be deployed do not rise to the level of "war in a constitutional sense."[63] One obvious benefit to legislative participation in decisions to resort to force in the first instance is that legislatures can constrain "overzealous executives by requiring evidence to justify wars."[64] As Tom Ginsburg notes, the Framers believed that congressional involvement in decisions related to force would slow down war-making except in true emergencies.[65]

A constitutional requirement of ex ante authorization is a powerful tool for legislatures because introducing troops on the ground often operates as a one-way ratchet. Once a state has committed troops to a conflict, legislatures have a hard time voting to withdraw those troops because doing so may be seen by the public as unpatriotic.[66] Congress generally uses its ex ante authority to enact laws that stipulate the settings in which and adversaries against whom the executive is authorized to use force. Today, these take the form of Authorizations for Use of Military Force (AUMFs). In 2018, Congress accorded the President authority akin to an AUMF for certain cyber operations, providing:

---

[62] Tom Ginsburg, *Chaining the Dog of War: Comparative Data*, 15 CHI. J. INT'L L. 138, 139 (2014).

[63] *See, e.g.*, U.S. Dep't of Justice, Memorandum from Assistant Attorney General Steven A. Engel to Counsel to the President, April 2018 Airstrikes Against Syrian Chemical-Weapons Facilities (May 31, 2018).

[64] Ginsburg, *supra* note 62, at 146.

[65] *Id.* at 142, 145; Yasuo Hasebe, *War Powers, in* OXFORD HANDBOOK OF COMPARATIVE CONSTITUTIONAL LAW 465 (Michel Rosenfeld & Andras Sajo eds., 2012) (noting that legislative approval for armed force provides legitimacy and popular support for the operations).

[66] *See, e.g.*, Mitchell v. Laird, 488 F.2d 611 (D.C. Cir. 1973) (discussing why members of Congress who opposed the continuation of the Vietnam War might nevertheless vote to appropriate money, to avoid abandoning the forces already fighting).

In the event that the National Command Authority [i.e., the President and the Secretary of Defense] determines that the Russian Federation, People's Republic of China, Democratic People's Republic of Korea, or Islamic Republic of Iran is conducting an active, systematic, and ongoing campaign of attacks against the Government or people of the United States in cyberspace, . . . the National Command Authority may authorize the Secretary of Defense, acting through the Commander of the United States Cyber Command, to take appropriate and proportional action in foreign cyberspace to disrupt, defeat, and deter such attacks . . . .[67]

When the Defense Department employs this authority, the Secretary of Defense must report to the congressional defense committees no later than forty-eight hours after the operation.[68]

Congress can also shape the Executive's use of force after it begins. Congress's power of the purse can provide significant leverage over how and where the Executive conducts those operations and the length of time for which the Executive can fight. Congress can conduct oversight for the duration of the conflict, to examine how the Executive is fighting the conflict, including whether it is exceeding its mandate, using resources wisely, and complying with international and domestic law.[69] Depending on the capacity of the congressional committees tasked with oversight responsibilities, legislators can hold the Executive accountable for illegal, incompetent, or unwise military and policy decisions. A legislature's ability to enhance its Executive's compliance with public law values—including international law—depends on a reliable flow of information between the Executive and the legislature; on the legislature's competence to understand the strategy, tactics, and tools that the Executive is using; and on adequate time to make informed decisions. The introduction of significant levels of cyber autonomy into the mix is likely to complicate these already-challenging tasks.

Burgeoning cyber autonomy may affect democratic accountability for the use of force and domestic checks and balances in three ways. First, it may alter the balance of power between Congress and the Executive, further empowering the latter at the expense of legislative input about the fact,

---

[67] John S. McCain National Defense Authorization Act for Fiscal Year 2019, Pub. L. No. 115-232, § 1642(a)(2), §1642(c), 132 Stat. 1636 (2018).

[68] *Id.*

[69] One salient example here is the U.S. Congress's effort to try to terminate President Ronald Reagan's funding of the Contras in Nicaragua. *See* Boland Amendment, Pub. L. No. 98-473, § 8066(a), 98 Stat. 1837 (1984).

timing, scope, and legality of particular uses of force or offensive cyber operations. Second, it may alter the balance among executive agencies. Third, it may alter power dynamics among different types of officials within those agencies. If obtaining the input of a diverse set of executive officials and securing a legislative role in decisions to use force helps improve the quality of decision-making, the overall effect of robust uses of cyber autonomy may be to increase the potential for "bad" conflicts between the United States and an adversary.[70]

4. The Effect of Cyber Autonomy on Congressional Oversight

There are several ways in which autonomous cyber capabilities might further empower the Executive at the expense of Congress.[71] First, Congress may suffer from information deficits about the existence and capabilities of the cyber systems, which generally operate within the national security black box. Assume that DOD develops autonomous cyber systems that can operate offensively or counteroffensively. An initial concern is that legislators are unaware that the autonomous systems exist. Although they sometimes appropriate money for specific programs, appropriations laws do not necessarily articulate in detail the types and nature of weapons that militaries are or are not authorized to develop. Legislators may also have difficulty obtaining information about executive cyber doctrines that will guide how the Executive will utilize its cyber tools—including autonomous one. Even though Congress has committees dedicated to overseeing the defense and intelligence agencies, and recently legislated with particularity in the cyber area, Congress had difficulty gaining access to a classified Trump-era U.S. executive policy that set out the approval process for conducting offensive cyber operations.[72] It stands to reason that Congress might also have

---

[70] *See* Ginsburg, *supra* note 62, at 145.

[71] The growing autonomy of cyber operations is only one aspect that poses a threat to legislative capacity and oversight. The increased precision of cyber tools means that they can produce a more potent effect on the intended victim, which could increase the risks of escalation. Further, the growth of the Internet of Things and the interconnectedness of many publicly and privately owned systems means that there are more ways for U.S. cyber operations to have cascading, unintended effects. As with the growing autonomy of cyber systems, both factors make it critical for Congress to retain an oversight role.

[72] Mark Pomerleau, *After Tug-of-War, White House Shows Cyber Memo to Congress*, FIFTH DOMAIN (Mar. 13, 2020) (describing a multimonth struggle to obtain access to National Security Presidential Memorandum 13).

problems obtaining information about the extent of the human role in those cyber operations. As a related matter, even if DOD shares information with legislators about its cyber capabilities or doctrines, legislators may have difficulty understanding particular cyber capabilities, including autonomous capabilities and the risks attendant thereto. As noted earlier, there are many reasons to think that the average legislator is not particularly savvy about technology.[73]

Even legislators with a basic understanding of cyber operations may not fully appreciate the risks of autonomous operations and may not be positioned to ask the right questions of the executive branch. Indeed, various executive officials involved in decision-making will not understand the capabilities and risks of complex autonomous cyber systems. In the context of electronic surveillance systems, for example, in 2013 the U.S. Director of National Intelligence (DNI) declassified a set of documents that revealed a failure to comply with judicial mandates. The DNI explained that the compliance problems

> stemmed in large part from the complexity of the technology employed in connection with the bulk telephony metadata collection program, interaction of that technology with other NSA systems, and a lack of a shared understanding among various NSA components about how certain aspects of the complex architecture supporting the program functioned. These gaps in understanding led, in turn, to unintentional misrepresentations in the way the collection was described to the FISC.[74]

If some intelligence officials within a single agency were unclear about how the technology supporting an electronic surveillance program worked, it is easy to imagine that legislators might struggle to understand very technical cyber tools that include significant levels of autonomy.

Second, there may be fewer opportunities temporally for members to weigh in on the wisdom of forcible responses. As noted previously, the Executive has taken the view that very few uses of force require congressional

---

[73] *See* Karen Hao, *Congress Wants to Protect You from Biased Algorithms, Deep Fakes, and Other Bad AI*, MIT TECH. REV. (Apr. 15, 2019) (noting that "only a handful of members of Congress have a deep enough technical grasp of data and machine learning to approach regulation in an appropriately nuanced manner").

[74] Office of the Director of National Intelligence, Press Release, *DNI Clapper Declassifies Intelligence Community Documents Regarding Collection Under Section 501 of the Foreign Intelligence Surveillance Act (FISA)* (Sept. 10, 2013).

pre-authorization. Purely defensive autonomous cyber operations—those that use autonomy only to identify and fend off hostile cyber operations within one's own system—are unlikely to implicate congressional prerogatives, as these settings will fall within the Executive's "repel attacks" power. If the only time ex ante congressional authorization for military operations is legally necessary is when the United States plans to deploy hundreds of thousands of troops abroad, cyber operations—whether human-in-the-loop or out-of-the-loop—will almost never reach the threshold of "war in a constitutional sense."[75] Hostile cyber exchanges, at least when the salvos remain within the cyber realm, are unlikely to pose an immediate and significant threat to U.S. troops and will not even trigger the Executive's obligation to notify Congress under the War Powers Resolution.

Yet autonomous cyber systems may pose a reasonable chance of escalation—whether intended or unintended—such that legislative input might be normatively desirable ex ante. And cyber capabilities that leave one's own system,[76] even in an act of self-defense, are more likely to implicate congressional prerogatives because they increase the chance of escalation and error. Further, autonomous systems "may operate at speeds that make it impossible for the operator to meaningfully intervene."[77] Thus, once the United States deploys an autonomous cyber tool that can reach outside its own system and inflict substantial harm, there will be no opportunity to consult with Congress on particular operations, even when such consultation might be normatively desirable.

Third, one of the more reliable roles for Congress during a conflict is providing oversight. Congress can help unearth how conflicts started, whether the Executive is achieving its military and strategic goals, and whether it is complying with domestic and international laws. Congress often relies on executive actors to provide information about the conflict, but it can also convene hearings of outside experts and collect open-source intelligence about the situation from journalists on the ground. Cyber hostilities, though, particularly those conducted by highly autonomous systems, will be far

---

[75] Matthew Waxman, *Cyber-Attacks and the Constitution*, HOOVER INST. (2020) ("[I]f war powers is a special constitutional category demanding strong legislative checks . . . mainly because of the risks to American blood, cyber-attacks would barely register at all, because those risks are so tiny and remote."); Eric Jensen, *Future War and the War Powers Resolution*, 29 EMORY INT'L L. REV. 499, 541 (2015) (noting that the War Powers Resolution's reporting threshold fails to encompass cyber operations).

[76] *See* Rain Liivoja et al., *Autonomous Cyber Capabilities Under International Law*, THE NATO COOPERATIVE CYBER DEFENCE CENTRE OF EXCELLENCE, at 12–13 (2019).

[77] *Id.* at 15.

harder to understand and oversee. Conducting forensic audits that recreate what happened during a cyber exchange and translate them into language that congressional overseers can understand will be more challenging than reviewing radar patterns or identifying the source of limpet mines found on oil tankers.[78] The use of artificial intelligence to facilitate autonomy will pose "AI black box" problems for legislators who seek to audit how the cyber operations played out. Further, there will be no "war zone" to which journalists or outside analysts can travel to talk to troops on the ground about what they are seeing. As a result, there will be far fewer open-source reports about what has transpired during these "invisible" cyber operations, unless they morph into kinetic conflicts.

Existing statutes require the U.S. military to report to the congressional defense committees within forty-eight hours of conducting a cyber operation determined to have a medium or high probability of political retaliation, detection, or collateral effects and intended to cause effects in an area in which the United States is not already involved in hostilities.[79] This kind of requirement is helpful, because it puts some members of Congress on notice of situations that might lead to conflict. But a situation between the United States and an adversary could escalate significantly within forty-eight hours, particularly if the states are using autonomous systems that are not adequately engineered to avoid escalation and minimize risks of misdirecting responses. Further, it is not yet clear how well these reporting rules are functioning and whether Congress is receiving the information that it needs to provide adequate oversight.[80]

5. The Effect of Cyber Autonomy on Interagency Dynamics

The use of autonomous cyber tools has the potential to affect the balance of power within the executive branch itself. One interesting question is whether the use of high levels of cyber autonomy will continue to push power out to the military as the creator and operator of these autonomous tools, or

---

[78] *Iran News: U.S. Says Mines Used in Tanker Attacks Bear "Striking Resemblance" to Weapons Touted by Tehran*, CBS News (June 19, 2019).

[79] 10 U.S.C. § 395 (2019).

[80] Robert Chesney, *The Domestic Legal Framework for US Military Cyber Operations* 15, Hoover Inst. Aegis Series Paper No. 2003 (2020).

whether it offers an unexpected opportunity to readjust and centralize the locus of some of the decision-making associated with these tools.

On its face, highly autonomous cyber tools might appear to empower militaries at the expense of other executive agencies with important equities in foreign policy decision-making, such as the State and Justice Departments. Interagency disagreements and negotiations can be very helpful in strength-testing government policies, as Chapter 1 details. But even if these other agencies are involved in discussions about cyber strategy, they likely lack the technological sophistication that military cyber operators possess and so may have difficulty understanding whether highly autonomous cyber tools advance or hinder certain policy objectives and what level of risk these sys-tems pose. Further, as with any military operation, those who sit closest to the point of execution have the greatest power to make last-minute decisions and adjustments. Although autonomous systems will take some of that control from those cyber operators, those operators nevertheless have more direct "eyes on" the operations and their effects. In the United States, Congress's recent legislative acts seem to have enabled this. As Matthew Waxman notes, "Congress has clarified the Defense Department's authority to conduct of-fensive cyber-operations, thereby strengthening its position within the ex-ecutive branch and facilitating action by alleviating legal doubts about its mandate."[81] Part II, however, will consider whether there are ways in which increased autonomy might (counterintuitively) reverse the flow to power to the military.

6. The Effect of Cyber Autonomy on Intra-agency Dynamics

Finally, within individual executive agencies, autonomous cyber tools, like other high-technology tools, will almost inevitably empower operators and computer scientists over lawyers. In contexts driven by high-technology problems, computer engineers and data scientists will become relatively more important to policymakers than they have been in the past, and senior officials may start to treat the input of technology experts as just as important to an international law or foreign policy decision as that of their lawyers.[82]

---

[81] *Id.* at 10–11 (referring to 2012 NDAA, Pub. L. No. 112-81, § 954 (2011)); 10 U.S.C. § 111 (2011); National Defense Authorization Act for Fiscal Year 2018, Pub. L. No. 115-91, §1633(a), §1633(b)(5) (B), 131 Stat. 1283 (2017).

[82] Ashley Deeks, *High-Tech International Law*, 88 Geo. Wash. L. Rev. 574, 647 (2020).

In my view, "It will be the data scientists who can suggest new text-as-data tools and interpret the results of existing models."[83] Data scientists who embrace and understand the problems that government policymakers, lawyers, and diplomats face will be influential in this setting. Among officials who are not cyber experts, military and civilian actors who are technologically literate will be empowered relative to those who disdain technology or are unable to grasp its basic capabilities, limitations, and risks.[84] Thus, lawyers and policymakers who seek to work with data scientists and programmers to understand autonomous cyber tools will gain power relative to their counterparts who cannot or will not do so.[85]

7. Summary

This section illustrated one looming manifestation of the double black box: the use of autonomous cyber operations. Even if states manage these operations very carefully, the potential exists for states to engage in unintended cyber hostile acts that might lead to armed conflict. At least in democracies, legislatures have historically had a role to play in checking executive branch military and foreign policy decisions, but that role today is increasingly narrow, due in part to the interplay between the classified nature of cyber operations and the introduction of AI into cyber systems. This means it is difficult to ensure that the Executive's use of these systems is effective, to hold individuals responsible for poorly conceived or designed cyber tools, and to find productive avenues in which to require the Executive to justify its decisions. Part II will take up the question of how Congress, the Executive, and other actors can establish appropriate parameters for the use and oversight of NSAI, including tools such as autonomous cyber weapons.

---

[83] *Id.* at 647.

[84] *See* Linell Letendre, *Lethal Autonomous Weapons Systems: Translating Geek Speak for Lawyers*, 96 INT'L L. STUD. 274 (2020).

[85] Deeks, *supra* note 82, at 647.

PART II
UNPACKING THE DOUBLE BLACK BOX

4

Using Traditional Checks in the
U.S. System

"It seems to me that we're always a lot better at developing technologies than we are the policies on how to use them."[1]

A. Introduction

Chapter 1 considered the existence and nature of the national security black box, a concept that reflects the difficulty that a range of actors confronts in overseeing and checking U.S. national security activities. This is true both for those entities on which the public has traditionally relied to serve as surrogates and for the less well-recognized actors who sometimes gain visibility into government activities behind the shield of classification and who have certain incentives to check the Executive's actions. Chapter 2 demonstrated the ways in which our national security agencies have already started to use advanced algorithms and explained why those tools will make it challenging for national security officials to meaningfully explain the basis for their decisions to those adversely affected by them—or even understand the basis for the results themselves. Chapter 3 introduced the idea of the double black box, arguing that it will be harder for both traditional and non-traditional providers of oversight to ensure that the government's use of national security AI comports with our public law values relative to their ability to check the Executive in settings that do not involve AI.

But the story cannot end there. Even if it will be a real challenge to confirm that the Executive's national security uses of AI are legal, competent, accountable, and justified, the United States must nevertheless confront that

---

[1] Morgan Chalfant, *Congress Told to Brace for "Robotic Soldiers"*, THE HILL (Mar. 1, 2017) (quoting House Armed Services Committee Chair Mac Thornberry (R-TX) during a hearing about twenty-first-century warfare).

challenge head on. The technology will be, by most accounts, a transformational one. As the United States, China, Russia, Israel, the United Kingdom, and a range of other states race forward, each state will feel pressure from the others to at least keep up with, if not surpass, their adversaries. This, in turn, puts pressure on government actors who genuinely want to adhere to their touchstones (ethical, responsible, accountable uses) as they develop and deploy AI, because proceeding with caution could slow AI development. Indeed, statements from some members of Congress and a key theme of the National Security Commission on AI's (NSCAI's) final report is that the United States is moving much too slowly in its work on national security AI.[2]

But a race that seeks a maximally potent national security tool without heeding whether that tool is effective and trustworthy—and whether it reflects U.S. values—has led us to undesirable outcomes in the past. For example, many believe that the U.S. government's decisions to use renditions, secret detention facilities, and waterboarding after the September 11 attacks were not necessary to ensure U.S. security and were neither wise nor legal. Some nonetheless fear that "pulling our punches" by regulating government or corporate national security AI will cause the United States to fall irreversibly behind. But scrutinizing the Executive to ensure lawful and competent AI development will reduce errors and improve the quality of the product.[3] Competent and accountable AI will work to the economic and security advantages of the United States, fostering confidence in U.S. users and attracting allies and buyers. As Michèle Flournoy and Avril Haines note, "[H]igh standards for robustness, assurance, interpretability, and governability can ultimately be a tremendous source of strategic advantage."[4]

---

[2] Eric Schmidt & Bob Work, *Final Report*, National Security Comm'n on AI (2019); Mohar Chatterjee, *The Pentagon's Endless Struggle with AI*, POLITICO (June 27, 2023) ("Rep. Seth Moulton (D-Mass.), who sits on the House Armed Services Committee, told Politico that the military has fallen 'way behind' on AI . . . ."). At the same time, Eric Schmidt, a co-chair of the NSCAI, noted, "The idea that everything the United States does with artificial intelligence has to be in line with American values is one of the most important themes the commission has uncovered during its research." Yasmin Tadjdeh, *National Security Commission on AI Releases Interim Report*, NAT'L DEF. (Nov. 4, 2019).

[3] *See, e.g.,* James Demsey, Testimony, House Committee on Government Reform (Aug. 3, 2024) ("Privacy protection, checks and balances, accountability and redress are not incompatible with effectively fighting terrorism. To the contrary, clear guidelines and oversight mechanisms are part of the solution."); Stephen Preston, CIA General Counsel, *CIA and the Rule of Law*, 6 J. NAT'L SECURITY L. & POL'Y 1 (2012) (stating that "an abiding respect for the rule of law is one of our country's greatest strengths, even against an enemy with only contempt for the law").

[4] Michèle Flournoy, Avril Haines & Gabrielle Chefitz, *Building Trust Through Testing* 5, WestExec Advisors (Oct. 2020). On the flip side, Angela Huyue Zhang, writing about China's business-friendly regulation of AI, notes that China's "leniency risks creating potential regulatory lags that could escalate into AI-induced accidents and even disasters." Angela Huyue Zhang, *The Promise and Perils of China's Regulation of Artificial Intelligence*, U.H.K. Faculty of Law Res. Paper No. 2024/02.

How, then, do we strike the right balance, particularly when partisan politics have become so potent? Unsurprisingly, there is no silver bullet. We must march ahead with the secrecy surrogates that we have—just as we have done for decades. The system of traditional and nontraditional checks provides the U.S. public with options and tools to help ensure that new AI systems comport with public law values; it will just require more work to maintain the tools' effectiveness. There are things those surrogates can do to improve the likelihood that the United States avoids bad decisions about when, where, and how to use national security AI, and about the nature of the AI it does use. This chapter emphasizes structural and procedural (rather than substantive) adjustments, on the theory that process rules are more likely to achieve consensus among groups with disparate views about the use of national security AI, and as a result are more likely to take root in this partisan era. In creating procedures that strengthen compliance with public law values, the Executive will be more likely to make intelligent substantive choices that reflect a wider range of input than that of the national security bureaucracy alone.[5]

The goal of the procedural proposals in this chapter is to help those overseeing U.S. national security decisions unearth the following types of information about national security AI, to lessen the opacity of the double black box. Our secrecy surrogates should seek to understand:

- Who—Which agencies are using the tools? Who approved that use?
- What—What types of AI-driven algorithms are national security agencies using, to make which kinds of predictions or decisions? Which military systems contain fully autonomous modes? What confidence levels will the Executive require of a tool before using it, and what error rates will the Executive accept?
- Where—Where are the intelligence, military, and homeland security agencies using these tools? Only outside the United States? Inside the territory only of our adversaries, or also our allies? Inside the United States? Against whom?
- When—In what settings are the agencies using these tools? Intelligence analysis, targeted killings, covert action, wartime? Are there situations

---

[5] Ashley Deeks & Kristen Eichensehr, *Frictionless Government and Foreign Relations*, 110 VA. L. REV. __ (forthcoming 2024) (discussing how to avoid groupthink in national security decision-making).

in which agencies have committed not to deploy these tools? Should those boundaries be wider (or narrower)?

- Why—Why has the Executive chosen to deploy AI in a particular setting, rather than rely only on human capabilities?[6] How does the use of AI tools enhance efficiency and accuracy? And will the Executive understand why a particular system made the decision it did?
- How—How well tested are the AI systems?[7] And how well trained are the users?

If our secrecy surrogates can obtain answers to these questions, they will be well positioned to promote lawful and effective uses of national security AI.

Note that some of these questions reflect a concern about the *use* of AI tools per se, while others reflect concern about the quality of the *outputs* of the AI tools. There may be some settings in which we only care about the latter, while in other cases the sheer fact of using AI to recommend an action might be inconsistent with a public law value. Concerns about legality might arise based on the very use of an AI system (because the statutory authority at issue requires a person to make the decision, say) or based on the output (as where the system's recommendation to strike a target would violate the laws of armed conflict (LOAC) if executed). Concerns about efficacy are largely concerns about the quality of AI systems' outputs. Concerns about accountability are largely motivated by worries about the implications of AI's use, regardless of output. The normative proposals contained in this chapter attempt to address both *use* and *output* concerns.[8]

Finally, for those skeptical that the United States should undertake any measures to regulate national security AI, it is worth recalling an important context in which the United States has bound itself to the mast, even in

---

[6] In 2020, the U.S. Intelligence Community committed to ask some of these types of questions of itself. In the Artificial Intelligence Ethics Framework for the Intelligence Community, the Executive produced a "living document intended to provide stakeholders with a reasoned approach to judgment." The document contains a range of questions about legal, obligations, ethical standards, testing, and documentation that the IC should ask and answer as it seeks to develop ethical AI tools. Office of the Director of National Intelligence, *Principles of Artificial Intelligence Ethics for the Intelligence Community* (2020).

[7] Flournoy, Haines & Chefitz, *supra* note 4.

[8] One could draw a loose comparison with the regulation of government contractors. In some cases, the Executive is not permitted to use contractors at all—as where an "inherently government function" is at issue. In other cases, it may not be inherently problematic to use a contractor for a project but we worry about that contractor's performance (or "output") because he may have different incentives than a federal employee would. *See, e.g.,* Jon Michael, *Privatization's Pretentions,* 77 U. Chi. L. Rev. 717, 718 (2010) (discussing how privatization allows "contractors to abuse their discretion, evade oversight, and generate unanticipated cost overruns").

situations in which its adversaries often do not follow the rules: LOAC. The United States requires its armed forces to comply with LOAC, which restricts how they fight armed conflicts and ensures that they adhere to certain moral values, even if the states or nonstate actors the United States is fighting choose to ignore LOAC.[9] That compliance has not hurt us in the conflicts we have fought. The United States presumably has no plans to deviate from LOAC if it ends up in an armed conflict with China. Likewise, it should not abandon its values when building and deploying national security AI, even if other states deploy AI systems that are illegal, immoral, or unaccountable.

Some proposals in this chapter highlight possible roles for Congress, including enacting a "framework statute" to structure the use of high-risk national security AI and creating reporting requirements akin to those that now exist for covert action and risky offensive cyber operations. Other proposals argue for the Executive to take certain actions on its own, such as creating regularized working groups within the Executive, staffed by policymakers, engineers, lawyers, and ethicists, that would oversee and review "high-risk algorithms" (i.e., those used in settings that could result in bodily harm or detention).[10] This might also include "red team" exercises that pit competing algorithms against each other to see which one is most effective, and to ensure that all are difficult to hack.[11] The chapter will urge the national security Executive to be radically transparent about the virtues and challenges of national security AI and its plans to address those challenges. It also will consider the courts' ability to insist that the Executive use only "explainable AI" and the ways in which the practices of whistleblowers, leakers, and journalists may evolve.

For some, the following proposals will seem like "weak tea," modest adjustments that may not be robust enough to meet the challenge of a tool that some see as revolutionary. For this camp, statutes such as the covert action statute and the War Powers Resolution (which serve as models for some

[9] Jennifer M. O'Conner, Speech, N.Y.U. Law Sch., *Applying the Law of Targeting to the Modern Battlefield*, JUST SECURITY (Nov. 28, 2016) ("We comply with the law of war because it is the law.... We will treat everyone lawfully and humanely, even when our foes do not do the same.").

[10] *Cf.* Andrew Tutt, *An FDA for Algorithms*, 69 ADMIN. L. REV. 1 (2017) (arguing for a new federal agency to approve certain dangerous or complex machine learning algorithms).

[11] For example, in 1976, President Ford's Foreign Intelligence Advisory Board sponsored three experiments in "competitive analysis" of the Soviet strategic threat that challenged the CIA's threat assessment. Stephen Flanagan, *Managing the Intelligence Community*, 10 INT'L SECURITY 58, 70–71 (1985). One strategy for guarding against misdesigned AI would be to run competitions between systems to see which performs better. *See also* Richard Danzig, *Technology Roulette*, CTR. FOR NEW AM. SECURITY 19 (June 2018) (suggesting periodic assessments by outside organizations of nascent technologies).

of the proposals that follow) have not had a significant restraining effect on the Executive. For others, the proposals may seem too optimistic, given the sclerotic state of the U.S. Congress and a very strong Executive that has limited incentives to self-constrain. However, these proposals are crafted with the goal of being both feasible—taking into account what we know about how the different branches and actors within them operate—and generally aligned with the actors' own incentives. As the introduction to this book noted, there is no silver bullet to the persistent challenge of government secrecy, and no national consensus about the direction that our government should take in its use of AI.

B. Congress as a Check

Congress's work on AI is at a nascent stage, especially as it relates to national security. Almost all of the laws that it has enacted as of April 2024 have been directed at the domestic uses or implications of AI and have been drafted at a high level of generality. For example, in the National Artificial Intelligence Initiative Act of 2020, Congress required the President to establish and implement the "National AI Initiative" to ensure continued U.S. leadership in AI research and development; "lead the world in the development and use of trustworthy [AI] systems in the public and private sectors"; and prepare the workforce for the integration of AI in all economic sectors.[12] On the international front, it instructed the President to "support opportunities for international cooperation with strategic allies, as appropriate, on the research and development, assessment, and resources for trustworthy [AI] systems."[13] Although indicative of the general direction that Congress would like to see AI use head, it hardly provided detailed prescriptions.

To date, Congress has enacted only a few laws directed specifically at national security AI. For example, in the 2019 National Defense Authorization Act (NDAA), Congress directed DOD to develop a detailed strategic plan to "develop, mature, adopt, and transition AI technologies into operational use."[14] The law required DOD to establish an AI strategy, define the term "AI,"

---

[12] 15 U.S.C. § 9411(a).

[13] *Id.*, § (b)(8).

[14] Pub. L. No. 115-232, § 238 (2018). That law also required DOD to "work with appropriate officials to develop appropriate ethical, legal, and other policies for the Department governing the development and use of artificial intelligence enabled systems and technologies in operational situations."

and accelerate its development and fielding of AI.[15] This law, too, was written at a high level of generality and did little to provide opportunities for oversight. Although Senate majority leader Chuck Schumer has called for a robust push for AI regulation, Congress has generally had a hard time drafting substantive rules to regulate social media, technology companies, and data privacy.[16] AI regulation—and in particular national security AI regulation—will be at least as hard.

That said, Congress's interest in and exposure to national security AI is growing. Congress as a body received its first classified briefing on AI in July 2023. According to news reports, Senators left that briefing "with increased concerns about the risks posed by the technology and no clear battle lines on a legislative plan to regulate the booming industry."[17] One member noted, "I just don't particularly know enough about AI yet to even understand what it is we're trying to regulate. There's probably some role to play in codifying how government uses it in defense realms and so forth, but . . . I think it's something we're still learning about."[18] Another member has sought to require DOD to establish a formal pathway for U.S. servicemembers to report potential AI errors and biases, including in combat.[19] Congress clearly is taking steps to educate itself about AI systems, as evidenced by programs such as Stanford University's AI boot camp for congressional staffers, but it has some distance to go.[20] This suggests that neutral framework legislation of the type proposed in the following section would be a good place to start. But Congress needs to act with alacrity if it wishes to avoid being presented with technological faits accompli.

Congress took some useful steps in the 2024 National Defense Authorization Act, reflecting its efforts to increase its facility with AI and the growing sense that AI will play a major role in U.S. defense. That Act authorized DOD to establish an AI bug bounty program.[21] It required

---

[15] The 2024 NDAA required DOD to update its AI policies and strategies and to issue guidance about how DOD will mitigate bias and monitor accountability for AI activity. P.L. 118-31, § 222.

[16] Ashley Deeks, *Facebook Unbound?*, 105 VA. L. REV. ONLINE 1 (2019) (explaining why "it has proven difficult for Congress and the courts (and the Executive) to weave a set of legal constraints around technology companies that offer us social media platforms, build advanced law enforcement tools, and employ machine learning algorithms to help us search, buy, and drive").

[17] Rebecca Klar, Rebecca Beitsch & Al Weaver, *Senators Grapple with Response to AI After First Briefing*, THE HILL (July 11, 2023) (noting that "lawmakers were split about how and even whether to seek to regulate AI").

[18] *Id.*

[19] Brandi Vincent, *House Lawmakers Want DOD to Create a Process for Reporting and Retiring Irresponsible AI*, DEFENSESCOOP (June 23, 2023).

[20] Stanford Univ., *Congressional Bootcamp on AI.*

[21] 2024 NDAA, *supra* note 15, § 6097.

DOD to "clarify guidance on the instances for and role of human intervention and oversight in the exercise of artificial intelligence algorithms for use
in the generation of offensive or lethal courses of action for tactical operations."[22] It established within the State Department a "Chief AI Officer."[23]
And it formalized and updated the structure of DOD's internal AI governing
council and mandated periodic reporting to the congressional armed services committees.[24]

These are good signs that Congress is waking up to its role. But there are
a number of statutory models that Congress could draw on to develop more
persistent visibility into and control over the actual national security AI systems that the Executive develops. Congress has enacted statutes that regulate
the use of foreign electronic surveillance and the introduction of U.S. forces
into hostilities, as well as statutes that require the Executive to report on
activities such as the use of covert action, offensive cyber operations, and
changes to the legal framework used to fight terrorism. Some of these statutes
contain substantive limitations on these operations, but most of them are
oriented toward procedural rules and information-forcing. These statutes
are intended to address the national security black box problem by bolstering
the likelihood that the regulated programs will be undertaken competently,
legally, and accountably.

1. Framework Statute for Approving High-Risk NSAI

Congress has enacted a number of laws that create a formalized process by
which the President must notify it of certain high-risk national security measures that he has chosen to take.[25] In some of these statutes, Congress creates
a substantive baseline standard for presidential action, such as the covert
action statute's requirement that the President find that a particular action
is "necessary to support identifiable foreign policy objectives of the United
States and is important to the national security of the United States."[26] That
statute also requires the President to share covert action findings with the
congressional leadership and the intelligence committees, generally before

---

[22] *Id.,* § 222.
[23] *Id.,* § 6303.
[24] *Id.,* § 1725.
[25] For the initial blog post proposing this idea, see Ashley Deeks, *Regulating National Security AI Like Covert Action* (July 25, 2023).
[26] 50 U.S.C. § 3093.

the action takes place. The War Powers Resolution requires the President to notify Congress within forty-eight hours when he introduces U.S. forces into hostilities without underlying congressional authorization to do so, and it requires him to remove those forces from hostilities within sixty days if Congress does not subsequently authorize their deployment.[27]

Like the War Powers Resolution, the covert action statute helps ensure that the President's use of a high-risk tool is legal and that policymakers have considered its use carefully. The statute also holds the President directly accountable for the decision to conduct a covert action. The requirement that he report a finding to select members of Congress before the action occurs provides some transparency to a discrete set of non-Executive actors, who can provide a reality check about the need for a covert approach and the risks if the U.S. role is revealed. And the requirement that the President attest that the use of a particular covert action is necessary to support a specific U.S. foreign policy objective helps ensure that the Executive has considered alternatives and found them inferior to the proposed covert action.

Several elements in the covert action statute, including a baseline standard, presidential authorization, and congressional reporting rules, would translate well into a statute that addresses high-risk uses of national security AI. The purpose of the statute would be to ensure that the President himself approves the deployment of such high-risk uses, that senior policymakers and lawyers in the executive branch have the opportunity to debate those uses, and that Congress is aware that the United States is using such tools.

The first thing a statute would need to do is to clearly define what types of AI tools would trigger the statute's requirements. The highest risk AI tools include those that could initiate an armed conflict, the use of nuclear weapons, or other forms of kinetic force without a human on the loop; those that produce recommendations to detain or kill people; and those that directly inform an official's decision to charge someone with a crime. In short, the statute should focus on tools that pose a "significant risk of loss of life or liberty" or "a reasonably foreseeable risk of serious damage to the diplomatic or military relations of the United States if the existence or use of the tool were disclosed without authorization."[28] The statute could provide that the President may not authorize the risk of a high-risk AI tool unless he first signs an "AI Determination" that briefly describes the tool, determines that the use

---

[27] War Powers Resolution, 50 U.S.C. § 1541 et seq.
[28] Compare 50 U.S.C. § 3093(d).

of such tool is necessary to promote U.S. national security, identifies which agency or agencies are authorized to use it, assesses that its use would not violate the Constitution, U.S. law, or international law, and concludes that the benefits of use outweigh the risks. There are other contexts in which agencies must reach agreement about risk levels, such as the National Intelligence Priorities Framework, a classified document created by the White House and national security agencies that prioritizes which countries and targets the IC will focus on and the risks entailed in exposure.[29]

The statute should also require that the President notify certain congressional committees within a short period of time that he has signed an AI Determination. As with the covert action statute, Congress could require that the President keep those committees "fully and currently informed" about the ongoing use of high-risk AI tools, including significant failures and significant changes in the tools' use.[30] Finally, Congress might consider a provision to the effect that "no use of high risk AI may be conducted which is intended to have or has a high likelihood of influencing United States political processes, public opinion, policies, or media."[31] This would limit the government's ability to use deepfakes, for example, where it was highly likely that the deepfakes would (even unintentionally) influence U.S. public opinion.

Congress could modify this proposal along various axes. For example, if Congress and the Executive together believed that requiring presidential sign-off was too onerous or time-consuming, an alternative would be to require Cabinet-level officials to sign AI Determinations for any high-risk AI that their agencies deploy and submit those Determinations to the relevant committees.[32] It could also restrict those officials from further delegating to subordinate officials the authority to sign a Determination.[33] Likewise, Congress could make the list of what AI tools would be covered more or less capacious. Further, DOD and the IC might require different

---

[29] Dir. of Nat'l Intel., *National Intelligence Priorities Framework*, IC Dir. 204. The European Union AI Act takes a risk-based approach to regulating AI. Euro. Comm'n, *AI Act* (Mar. 4, 2024).

[30] Compare 50 U.S.C. § 3093(b).

[31] Compare 50 U.S.C. § 3093(f).

[32] Congress has required cabinet-level certifications in the past. For instance, in the Ike Skelton National Defense Authorization Act for Fiscal Year 2011, Pub. L. No. 111-383, § 1033(b)(5), 124 Stat. 4137, 4352 (2011), Congress required the Secretary of Defense to certify certain facts before authorizing transfers of detainees out of the Guantanamo Bay Detention Facility. *See generally* Comment, *Certification as Sabotage: Lessons From Guantanamo Bay*, 127 YALE L.J. 1416 (2018).

[33] Congress has restricted agencies' power to subdelegate decisions before. *See, e.g.,* 10 U.S.C. § 127e (prohibiting the Secretary of Defense from delegating decisions about providing financial support to foreign proxy forces).

framework statutes, given that they have different missions, underlying statutory authorities, and oversight committees.

One advantage to a framework statute like this is that it would likely prompt the Executive to establish an interagency process to draft the AI Determinations and review the legality of their contents. In the covert action setting, various administrations have established an interagency lawyers' group to review draft findings, which helps ensure that the proposed actions do not violate U.S. law.[34] A framework statute like this for national security AI would ensure that the President knows when his national security agencies are deploying the most sensitive, powerful AI tools to make battlefield and intelligence decisions, and ensure that the tools have passed interagency review as well.

2. Reporting to Congress

Even if Congress does not see the need for or cannot agree on a framework statute, it would be well-advised to enact legislation requiring the Executive to report to it about its use of national security AI. There are many models for national security reporting to Congress, including reporting on offensive cyber operations, forty-eight-hour and six-month War Powers reports, annual reports on the use of the Foreign Intelligence Surveillance Act, and notification requirements for changes to the legal framework for the use of military force,[35] as well as the covert action reporting just discussed. In general, Congress relies heavily on reporting from the Executive to position itself to conduct oversight and determine when further legislation is needed, including where Congress wishes to alter the Executive's policies. Congress's national security reporting requirements tend to focus on executive activities

---

[34] See, e.g., Caroline Krass, Questions for the Record Related to Her Nomination to Become CIA General Counsel 3 (2014) ("When reviewing covert action activities, the CIA General Counsel works with senior lawyers from the other departments and agencies, including those at the Justice, State, and Defense Departments, both to ensure that the proposed covert action activity does not violate U.S. law and to identify any potential violations of international law.").

[35] 50 U.S.C. § 1549 (stating that "the President shall submit to the appropriate congressional committees a report on the legal and policy frameworks for the United States' use of military force and related national security operations, . . . including a list of all foreign forces, irregular forces, groups, or individuals for which a determination has been made that force could legally be used under the [2001] Authorization for Use of Military Force . . . and a description of whether force has been used").

that pose a risk of (or indeed constitute) armed conflict, expose U.S. forces to harm, or invite foreign tensions with allies or adversaries.

One recent reporting requirement for offensive cyber operations could serve as a useful model for AI reporting. In 2019, Congress began to require the Secretary of Defense to submit to the congressional defense committees "notice in writing of any sensitive military cyber operation conducted under this title no later than 48 hours following such operation."[36] The statute defines "sensitive military cyber operations" to mean either an offensive or defensive cyber operation that is carried out by the U.S. armed forces; that is intended to achieve a cyber effect against a foreign terrorist organization or a country with which the United States is not involved in hostilities; and that is determined to have a medium or high collateral effects estimate, a medium or high intelligence gain or loss, medium or high probability of political re- taliation, or a medium or high probability of unintended detection.[37] The statute also makes clear that it does not apply to cyber activities undertaken as covert action.

There are other congressional reporting requirements for military cyber operations as well. Title 10 U.S.C. § 484 requires DOD to provide quarterly cyber operations briefings on "all offensive and significant defensive military operations in cyberspace, including clandestine cyber activities, carried out by the Department of Defense during the immediately preceding quarter."[38] That briefing must describe operations broken down by geographic area or functional command and an update on authorities and legal issues appli- cable to operations, including any presidential directives and delegations of authority received since the last update. Title 10 U.S.C. § 396(a)(1) requires quarterly briefings to the armed services committees regarding application of DOD's weapons review process to "a cyber capability that is intended for use as a weapon."[39] And section 396(a)(2) imposes a forty-eight-hour notifi- cation requirement whenever "any cyber capability that has been approved for [use as a weapon] under international law by a military department" is actually used as a weapon.[40]

Robert Chesney has noted that the notification process for offensive cyber operations is "akin to the more familiar one used for covert action" but that,

[36]   10 U.S.C. § 395(a).
[37]   10 U.S.C. § 395(c)(1)(C).
[38]   10 U.S.C. § 484(a).
[39]   10 U.S.C. § 396(a)(1).
[40]   10 U.S.C. § 396(a)(2).

unlike with the covert action statute, it does not require the kind of interagency involvement that happens with covert action.[41] He writes, "Given that such circumstances are likely to be of some diplomatic and legal sensitivity, . . . it is easy to see why Congress wanted to ensure some customized form of notification requirement for them."[42] This set of reporting requirements could readily be translated into a statute that requires similar notifications about when the Executive approves the use of a risky national security AI system, when the Executive uses such systems, and whether problems arose during the process of approving and deploying those systems. Ensuring that Congress is aware of what high-risk systems the Executive is using—and requiring reporting on when and where those uses occurred—will force the Executive to explain and justify its decisions, allow Congress to identify which executive officials approved particular operations, understand the legal framework for the systems' use, and answer the other types of questions listed in section A of this chapter. Reporting requirements are the easiest way for a traditional secrecy surrogate to gain insight into the double black box.

In addition to requiring reporting, Congress should convene both closed and open hearings about the Executive's use of national security AI. Most obviously, these hearings can extract information about the range of questions listed previously. Less obviously, different congressional committees can use these hearings strategically, to ensure that agencies whose missions are affected by the government's use of AI but that do not use those systems themselves possess information that will help them engage in interagency checks and balances. For example, the Senate Foreign Relations Committee could convene a hearing about AI's interplay with international law at which State Department officials will testify. In preparation for that testimony, the State Department necessarily will engage with the other agencies that are using AI, thus increasing the State Department's knowledge about AI operations and trends.

---

[41] Robert Chesney, *Military Cyber Operations: The New NDAA Tailors the 48-Hour Notification Requirement*, LAWFARE (Dec. 18, 2019).

[42] *Id.* ("The underlying reason to want congressional oversight is the general concern that such operations may generate unintended-but-painful consequences, just as in the covert-action oversight paradigm. And in this context, that would include situations in which the operation might cause serious repercussions with another state, harm to third parties, disruption of intelligence-collection equities or general embarrassment to the United States—that is, precisely the categories identified above.").

3. Joint Committee on AI

Congress occasionally has created joint committees, composed of Republican and Democratic members from both the House and the Senate. The Joint Committee on Taxation, for example, assists majority and minority members from both houses to develop tax legislation, though it does not propose bills itself.[43] It also investigates aspects of the federal tax system and prepares revenue impacts for tax legislation.[44] The creation of the Committee responded to "the need for . . . a procedure by which the Congress could be better advised as to the systems and methods employed in the administration of the internal revenue laws with a view to the needs for legislation in the future, simplification and clarification of administration, and generally a closer understanding of the detailed problems with which both the taxpayer and the Bureau of Internal Revenue are confronted."[45]

Congress should consider creating a Joint Committee on Artificial Intelligence, including a subcommittee that is focused on national security–related AI.[46] The Committee, which should have a permanent staff, could serve as an in-house think tank that would provide standing expertise on AI technologies and their societal impacts. It would allow Congress to rely more heavily on its own expertise rather than that of the executive branch as it considers legislation and oversight actions.[47] AI systems cut across a range of committees, including the Intelligence, Armed Services, Foreign Affairs, and Homeland Security Committees; AI technology is complex (as prior chapters have revealed); and Congress already is confronting a host of calls for AI regulation. All of these factors make AI well suited for a Joint Committee.

---

[43] Congress of the United States, The Joint Committee on Taxation, About.

[44] *Id.*

[45] Congress of the United States, The Joint Committee on Taxation, History.

[46] In 1990, Harold Koh proposed that Congress create a Joint Committee on National Security, though Congress has not yet done so. HAROLD KOH, THE NATIONAL SECURITY CONSTITUTION: SHARING POWER AFTER THE IRAN-CONTRA AFFAIR 169–71 (1990).

[47] *See* George Yin, *How Codification of the Tax Statutes and the Emergence of the Staff of the Joint Committee on Taxation Helped Change the Nature of the Legislative Process*, 71 TAX L. REV. 723 (2018).

4. Expert Oversight Board

Another option for Congress is to create a new oversight body that is expert in AI and that provides oversight and advice to national security agencies about their use of high-risk AI. Congress could model such a body on the Privacy and Civil Liberties Oversight Board (PCLOB), which is an independent agency that "continually review[s] the implementation of Executive Branch policies, procedures, regulations, and information-sharing practices relating to efforts to protect the nation from terrorism, in order to ensure that privacy and civil liberties are protected."[48] Its five members are Senate-confirmed, it has bipartisan membership, and it handles classified information.[49] It also reviews proposed legislation and regulations, reports to Congress twice a year, and convenes public fora to prompt public discussions about electronic surveillance programs.[50] A comparable AI-focused oversight body could be staffed by computer scientists, ethicists, and lawyers; could review and audit the types of high-risk AI that intelligence, defense, and homeland security agencies are developing or using; and could provide objective advice about the quality and risks of the AI systems it reviews.[51] Although this body would still be located in the executive branch, it would have independence and a singular mission that could fruitfully provide a check on the agencies' use of high-risk AI.

5. Mandating Auditable or Explainable AI (xAI)

Chapter 2 asked whether xAI was a solution to the algorithmic black box. It noted that explainability will bolster user confidence in national security AI systems, but it concluded that xAI is a work in progress and only a partial step

---

[48] U.S. Privacy and Civil Liberties Oversight Board, History and Mission.

[49] Bodies like this are quite common in European countries. *See* Norwegian Parliamentary Oversight Committee on Intelligence and Security Services, Brief Overview of Intelligence and Security Oversight Bodies in Certain Countries (2022); UK Investigatory Powers Commissioner's Office, The Equities Process.

[50] Press Release, *Privacy and Civil Liberties Oversight Board to Hold Public Forum on FISA Section 702 with General Nakasone to Keynote*, PCLOB (Dec. 14, 2022).

[51] For a discussion of third-party audits of AI systems, see Inioluwa Raji et al., *Outsider Oversight: Designing a Third Party Audit Ecosystem for AI Governance*, AIES 2022. *See also* DARRELL WEST & JOHN ALLEN, TURNING POINT: POLICYMAKING IN THE ERA OF ARTIFICIAL INTELLIGENCE 183 (2020) (arguing that "software designers should annotate their AI and have AI audit trails that explain how particular algorithms are put together or what kinds of choices are made during the development process").

toward achieving our public law values. That said, there are good reasons for Congress to urge the Executive to adopt AI tools that are explainable or auditable.

A legislative requirement for xAI could take several forms. In mid-2023, Senate Majority Leader Chuck Schumer proposed a framework for AI regulation that included a call for explainability, by which he meant that citizens should be able to ask why an AI system chose one answer over another.[52] (His proposal was not focused on national security AI.) At the same time, Schumer acknowledged that xAI is a thorny and technically complicated problem, and commentators have argued that requiring all AI systems to be explainable would force companies to stop using very complex models (including large-language models).[53]

Congress could address the explainability of national security AI directly by requiring U.S. national security agencies to only use AI that is sufficiently explainable to or auditable by its users, without mandating a particular form or format for those explanations. The Executive might support this approach: DOD's 2020 Ethical Principles state that DOD's "AI capabilities will be developed and deployed such that relevant personnel possess an appropriate understanding of the technology, development processes, and operational methods applicable to AI capabilities, including with transparent and auditable methodologies, data sources, and design procedure and documentation."[54] One reason DOD already has incentives to be sure that it understands its systems is that "[r]isks of sabotage and emergent effects from interaction will be greater with systems that have more autonomy and operate in more populated and interactive technological and physical environments."[55] As a result, those systems must be "even better understood and better controlled than their predecessors."[56]

If Congress enacts reporting requirements related to high-risk AI, ensuring that military and intelligence AI is auditable or explainable to relevant audiences (including the full range of executive officials in the decision-making chain and members of Congress) will help Congress understand that reporting, press the Executive to reveal the cause of any AI accidents

---

[52] Will Henshall, *Chuck Schumer Wants AI to Be Explainable. It's Harder Than It Sounds*, TIME (June 23, 2023).

[53] *Id.*

[54] U.S. Dep't of Defense, Ethical Principles for Artificial Intelligence (Feb. 2020).

[55] Danzig, *supra* note 11 at 19.

[56] *Id.*

that may transpire, and test government claims about the systems' relia-bility.[57] Requiring auditable or explainable national security AI will also help a wider range of national security officials understand and engage with the AI programs of their fellow agencies.

Each of these four proposals is intentionally procedural, in keeping with the relatively neutral nature of public law values, and none takes (or requires members of Congress to take) substantive positions on what the government should or should not use AI to accomplish. If Congress begins to build greater substantive consensus around AI than currently exists, though, it might pursue additional ideas along the following lines.

6. Mandating Negative Security Assurances

In the nuclear setting, the United States has long adopted a policy that it would not use nuclear weapons against non-nuclear weapons states that are parties to the Nuclear Non-Proliferation Treaty (NPT) and that comply with their nuclear non-proliferation obligations. In 2022, the Biden admin-istration confirmed these "negative security assurances," which have been in place since 1978.[58] One key reason for this policy is to reduce the incentive for non-nuclear weapon states to pursue nuclear weapons.

Congress could consider asserting a U.S. policy not to use certain forms of high-risk AI, such as lethal autonomous weapon systems (LAWS), against states that have not developed such systems. There is no equivalent to the NPT that prohibits states from possessing or using LAWS, so a U.S. com-mitment could not be tied to treaty adherence or compliance. Nevertheless, the United States presumably has reasonably good intelligence about which states are pursuing such systems. Such a commitment might dissuade certain

---

[57] Ashley Deeks, *Will Cyber Autonomy Undercut Democratic Accountability?*, 96 INT'L L. STUD. 464, 489 (2020) [hereafter Deeks, *Democratic Accountability*] ("Requiring executives to produce algorithms that are more transparent might also make it easier for legislators to hold executive ac-tors accountable because transparent algorithms might be easier to audit after the fact than human decisionmakers."); Ashley Deeks, *The Judicial Demand for Explainable Artificial Intelligence*, 119 COLUM. L. REV. 1829, 1849 (2019) [hereafter Deeks, *Judicial Demand*] ("Congress may demand and shape the use of xAI across industries or within government via legislation, and it may also demand the use of xAI in briefings by executive agencies, including the intelligence community. . . . That statute may capture the basic values that Congress wants xAI to advance.").

[58] The 2022 Nuclear Posture Review states, "The United States continues to adhere to a negative se-curity assurance that it will not use or threaten to use nuclear weapons against non-nuclear weapons states party to the Treaty on the Nonproliferation of Nuclear Weapons that are in compliance with their nuclear non-proliferation obligations." 2022 Nuclear Posture Review.

states with relatively sophisticated military technology to forgo pursuing LAWS, which would in turn reduce proliferation risks and threats to U.S. forces.

7. Prohibiting AI in Nuclear Command and Control

In June 2023, several Senators released a draft bill that would prohibit the Executive from spending federal funds to use an autonomous weapons system that is not subject to meaningful human control to launch a nuclear weapon or select or engage targets for the purposes of launching a nuclear weapon.[59] The bill would apply to any use of an autonomous system to launch a nuclear weapon, even where the United States was acting defensively after having been struck first.

Current U.S. policy precludes the introduction of AI into nuclear command and control systems.[60] In 2022, the United States, the United Kingdom, and France affirmed that they would "maintain human control and involvement for all actions critical to informing and executing sovereign decisions concerning nuclear weapons employment."[61] In February 2023, the U.S. government tabled a "Political Declaration on Responsible Military Use of Artificial Intelligence and Autonomy," containing that same language.[62] But Congress might want to ensure that this remains U.S. law, not simply a U.S. policy that a new administration easily could change.

A proposal such as the June 2023 bill would invite constitutional pushback from the Executive, which staunchly defends the President's ability to make tactical or operational military decisions without direction from Congress. Congress has responses to this argument, including that a bill like this would

---

[59] Block Nuclear Launch by Autonomous Artificial Intelligence Act of 2023, Sen. Markey (118th Cong.). This discussion is drawn from Ashley Deeks & Matthew Waxman, *Can Congress Bar Fully Autonomous Nuclear Command and Control?*, LAWFARE (June 5, 2023).

[60] Dep't Sec'y of Defense Kathleen Hicks, *The State of AI in the Department of Defense*, U.S. Dep't of Defense (Nov. 2, 2023) ("[I]n the 2022 Nuclear Posture Review the United States made clear that in all cases, we will maintain a human 'in the loop' for all actions critical to informing and executing decisions by the President to initiate or terminate nuclear weapons.").

[61] 2020 Rev. Con. of Parties to the Treaty on the Non-Proliferation of Nuclear Weapons, Principles and Responsible Practices for Nuclear Weapons States, NPT/Conf.2020/WP.70 (July 29, 2022), ¶ 5(vii). *See also* U.K. House of Lords, *Proceed with Caution: Artificial Intelligence in Weapon Systems* 4 (2023) (urging U.K. government to prohibit the use of AI in nuclear command and control).

[62] U.S. Dep't of State, Political Declaration on Responsible Military Use of Artificial Intelligence and Autonomy. The United States removed this provision from a later draft of the Declaration, apparently at the request of one or more states.

constitute the exercise of a lesser-included power to decide what types of nuclear weapon systems the President may spend money on. In any event, a colleague and I previously suggested a somewhat different approach that would put Congress on stronger constitutional ground. We wrote, "Instead of prohibiting the use of funds to *use* an autonomous nuclear launch system, Congress might prohibit the spending of funds to *develop* one. This would help reframe the issue as one of Congress's power—by virtue of its exclusive Article I powers to create military forces—to decide what weapon systems should or shouldn't be in the military arsenal, rather than an issue of Congress's power to limit how the president may use systems that are otherwise in that arsenal."[63] A key advantage to this approach is that it would hold the President personally accountable for the decision to use nuclear weapons by precluding his ability to delegate such decision-making to a machine.

A number of scholars who have written about national security AI have proposed other approaches that Congress could take.[64] This section's discussion is not intended to suggest that those ideas are flawed; instead, it focuses on procedures that will advance public law values and shed light on the double black box, rather than try to impose particular substantive outcomes on the shape of national security AI.

C. Courts as a Check

As Chapter 1 explained, federal courts generally can play only a modest role in penetrating the national security black box. Because many intelligence and military activities are never challenged in litigation, courts only infrequently have occasion to evaluate (and sometimes halt) these executive actions. To date, courts have not played a robust role in navigating the algorithmic black box, either, though that may change soon. As companies and the U.S. government increasingly employ battalions of AI systems, the

---

[63] Deeks & Waxman, *supra* note 59 (emphasis added).
[64] JAMES BAKER, THE CENTAUR'S DILEMMA: NATIONAL SECURITY LAW FOR THE COMING AI REVOLUTION (2020) (proposing to update the Defense Production Act); David Engstrom et al., *Government by Algorithm: Artificial Intelligence in Federal Administrative Agencies* 7, Admin. Conf. of the United States (Feb. 2020) (proposing to "require agencies to engage in prospective 'benchmarking' of AI tools by reserving a random hold-out sample of cases for human decision, thus providing critical information to smoke out when an algorithm has gone astray or 'automation bias' has led decision-makers to excessively defer to an algorithm"); Richard Fontaine & Loren DeJonge Schulman, *Congress's Hidden Strengths*, CTR. FOR NEW AM. SECURITY (July 30, 2020) (urging Congress to use informal oversight tools).

number of AI-related cases in U.S. courts is certain to grow exponentially. As a result, the courts themselves will be important actors in the machine learning ecosystem that will decide when, how, and in what form to develop xAI.[65] Depending on the case, courts will need to consider a range of questions: Who is the audience for the explanation? How simple or complex should the explanation be? What structure or form should the xAI take? Should it be lines of code, or visual presentations, or manipulable programs?[66] What factors should the explanation focus on? As they seek to decision those cases, they are likely to demand meaningful explanations for algorithmic decisions, recommendations, or predictions.[67] By virtue of this demand for explanations, judges have the potential to play a key role in shaping the direction that xAI takes.[68]

Other AI-related cases will not be about AI systems' explainability. Most of the underlying doctrines and statutes that will be at issue in non-national security cases that implicate AI, such as fraud, product liability, intellectual property protections, the Computer Fraud and Abuse Act, and the Administrative Procedure Act, are unlikely to apply directly in national security settings. However, courts may reach decisions in commercial or unclassified government cases that either bind the Executive in its classified operations as well or at least signal to the government how it should approach legal questions that its classified AI tools may implicate. In short, courts are unlikely to play a robust checking function on the double black box, but as unclassified AI-related legal doctrines develop, those doctrines will cast light on how the national security executive should consider operating and may indirectly constrain its behavior.

One court in particular could play a meaningful role in checking the IC's AI/ML tools and requiring explanations for their recommendations: the Foreign Intelligence Surveillance Court. To obtain authorization to conduct electronic surveillance on someone inside the United States for intelligence purposes, the U.S. government must demonstrate to the FISC that there is

---

[65] This discussion is drawn from Deeks, *Judicial Demand, supra* note 57.

[66] Sandra Wachter, Brent Mittelstadt & Chris Russell, *Counterfactual Explanations Without Opening the Black Box: Automated Decisions and the GDPR*, 31 HARV. J.L. & TECH. 841, 872 (2018) (noting that the algorithm's creator could disclose the algorithm's source code, formula, weights, and full set of variables).

[67] *See* Deeks, *Judicial Demand, supra* note 57, at 1830. In the national security context, judges frequently must decide what types of classified explanations by the executive branch are sufficient. Ashley Deeks, *Secret Reason-Giving*, 129 YALE L.J. 612 (2020) (discussing secret reason-giving in the context of foreign surveillance, asset freezes, state secrets, and FOIA).

[68] Deeks, *Judicial Demand, supra* note 57, at 1830.

probable cause that a person is an agent of a foreign power. If the IC relies heavily on AI/ML systems to make that case, the FISC undoubtedly will require information from the IC about those systems, including the data on which they were trained, the parameters they contain, and their error rates. These cases will only be a small percentage of the situations in which the U.S. government uses these tools, though.

D. Internal Executive Checks

Some will resist the idea that the executive branch can serve as a check on itself. After all, the key concern behind the double black box is that the Executive will use AI tools behind the veil of secrecy in a way that prevents us from knowing whether those uses comply with public law values. However, this fails to appreciate that the Executive is comprised of a wide range of actors who will have different perspectives on what uses of AI are acceptable. Recall that the double black box itself looks different for different actors: some executive officials (such as agency lawyers or policymakers from the State, Treasury, or Justice Departments) have only a hazy sense of what types of national security AI the government is using, but their jobs may require them to seek out and understand those uses. That process itself may foster reason-giving, increased AI quality, and accountability for the AI owner.

Indeed, to date, the only actor that has imposed substantive rules or procedures on the Executive's development and use of national security AI is the Executive itself. DOD, the Intelligence Community, and DHS have issued public policies about their use of AI.[69] The IC put out a list of ethics- and safety-driven questions that it expects its AI developers to ask.[70] And DOD has issued a Responsible AI Strategy and Implementation Pathway that sets out lines of effort for the Department as it moves to accelerate AI adoption.[71] In 2023, President Biden issued a lengthy executive order on AI, one part of which mandated an interagency process to provide a proposed National Security Memorandum by July 2024 on the governance of AI for

---

[69] *See, e.g.*, U.S. Dep't of Homeland Sec'y, *Acquisition and Use of Artificial Intelligence and Machine Learning Technologies by DHS Components* (Aug. 8, 2023).

[70] Office of the Director of National Intelligence, *Principles of Artificial Intelligence Ethics for the Intelligence Community* (2020).

[71] U.S. Dep't of Defense, *Responsible Artificial Intelligence Strategy and Implementation Pathway* (June 2022).

military and intelligence purposes.[72] These efforts are commendable first steps toward legal, efficient, accountable uses of AI, but they do not yet provide the level of detail that will allow appropriate actors in other agencies to peer inside the black box.

But it will be key for those inside the executive branch who are given the opportunity to do so to understand what they are looking at. Many who have written about AI have urged the government to improve its ability to recruit, train, and retain AI experts.[73] However, the government should also encourage nontechnical experts, including policymakers, lawyers, diplomats, and budget experts, to acquire basic AI skills so that they are better poised to use those tools in their own jobs and engage their national security counterparts about the tools those counterparts are using. As the 2020 First Quarter NSCAI report states, "Building a federal workforce that designs, develops, and fields AI technologies for national security in an ethical and responsible manner requires everyone within the national security enterprise to have a foundational understanding as to what constitutes ethical and responsible AI, including a baseline awareness of the risks and limitations associated with AI systems."[74] The report notes that legal, ethics, and oversight personnel as well as technologists "require more in-depth and tailored training to ensure they are adequately knowledgeable about the responsible and ethical considerations of AI."[75] In its 2020 Second Quarter report, NSCAI specifically argues that the State Department "should expand training on AI and emerging technology for personnel at all levels across professional areas."[76] Although NSCAI seems to urge this approach so that U.S. diplomats are better able to persuade their counterparts that the U.S. approach to AI is preferable to China's,[77] having nonmilitary, non-intelligence officials conversant in AI means that they will also be able to better serve as interagency checks as the tools are built and deployed.

---

[72] White House, Executive Order on the Safe, Secure, and Trustworthy Development and Use of Artificial Intelligence, § 4.8 (Oct. 30, 2023). News reports indicate that President Biden's team sent him a classified proposed Memorandum for his review in July 2024, but as of September 2024 no part of that Memorandum is public. *See* Alexandra Kelley, *Memo on AI's National-Security Implications Heads for Biden's Desk*, DEFENSE ONE (July 26, 2024).

[73] WEST & ALLEN, *supra* note 51, at 184.

[74] National Security Commission on AI, First Quarter Recommendations 69 (Mar. 2020).

[75] *Id.*

[76] National Security Commission on AI, Second Quarter Recommendations, at vii (2020).

[77] *Id.* at 79 (noting that U.S. diplomats must "marshal coalitions of like-minded partners to shape standards, norms, and commerce").

1. Interagency Policy and Legal Processes

One critical way that the Executive tries to take into account the full range of interests when it sets policy is by employing the interagency process. Presidents establish processes, often run by the National Security Council, that escalate in seniority and include an interagency policy committee (at the Assistant Secretary level), a Deputies' Committee (at the level of Deputy Secretary), a Principals' Committee (heads of departments and agencies), and the National Security Council itself, headed by the President and attended by his national security Cabinet.[78] "The primary motivation for the establishment of the National Security Council after World War II was the recognition that the nation's foreign policy interests could not be pursued exclusively through the efforts of executive departments acting separately."[79] It is through these interagency processes that an administration develops, coordinates, and evaluates the policies of the Executive as a whole and, in some cases, the national security agencies individually.

If, as the prior section suggests, Congress enacts an AI framework statute, the President should establish an interagency process similar to the kind it has developed for other high-risk operations to address the statutory requirements. One model is covert action: for high-risk AI, an interagency policy group could develop a draft Determination and a lawyers' group could evaluate it just as they evaluate draft findings for covert action.[80] This process would be a one-and-done—once the President signs the "AI Determination," the CIA or DOD would proceed to deploy the high-risk tool without coming back to the interagency unless and until it becomes necessary to amend the Determination. This approach would require State, Justice, Commerce, and Treasury officials to get smarter about AI to stay in the loop. There have been some recent, promising signs, including the establishment within the State Department of an Office of the Special Envoy for Critical and Emerging Technology[81] and a more prominent role for the Arms Control Bureau in leading multilateral discussions about AI standards.[82]

---

[78] For the Biden administration's version of this document, see White House, National Security Memorandum 2, *Memorandum on Renewing the National Security Council System*.

[79] John Deutsch, Arnold Kanter & Brent Scowcroft, *Strengthening the National Security Interagency Process, in* KEEPING THE EDGE 265 (A. Carter & J. White eds., 2000).

[80] *See* Krass, *supra* note 34.

[81] U.S. Dep't of State, Office of the Special Envoy for Critical and Emerging Technology.

[82] U.S. Dep't of State, Keynote Remarks by Amb. Bonnie Jenkins to the Summit on Responsible Artificial Intelligence in the Military Domain (Feb. 16, 2023).

Even if Congress does not enact a framework statute, the Executive should create an interagency process for reviewing high-risk AI tools. The Executive could model that process on those set up by Presidents Obama and Biden around the use of targeted killings[83] and offensive cyber operations.[84] In both cases, these presidential policies were memorialized in blanket policy documents negotiated in the interagency and signed by the President.[85] They reportedly established an understanding of which kinds of operations agencies may undertake without further interagency process and which ones must come back through the interagency (or the National Security Council, or the President) for notice or approval.[86] High-risk military or intelligence AI bears several similarities to targeted killings and offensive cyber operations: all occur within the national security black box, all pose significant risks to U.S. foreign policy (even when successful), all require attention to the relevant international and domestic legal frameworks, and all raise questions about whether the United States should notify the state in whose territory the United States employs the tool.

In order for all members of the interagency review team to understand the high-risk system they are reviewing, the officials representing their agencies on that team should be required to undertake an intensive crash course on AI. Further, the agency bringing forward the high-risk system should create a "baseball card" for the interagency group that explains how the system works and has performed in prior testing, as well as the potential risks if the system fails to operate as anticipated.[87] Establishing such a process could bolster public trust (both domestic and foreign), enhance legal compliance, ensure rigor in the deployment process, broaden the expectation of reason-giving (especially if the President must approve the use of a particular tool),

---

[83] Presidential Policy Memorandum Governing Direct Action Counterterrorism Operations Outside Areas of Active Hostilities (n.d.).

[84] U.S. offensive cyber operations policies under Presidents Obama, Trump, and Biden remain classified, though President Obama's policy was leaked. News reports suggest that these policies were shaped by the interagency before the Presidents approved them. *See* Suzanne Smalley, *Biden Set to Approve Expansive Authorities for Pentagon to Carry Out Cyber Operations*, CYBERSCOOP (Nov. 17, 2022).

[85] *See id.* (describing President Biden's offensive cyber operations policy); Charlie Savage, *Biden Rules Tighten Limits on Drone Strikes*, N.Y. TIMES (July 1, 2023) (describing the Biden policy, including the requirement that the President approve specific strikes outside area of active hostilities).

[86] Smalley, *supra* note 84 (noting that the final version supposedly "will include provisions requiring the White House to receive details of cyber operation plans from DOD well in advance of operations").

[87] *See* Flournoy, Haines & Chefitz, *supra* note 4, at 3 ("[D]eveloping an effective TEVV approach that is sufficiently predictive of performance is critical to building the trust in these systems necessary to deploy and leverage these capabilities at scale.").

enhance accountability (because it will be clear which actors approved the system's use), and improve the quality of systems (by widening the group that can spot errors).[88] The defense and intelligence agencies likely will resist such an idea, arguing that they generally do not vet their tools with other agencies. However, as with targeted killings and offensive cyber tools, AI systems are novel, high-risk national security tools whose use will be very controversial both inside and outside the United States, at least in the near term. As a result, a broader set of U.S. national security experts should be involved in early decisions about whether, when, and how to use these systems.

The use of national security AI will raise a range of difficult international and domestic legal questions as well as those policy questions. For example, if a statute requires the Secretary of Defense to sign off on a particular operation before DOD undertakes it, does that preclude DOD from using an autonomous system to perform that operation? Would the use of a deepfake that purports to show prisoners of war held by the United States criticizing their own government violate the Geneva Conventions prohibition on exposing POWs to "public curiosity"?[89] If Russia hacks a U.S. autonomous naval drone and uses it to attack a Ukrainian warship, does the United States bear any responsibility? If the CIA wants to use a deepfake to make it look as if a famous U.S.-Iranian dual national is praising a U.S. policy, does that implicate the First Amendment? Could DOD invoke the U.S. Constitution's Taking Clause to seize a high-value algorithm developed by a U.S. company?[90]

Policymakers should ensure that they include their agency lawyers in AI development. The White House should encourage DOD, the CIA, and the Office of the Director of National Intelligence's lawyers to bring to the interagency lawyers' group difficult AI-related questions, to ensure that the questions are evaluated by lawyers who bring a range of expertise to the table. Agency lawyers should see the interagency lawyers' group as an ally. At the same time, the interagency group must operate at the "speed of relevance," so that it provides guidance to policymakers quickly and does not let hard questions languish.[91]

---

[88] For another proposal to involve the interagency in the review of an AI tool, see Daniel Byman et al., *The Case for a Deepfake Equities Process*, LAWFARE (May 24, 2023) (envisioning an interagency process to determine when agencies may use deepfakes).

[89] Geneva Convention (III) Relative to the Treatment of Prisoners of War, art. 13 (Aug. 12, 1949).

[90] *See* James Baker, *Artificial Intelligence and National Security Law: A Dangerous Nonchalance*, Starr Forum (May 25, 2018).

[91] *See, e.g.*, U.S. Dep't of Defense, Remarks by Secretary Mattis on the National Defense Strategy (Jan. 19, 2018) (stating that the strategy "provides clear direction for significant change at the speed of relevance").

2. Dissent Channel

The Dissent Channel is a mechanism by which Foreign Service Officers may communicate directly to the Secretary of State their concerns about the direction U.S. policy is taking.[92] According to the Foreign Affairs Manual, the "Dissent Channel was created to allow its users the opportunity to bring dissenting or alternative views on substantive foreign policy issues, when such views cannot be communicated in a full and timely manner through regular operating channels or procedures, to the attention of the Secretary of State and other senior State Department officials in a manner which protects the author from any penalty, reprisal, or recrimination."[93] Created during the Vietnam War, members of the Foreign Service have used it to object to operations during that war, U.S. strategy toward the Soviet Union, U.S. recognition of a corrupt Guatemalan dictator, and President Trump's travel ban, among other policies.[94] Creating a comparable channel for U.S. employees to report concerns about government uses of AI would be a way to ensure that senior executive officials have visibility into AI incidents in the field (or deep in the bowels of an agency).

Congress could create the equivalent of a Dissent Channel via legislation, but the Executive could also decide on its own to create a Dissent Channel inside each agency that will use high-risk AI (including DOD, DHS, and the IC).[95] Doing so would give officials within those departments who wanted to elevate their concerns a clear channel in which to do so. The President could also require that each agency share Dissent Channel communications with the National Security Council, to better allow NSC to track AI developments inside agencies.[96]

One downside of such a channel is that, unless carefully managed, dissenters may be treated as whistleblowers, who often suffer retaliation for their acts. Because the AI systems at issue are very likely to be classified, it would be difficult to create an anonymous hotline for agency employees to call. If such concerns make additional agency-specific Dissent Channels

---

[92] Foreign Aff. Manual, 2 FAM 070 Dissent Channel (2018).

[93] 2 FAM 071.1.

[94] Nate Jones, Tom Blanton & Emma Sarfty eds., *Department of State's Dissent Channel Revealed*, Nat'l Security Archive (Mar. 15, 2018).

[95] *See* Neal Katyal, *Internal Separation of Powers: Checking Today's Most Dangerous Branch from Within*, 115 YALE L.J. 2314, 2329 (2006) (suggesting replication of the Dissent Channel outside the State Department and possibly permitting employees to dissent outside their agency).

[96] *See* Deeks & Eichensehr, *supra* note 5 (manuscript at 43).

likely to go unused, the Defense Department, DHS, and the IC could enforce the production of dissent. As a colleague and I wrote elsewhere:

> One way any given set of actors can bolster checks is to require some subset of their group to dissent. The idea of enforcing dissent to foster better outcomes is not a new one. It has analogues in religious traditions, particularly the Catholic Church's practice of appointing a "devil's advocate" to argue against the canonization of a particular saint.... Frederick Schauer has urged that "[i]f we think ... that ... it is essential to challenge accepted ideas as a way of advancing knowledge or avoiding intellectual complacency, then it is important not only to protect the challengers, but to ensure that such challengers exist ... and thus, if necessary, to take affirmative steps to create those institutions to ensure that there actually will be challenges."[97]

Translating this to the AI realm, agencies could establish AI "red teams" to ensure that some set of actors argues vigorously against the use of a particular risky AI tool and games out various scenarios in which the tool could produce harmful outcomes. The Defense Department and the IC often use red-teaming to challenge their own norms and assumptions and so have extensive experience that they could direct toward this challenge.[98]

One important counterargument to increasing checks on or within the Executive is the concern that these checks will render the United States too slow and cautious and, as a result, will force the United States to surrender its apparent lead in AI to China. Several AI reports bemoan excessive bureaucracy and call for a more streamlined approach to adopting military AI. NSCAI's 2020 First Quarter report, for example, worries that "successful AI application is threatened by bureaucratic impediments and inertia" and that "top-down leadership is needed to overcome organizational barriers and create strategic change."[99] But most of the Committee's concerns are focused on bureaucratic constraints related to acquisitions and recruitment

---

[97] *Id.* at 42, quoting Frederick Schauer, *Transparency in Three Dimensions*, 2011 U. ILL. L. REV. 1339, 1355.

[98] *See, e.g.*, Defense Science Board, *The Role and Status of DoD Red Teaming Activities* 1–3 (Sept. 2003) (noting that red teams can challenge operational concepts to discover weaknesses, temper complacency, serve as surrogate adversaries, and deepen understanding of available options); Micah Zenko, *Inside the CIA Red Cell*, FOREIGN POL'Y (Oct. 15, 2015) (describing "red team" inside the CIA).

[99] NSCAI, *supra* note 74, at 15. *See also* WEST & ALLEN, *supra* note 51, at 192 (arguing for "flattening organizations so that decisions are made closer to the front lines").

challenges.[100] Nothing proposed in this chapter would increase those types of bureaucratic impediments. Indeed, NSCAI urges a range of substantive policies that are consistent with this chapter, noting:

> Public trust will hinge on justified assurance that government use of AI will respect privacy, civil liberties, and civil rights. The government must earn that trust and ensure that its use of AI tools is effective, legitimate, and lawful. This imperative calls for developing AI tools to enhance oversight and auditing, increasing public transparency about AI use, and building AI systems that advance the goals of privacy preservation and fairness. . . . The government should strengthen oversight and governance mechanisms and establish a task force to assess evolving concerns about AI and privacy, civil liberties, and civil rights.[101]

This chapter proposes a range of checks by traditional secrecy surrogates that would help the government earn the trust that the report calls for, while remaining sensitive to classification concerns and avoiding unduly onerous regulations that could bring interagency policymaking to a standstill.

3. Coding the Laws of Armed Conflict

The U.S. military, like its peers, will use AI tools in settings that implicate LOAC.[102] At the most ambitious end of the spectrum, militaries are pursuing broad autonomy for machines to make kinetic decisions.[103] At the more

---

[100] NSCAI, *supra* note 74, at 21 et seq. *See also* Schmidt & Work, *supra* note 2, at 64 (worrying that bureaucracy deters start-ups from working with DOD); *id.* at 375 (worrying that highly skilled technologists inside government face bureaucratic hurdles in sharing source code or downloading data sets).

[101] Schmidt & Work, *supra* note 2, at 11.

[102] This discussion draws from Ashley Deeks, *Coding the Law of Armed Conflict: First Steps*, in THE FUTURE LAW OF ARMED CONFLICT (M. Waxman & T. Oakley eds., 2022). *See also* Hans Vreeland, *Targeting the Islamic State, or Why the Military Should Invest in Artificial Intelligence*, WAR ON THE ROCKS (May 16, 2019) (discussing ways that AI will provide advantages in identifying targets); Johan Schubert et al., *Artificial Intelligence for Decision Support in Command and Control Systems* (23rd Int'l Command and Control Res. & Tech. Symp., Nov. 2018) (discussing advantages of incorporating AI into command and control systems).

[103] *See, e.g.*, Paul Scharre, *The Perilous Coming Age of AI Warfare*, FOREIGN POL'Y (Feb. 29, 2024); John Cherry & Christopher Korpela, *Enhanced Distinction: The Need for a More Focused Autonomous Weapons Targeting Discussion at the LAWS GGE*, ICRC BLOG (Mar. 28, 2019) (stating that "the U.S. government is currently researching and developing autonomous weapon systems with manual or automatic safeguards or locks in the case of weapon malfunction, the possibility of human intervention during operations, and real-time operating systems status updates provided to commanders").

modest end of the spectrum, militaries may develop algorithms that predict whether a detainee poses a serious threat, which neighborhoods to patrol, and whether someone is a civilian or an enemy combatant. The need to encode LOAC directly into an AI/ML algorithm is strongest in the case of fully autonomous weapons, but coding in the second set of cases should still be responsive to LOAC. Even if states intend to retain "meaningful human judgment" or "appropriate levels of human judgment" over military decisions, military operators will be well served if the algorithmic predictions or recommendations that guide those decisions fall within designated legal parameters.[104] Coding the law into AI systems is one way to help ensure that U.S. activities comply with the law.

The growing interest in relying on algorithms to support—and in some cases to supplant—human decision-making raises hard questions, including whether it is even possible to translate relatively indeterminate legal concepts into computer code and what choices governments need to make as they produce these algorithmic tools. Skeptics argue that it would be very difficult to encode key LOAC rules such as distinction and proportionality into lethal autonomous systems.[105] Lethal autonomous systems will be hard to engineer with embedded legal safeguards because their programmers necessarily must encode all applicable rules of LOAC into them; there will be no human to intercede between system decision and execution to ensure LOAC compliance. Many of the arguments about the impossibility of coding LOAC into lethal autonomous systems are cursory, though, and most concerns are directed at fully autonomous systems. There is a range of more modest predictive algorithms that will also facilitate military operations, which are nearer at hand.

Consider a system that processes video feeds and predicts whether a particular person on the battlefield is a member of the armed forces, civilian, medic, or unlawful combatant. Another example is an algorithm that predicts

---

[104] Lisa Shay et al., *Do Robots Dream of Electric Law? An Experiment in the Law as Algorithm*, in ROBOT LAW 274, 298 (Ryan Calo, A. Michael Froomkin & Ian Kerr eds., 2016) ("There is an increasing need for law in algorithmic forms, and with it, myriad challenges.").

[105] *See* Ulrike Esther Franke, *Flash Wars: Where Could an Autonomous Weapons Revolution Lead Us?*, EUR. COUNCIL ON FOREIGN REL. (Nov. 22, 2018) ("[S]ome particularly optimistic developers suggest that it may even be possible to programme laws of war into autonomous systems, such as rules of engagement, humanitarian laws, or proportionality. However, optimism on this front has faded in recent years."); Dustin Lewis, Gabriella Blum & Naz Madirzadeh, *War-Algorithm Accountability*, at ii (Aug. 2016) ("[E]ven among leading scientists, uncertainty prevails as to the technological limits."); Seumas Miller, *Machine Learning, Ethics and Law*, 23 AUSTL. J. INFO. SYS. 1, 10 (2019) (arguing that robots' failure to be able to recognize moral properties and our inability to reduce moral principles to code means that we cannot enshrine LOAC in robots).

whether someone poses an imperative threat to security, such that it would be lawful to detain him. Militaries might be inclined to develop algorithms in this and a host of other settings in which they (1) have large quantities of data; (2) must make the same kind of decision repeatedly; and (3) face uncertainty about the nature, identity, or intentions of a particular actor or object. Machine learning algorithms might improve existing processes. First, assuming the ability to create a robust database of information, the algorithms can take into account all of the information in the system, not just the information in the military decision maker's head at the time. Second, in the detention setting, these algorithms might be able to identify connections that humans might not otherwise see, such as preexisting relationships among detainees. Third, algorithms can be programmed to take into account only relevant information.[106] Those building the algorithms can embed basic legal parameters ex ante by telling the algorithm what features will be relevant to the legal questions to come and excluding irrelevant features.

It will be desirable for the military to develop predictive algorithms that are sensitive to the human user's legal framework ex ante and that assist the decision maker in her legally infused decision ex post.[107] If these are the settings in which the military will use predictive algorithms and machine learning in the near to midterm, perhaps the concept of "coding the law" is not quite right. Instead of "coding LOAC" into the algorithm in its entirely, the process could consist of three phases: (1) identifying the applicable law; (2) crafting and training the algorithm to produce a recommendation relevant to that legal framework; and (3) interpreting the algorithmic predictions through the lens of that law. The first and second steps of that process will overlap with a state's efforts to test, evaluate, verify, and validate the systems and to ensure that the system will not violate LOAC (a process envisioned by Article 36 of Additional Protocol I to the Geneva Conventions and generally considered to be required under customary international law).[108]

---

[106] This assumes that it is possible to avoid programming biases into these algorithmic systems.

[107] Annemarie Vazquez, *LAWS and Lawyers: Lethal Autonomous Weapons Bring LOAC Issues to the Design Table, and Judge Advocates Need to Be There*, 228 MIL. L. REV. 89, 106 (2020) ("[E]xperts familiar with advising commanders on LOAC issues in military operations must be present during design to help equip LAWs' learners with lawful and reliable parameters when their models are trained.").

[108] *See* Tobias Vestner & Altea Rossi, *Legal Reviews of War Algorithms*, 97 INT'L LEGAL STUD. 509, 513 (2021) (arguing that "for military systems that embed AI, as the law is translated into technical specifications, technical and legal assessments ultimately conflate into one" such that states must conduct legal reviews as part of the TEVV process).

If militaries pursue these kinds of predictive algorithms, we may see four systemic changes. The first change is that highly autonomous tools, including cyber tools, may empower militaries at the expense of other executive agencies that have important equities in foreign policy decisions.[109] Second, we may see a shift of power *within* agencies: computer and data scientists will become relatively more important to policymakers than they have been previously. Senior officials may treat their input as key to foreign policy decisions, competing with advice from more traditional advisers. This should serve as a wake-up call to policymakers, lawyers, and diplomats that they need to grasp the capabilities, limitations, and risks of national security AI if they wish to retain a seat at their agency's decision-making table.[110]

Third, and in tension with the first change, is the possibility that the use of increasingly autonomous systems could reverse this flow of power to militaries. Ironically, increased autonomy in warfighting tasks could offer the chance to centralize some decision-making, as the process of building machine learning algorithms for warfighting systems seeks to incorporate the commander's intent in advance and remain sensitive to legal constraints.[111] Forcing government officials to agree about how to interpret certain LOAC concepts may enhance U.S. compliance with international law. DOD likely would perceive this potential centralization of decision-making as unattractive and will resist sharing the authority to make algorithmic choices about autonomous cyber tools. Interagency lawyers might also struggle to agree on which features to incorporate into those tools. On the other hand, obtaining interagency acceptance of autonomous cyber tools would bolster the military's confidence about their use and would help the State Department's diplomats and lawyers assuage allies' concerns about the U.S. use of these tools.

Fourth, the process of developing national security AI could prompt militaries to re-evaluate how they currently undertake human-only LOAC analyses. Confronting questions about what specific features should feed into a detention or targeting decision and contemplating responses to quantitative recommendations raises questions about humans' own LOAC "algorithms." Each military officer has his or her own personal algorithms, which may lead one actor to approve a strike and another to decline to do

---

[109] Deeks, *Democratic Accountability, supra* note 57, at 493.
[110] *Id.* at 495.
[111] *Id.* at 494.

so. Machine learning-driven efforts to quantify the features and confidence levels surrounding LOAC decisions may force military actors to question and more clearly articulate what drives their noncomputerized military decisions. As Sergot et al. wrote, "Representation in logical form helps to identify and eliminate unintended ambiguity and imprecision."[112] Codifying military predictive algorithms might not only reduce imprecision in computer-assisted military decision-making: it might also reduce imprecision in human-only decision-making. For now, it is prudent to leave lawyers in the loop, even as the pace of war narrows the window for that final legal intervention.

4. Collecting Classified Sentiment about AI

As discussed earlier in this chapter, most of the contemporary discussion about how Congress and the Executive might regulate and derisk AI is focused on unclassified manifestations of AI tools.[113] Government actors are concerned about how AI tools such as ChatGPT will help malicious actors commit fraud and spread propaganda and misinformation, and about the prospect that AI will replace people's jobs. One set of responses to AI development may be legislative, informed by congressional hearings and lobbying on Capitol Hill by companies that produce AI systems. Another could be technocratic, led by actors like the Justice Department, the Federal Trade Commission, and the National Institute of Standards and Technology. A third—ambitious—approach, one proposed by Rep. Ted Lieu (D-CA), could be a combination of the first two: a congressionally created government commission to assess AI risks and potentially a new federal agency to oversee AI.

A fourth response, which could inform the substance of any of the first three approaches, would be to ask the public how it wants the government to protect it against AI's various risks and misuses. In 2023, the Department of Commerce took a first step in that direction, putting out a "request for comment" on how Commerce could regulate AI systems to assure users that

---

[112] M.J. Sergot et al., *The British Nationality Act as a Logic Program*, 29 Comm. ACM 370, 371 (May 1986).
[113] This section is drawn from Ashley Deeks, *Who's Tackling Classified AI?*, Lawfare (Apr. 17, 2023).

the systems are legal, effective, and safe.[114] The idea of opening up the conversation to the public is appealing. These systems affect all of us, and the public (including computer scientists, ethicists, lawyers, and policymakers, as well as those who have experienced AI errors or fraud) could usefully contribute examples of inspiring or terrible uses of AI systems, insights about what types of regulations have worked well in comparable technologies or societies, and broader reflections about the kind of society we do and don't want to live in.[115]

A 2023 *New York Times* opinion piece asked whether democracy and AI can fix each other.[116] The premise was that views on AI are highly polarized, with some individuals confident that AI will enhance human existence and others fearful that AI will undercut democracy and, ultimately, humanity itself. The author argued that AI "can make democracy work better by surfacing ideas from everyone, not just the loudest" speakers and "can find surprising points of agreement among seeming antagonists and summarize and digest public opinion in a way that's useful to government officials."[117] Some software companies (such as Pol.is) and some governments (such as Taiwan's) have begun to employ this approach, using AI tools and moderators to facilitate a consultative process among citizens to solicit and digest public opinion and narrow areas of difference.[118] The motivating idea is that it is possible to develop agreement on deadlocked issues by breaking down topics into discrete propositions and identifying areas where different sides can agree. Participants can redraft and refine the propositions in respond to continued divides, with the goal of reaching consensus.

As U.S. national security agencies are introducing a range of tools into their work, they surely are asking themselves difficult questions about what types of tools they should embrace or reject. To the credit of DOD, the IC, and DHS, they have committed to AI policies that reflect basic public law values: reliability, safety, accountability, lack of bias, and so on. But because

---

[114] U.S. Dep't of Commerce, National Telecommunications and Information Administration, AI Accountability Policy Request for Comment (Apr. 7, 2023).

[115] In 2023, a scholar used survey data to assess how comfortable the public was with the government's use of facial recognition in different contexts. He found that people were generally comfortable with government use to investigate serious crimes, enhance the security of controlled spaces, and in some cases increase efficiency of identify verification, but were particularly uncomfortable with abuse by officials for private purposes. Matthew Kugler, *Public Perceptions Can Guide Regulation of Public Facial Recognition*, 25 SCI. & TECH. L. REV. 1, 6 (2023).

[116] Peter Coy, *Can A.I. and Democracy Fix Each Other?*, N.Y. TIMES (Apr. 5, 2023).

[117] *Id.*

[118] Audrey Tang, *A Strong Democracy Is a Digital Democracy*, N.Y. TIMES (Oct. 15, 2019).

those principles and policies are written at a high level of generality, they will not answer many of the hard questions that will arise as these agencies consider what AI tools to use to defend the United States. Should the CIA be willing to use deepfakes to affect foreign elections? If the Defense Department decides to use ChatGPT-like tools to conduct deception operations against a set of foreign users, how will it ensure that those tools won't spread and "blow back" into the United States? What level of large language model "hallucination" should U.S. national security agencies be willing to tolerate? Are there some uses of AI that these agencies should take off the table, even if we know that our adversaries won't?

Many of these questions are easier to ask than to answer. One place to start is to obtain the views of a wide range of national security experts who spend their working hours behind the veil of secrecy. Using tools that operate like Pol.is, the executive branch could first give all participants basic training in different types of AI, what AI systems can and cannot do, and how they have been used in the real world. The executive could pose a range of questions about possible uses of national security AI, including realistic hypotheticals, for relevant officials within the Departments of Defense, Justice, Homeland Security, and State, as well as the intelligence community, to wrestle with. Moderators could then try to work toward consensus positions on various potential uses (or nonuses) of AI and share their findings with senior national security policymakers.

One initial objection is that this exercise would let the fox guard the henhouse rather than serving as a check on unwise or unlawful policies. However, the national security bureaucracy is surprisingly diverse in terms of experience, perspective, political persuasion, and training. A career Foreign Service Officer and a CIA field agent will not see issues identically. Nor will a Defense Department cyber specialist and a Justice Department lawyer in the National Security Division. Further, this would be a way to assemble a large number and wide range of views about classified uses of AI, which is otherwise difficult to collect input on. Views of executive branch officials are not the only input worth obtaining: Congress and the Executive will surely hear from technology companies, foreign allies, and nongovernmental organizations. But gaining views from national security professionals—be they intelligence analysts, diplomats, computer scientists, or military operators—would be invaluable as we shape a national approach to national security AI.[119]

---

[119] As discussed in the next chapter, the United States could pursue a similar approach with NATO member state officials.

5. Radical Transparency about the Challenges of AI

What else can the Executive do to ensure that the public accepts and trusts its use of high-risk national security AI? In a range of past cases, the government has developed and used policies in deep secret but then faced harsh criticism when those policies came to light. This includes the post–September 11 detention and interrogation programs, as well as warrantless wiretapping and the use of section 215 of the PATRIOT Act to collect bulk telephonic metadata on U.S. citizens. One (ironic) consequence of the U.S. efforts to keep these programs so secret is that they faced a particularly harsh spotlight when they became public.[120] The secrecy allowed the government to continue programs that would have lacked support among various pockets of U.S. citizens had they been known, and it also arguably intensified the legal and policy criticisms that followed.[121]

One way to manage this spotlight is to confront it directly by explaining the law and policies that undergird these operations. Officials in the second term of the George W. Bush administration and in the Obama administration eventually pursued this approach. By outlining the governing law, policies, and principles, the administrations reduced the challenges to and skepticism about some of these programs.[122] (The government also terminated the use of some of the post–September 11 programs entirely, such as the use of harsh interrogation techniques[123] and secret sites.[124])

This move toward greater transparency—at a level of generality that does not reveal operational details—should resonate with the military and intelligence community as they embark on the use of artificial intelligence and autonomy. Although the goal of many algorithms is to increase the reliability of government prediction and decrease decisional biases, this book has shown that machine learning–driven decision-making raises thorny questions about the transparency of and values embedded in the algorithms, the ability of the government to use algorithms in a manner consistent with legal rules, and the difficulty in deciding whom to hold accountable for decisions based

---

[120] This section is drawn from Ashley Deeks, *Predicting Enemies*, 104 VA. L. REV. 1529 (2018).

[121] *See* President John F. Kennedy, *The President and the Press: Address before the American Newspaper Publishers' Association* (Apr. 27, 1961) (arguing that "the dangers of excessive and unwarranted concealment of pertinent facts far outweighed the dangers which are cited to justify it").

[122] Yoni Eshpar, *Legal Transparency as a National Security Strategy*, 5 MIL. & STRATEGIC AFF. 3, 11–12 (2013) (noting that "criticism of the administration's legal and ethical record by the Congress, the media, and human rights organizations remained limited for most of Obama's first term").

[123] Exec. Order No. 13,491, 3 C.F.R. 2009 Comp. 199 (2010).

[124] *Id.* at 201 (ordering the CIA to close any detention facilities it was operating).

on those algorithms. Detention and targeting are two of the areas in which the military is likely to use machine learning. The lack of transparency—about what types and quality of data the military is using; about whether and how the military will attempt to build legal requirements into computer code; and about how the military will address automation bias to avoid relying on predictive algorithms where the situation does not warrant it—has the potential to undercut public U.S. support for these tools if they ultimately lead to costly errors or accelerate interstate conflict.

Faced with looming developments in artificial intelligence, DOD and the IC should build on the lesson that the George W. Bush and Obama administrations ultimately learned: there are advantages to be gained by publicly confronting the fact that new tools pose difficult challenges and trade-offs, by giving reasons for their use, and by clarifying how the tools are used, by whom, and pursuant to what legal rules. As it has in the past, the government can pursue a significant level of transparency in the national security space without imposing undue costs on how military programs function.[125] As President Obama noted when releasing his legal and policy frameworks related to the U.S. use of military force and other national security operations:

> Decisions regarding war and peace are among the most important any President faces. It is critical, therefore, that such decisions are made pursuant to a policy and legal framework that affords clear guidance internally, reduces the risk of an ill-considered decision, and enables the disclosure of as much information as possible to the public, consistent with national security and the proper functioning of the Government, so that an informed public can scrutinize our actions and hold us to account.[126]

Although legal transparency about those policies did not persuade all critics that the United States' interpretations of the law were the best possible interpretations, the United States' decision to clearly assert its legal positions forced the government to engage in a genuine dialogue with its critics, while also clarifying U.S. views among executive branch officials. In short, the government decided that transparency about its legal and policy claims

---

[125] For examples, see Deeks, *supra* note 120, at 1582–87.
[126] The White House, Report on the Legal and Policy Frameworks Guiding the United States' Use of Military Force and Related National Security Operations, at i (2016).

would redound to its strategic advantage.[127] Taking this route may require declassifying certain information—or resisting the instinct to classify it in the first place—but there are good reasons to think that this approach will pay dividends in the longer term.

One important precedent for AI-related transparency already exists. In 2012, the Department of Defense published a directive related to weapons autonomy. The Directive established "guidelines designed to minimize the probability and consequences of failures in autonomous and semi-autonomous weapon systems that could lead to unintended engagements."[128] It also set out the basic requirement that autonomous and semi-autonomous weapons systems "shall be designed to allow commanders and operators to exercise appropriate levels of human judgment over the use of force."[129] In the context of ongoing debates about whether, when, and how states should be allowed to deploy fully autonomous weapons systems on the battlefield, this Directive reflected an effort to lower public anxiety by signaling that the Defense Department required high-level approvals for developing and fielding autonomous weapon systems. A 2023 update to that policy retained this requirement.[130] The Directive generally demonstrated an effort by the United States to take the lead among states in setting out a public policy on the issue.[131]

The United States should adopt a similar approach to its use of national security AI more generally. The government's instinct often is to hunker down and hide behind classification,[132] judicial deference, and the standing and political question doctrines. It should fight those instincts, just as it did when

---

[127] President Barack Obama, Remarks by the President on Review of Signals Intelligence, Address to the U.S. Dep't of Justice (Jan. 17, 2014) ("[O]ur global leadership demands that we balance our security requirements against our need to maintain the trust and cooperation among people and leaders around the world. For that reason, the new presidential directive that I've issued today will clearly prescribe what we do, and do not do, when it comes to our overseas surveillance."); Robert S. Litt, Gen. Counsel, Office of the Dir. of Nat'l Intelligence, Keynote Remarks at American University Washington College of Law: Freedom of Information Day Celebration (Mar. 18, 2014) ("[P]ublic confidence in the way that we conduct our admittedly secret activities is essential if we are to continue to be able to anticipate and respond to the many threats to our nation.").

[128] U.S. Dep't of Defense, Directive, No. 3000.09, Autonomy in Weapon Systems, ¶ 1(b) (Nov. 21, 2012).

[129] Id., ¶ 4(a).

[130] U.S. Dep't of Defense, Directive, No. 3000.09, Autonomy in Weapon Systems, § 1(c) (Jan. 25, 2023).

[131] See, e.g., Lewis, Blum & Modirzadeh, supra note 105, at 26 (noting that the Directive is "one of the most technically specific state approaches to autonomy in relation to weapons systems").

[132] See, e.g., David Pozen, The Mosaic Theory, National Security, and the Freedom of Information Act, 115 YALE L.J. 628, 635 (2005) ("Defense and intelligence agencies have been among the most vocal critics of FOIA and have typically had the lowest disclosure rates.") (citations omitted).

it chose to release its autonomous weapons policy.[133] Pursuing a transparent approach to predictive algorithms would mean explaining to the public why the government has decided to use machine learning tools to facilitate its decision-making. It also would entail a public discussion about what the costs and benefits are to using these tools and how the military will attempt to mitigate those costs. Further, it would require the military to explain how it intends to ensure that its use of predictive algorithms is consistent with— and possibly even helps it improve its compliance with—its international law obligations. Although the military and the intelligence community will not reveal the actual content of their algorithms, this type of transparency will help those agencies address future critiques. This is particularly true if the agencies explain how they test the quality of its data, avoid training algorithms on biased data, and train users to avoid falling prey to undue automation biases.[134]

One advantage to be gained by some level of transparency surrounding the use of national security AI relates to the quality of decision-making. Opening up decisions about the use of algorithms can lead to higher quality decisions because a wider range of actors will contribute knowledge and expertise. The government can produce sounder policy and legal frameworks by bringing in a wider number of stakeholders inside the U.S. government, including the Departments of Justice and State. Allies and private-sector computer scientists likewise will be better positioned to help the United States improve its use of algorithms. By initiating conversations with its military allies about predictive algorithms, the United States might not only learn from the experiences of peers that are working on these issues but may also have the chance to influence allies' doctrines.[135]

---

[133] A 2017 update to a U.S. Army and Marine Corps manual indicates a growing understanding within the military that the public closely monitors its fighting in certain contexts. U.S. Dep't of the Army & U.S. Marine Corps, ATP 3-06/MCTP 12-10B, Urban Operations 1–90 (2017) ("Soldiers/ Marines are likely to have their [urban warfare] activities recorded in real time and shared instantly both locally and globally. In sum, friendly forces must have an expectation of observation for many of their activities and must employ information operations to deal with this reality effectively. Their challenge is to balance transparency with operations security....").

[134] See Eshpar, supra note 122, at 18 ("Military officials and security experts have the power to convey the fact that obeying the law and maintaining values are first-rate strategic assets.").

[135] See Heather M. Roff & P.W. Singer, The Next President Will Decide the Fate of Killer Robots— And the Future of War, WIRED (Sept. 6, 2016) (arguing in the autonomous weapons context that the United States should "try to build consensus among its partners and allies about what shared policies in this area ought to be.... This is valuable not just for each individual nation and the broader alliance, but also to create a key building block for the bigger global debate.").

Another advantage is that the United States can better shape the direction of the law related to AI use. For instance, the United States might be able to persuade allies to say more publicly about their own approaches, thus evincing more examples of state practice and shaping the nature of the international discussion about these tools. The U.S. government has pursued this approach in the cyber context. As a former State Department Legal Adviser put it:

> States should publicly state their views on how existing international law applies to State conduct in cyberspace to the greatest extent possible in international and domestic forums. Specific cyber incidents provide States with opportunities to do this, but it is equally important—and often easier—for States to articulate public views outside of the context of specific cyber operations or incidents. Stating such views publicly will help give rise to more settled expectations of State behavior and thereby contribute to greater predictability and stability in cyberspace.[136]

Translating this approach to the algorithmic context, the United States could, for example, articulate how its use of predictive algorithms interacts with international law requirements, whether by attempting to code international law restrictions into the algorithms (as discussed previously) or by ensuring that human decision makers continue to evaluate certain detention and targeting decisions without using algorithms. This would emphasize the U.S. government's commitment to international law compliance and stabilize other states' expectations.[137] Senior officials should also give speeches reflecting these approaches. The Defense Science Board recommended something similar, urging the Undersecretary of Defense for Policy to "routinely engage the public to build confidence that the Department is acting in accordance with applicable treaties and the Department's policies."[138]

A third advantage to strategic transparency is that it offers the U.S. government the opportunity to diffuse objections and arguments at an early stage.

---

[136] Brian J. Egan, Legal Adviser, U.S. Dep't of State, International Law and Stability in Cyberspace, Remarks Before the Berkeley Center for Law and Technology (Nov. 10, 2016), *in* 35 BERKELEY J. INT'L L. 169, 172 (2017).

[137] *See* Stephen Smith, Austl. Minister of Def., Address to the Third Plenary Session of the 12th International Institute for Strategic Studies' Shangri-La Dialogue on Military Modernization and Strategic Transparency (June 1, 2013) (describing how a military's transparency about its strategic intentions, defense policy, capabilities, and modernization can build confidence and reduce insecurity between states).

[138] U.S. Dep't of Defense, Defense Science Board, *Summer Study on Autonomy* 41 (June 2016).

Several audiences are important here: Congress, the courts, U.S. allies, and nongovernmental organizations. Strategic transparency would help the government bring Congress into its corner. The government could learn an important lesson in how *not* to proceed by reviewing the unfavorable treatment that Facebook and Google lawyers received during congressional testimony because of their companies' opaque use of algorithms and the far more favorable reception that the OpenAI CEO received, likely due to his transparency about the concerns that AI poses and his purported receptivity to government regulation.[139] Being forthcoming with Congress about the tools on the table and the military and intelligence advantages that attach to the use of predictive algorithms—including in the targeting context—will reduce that kind of backlash.

The courts are another important audience. When the Executive is clear about which underlying laws and procedures govern its activities, the Executive tends to receive greater deference from the courts.[140] Setting forth a clear legal basis and standards for the use of national security AI may also help inoculate the government against future litigation, or will at least flesh out the most salient legal critiques at early stages of the government's development of these tools. Additionally, a more open approach to discussing the use of these technologies with nongovernmental organizations might mitigate some of their most intense critiques and foreclose their efforts to use litigation to change the government's practices, particularly if they believe the government has taken some of their concerns into account.

All this is not to argue that the government should be completely transparent about the content of its algorithms. As in other areas of national security, there are legitimate concerns that full disclosure of the workings of AI systems will disclose too much information to actors who seek to harm us. Some aspects of the double black box will necessarily remain. Thus, observers almost surely will not be able to directly review whether the

---

[139] *See, e.g.,* Hamza Shaban, Craig Timberg & Elizabeth Dwoskin, *Facebook, Google and Twitter Testified on Capitol Hill. Here's What They Said,* WASH. POST (Oct. 31, 2017) (describing aggressive questioning by Senators about companies' lack of transparency about their business models and the manipulation they experienced during 2016 election); Cecilia Kang, *OpenAI's Sam Altman Urges Regulation in Senate Hearing,* N.Y. TIMES (May 16, 2023).

[140] *See* Derek Jinks & Neal Kumar Katyal, *Disregarding Foreign Relations Law,* 116 YALE L.J. 1230, 1247–49 (2007) (arguing that courts should only defer to the Executive where the Executive has engaged in a deliberative process that produced reasoned analysis); Dawn Johnsen, *Judicial Deference to President Trump,* TAKE CARE (May 8, 2017) ("[J]udicial deference generally embodies assumptions that the president's actions reflect regular processes behind-the-scenes, that the decisions are informed by expertise and judgment and are made in good faith.").

military has avoided training its algorithms on biased data or used sufficiently high-quality data for such training. Only the government itself will be able to judge those decisions. Nevertheless, publicly articulating the standards and processes to which the government will hold itself can play a significant role in prompting care inside the executive branch about the use of national security AI. Making public some of these internal executive debates will have some costs, including "practical costs on the speed of adoption of machine learning technologies."[141] But these short-term costs are outweighed by the benefits of obtaining public buy-in.[142] The government should give public reasons for its use of predictive algorithms and measured explanations about how it intends to use them, to produce some of the same advantages that courts and administrative agencies derive from public reason-giving.[143]

E. Whistleblowers, Leakers, and Journalists as Checks

Recall from Chapter 1 that a whistleblower is someone who reveals what she views as evidence of executive waste, fraud, abuse, or illegality to someone identified by statute as an appropriate recipient of that complaint. A leaker is someone inside the executive branch who discloses classified information without authorization, often with the expectation of anonymity.[144] Whistleblowing in agencies that deal with classified information is particularly challenging, which means that whistleblowers have played a relatively modest role in checking the national security Executive.[145]

---

[141] Tim Hwang, *Shaping the Terrain of AI Competition* 14, CTR. FOR SECURITY & EMERGING TECH. (June 2020).

[142] *Id.* ("The approach of forcing AI-driven systems on the public or hiding its deployment risks a backlash that may hinder the implementation of the technology."); David Kris, *Lessons for the Next Twenty Years: What the Two Decades Since 9/11 Have Taught Us About the Future of Foreign Intelligence Surveillance Law*, 12 J. NAT'L SECURITY L. & POL'Y 109 (2021) ("[W]hen a moment of political consensus does arrive, huge change is possible. The advent of intelligence under law in the mid-1970s, and the pro-surveillance reforms after 9/11, were profound. There is, however, often a significant tension between acting fast and building consensus.").

[143] *See* Deeks, *supra* note 120, at 1578.

[144] *See, e.g.*, Whistleblower Protection Act of 1989, Pub. L. No. 101-12, 103 Stat. 16 (codified as amended in scattered sections of 5 U.S.C.); Whistleblower Protection Enhancement Act of 2012, Pub. L. No. 112-199, 126 Stat. 1465; Intelligence Community Whistleblower Protection Act of 1998, Pub. L. No. 105-272, §§ 701–02, 112 Stat. 2396, 2413–17 (codified as amended at 5 U.S.C. § 8H, 50 U.S.C. § 3033(k)(5), and 50 U.S.C. § 3517); Whistleblower Protection for Contractor and Grantee Employees, Pub. L. No. 114-261, 130 Stat. 1362 (2016).

[145] For a discussion of gaps in IC whistleblower protections, see Irvin McCullough & Kel McClanahan, *SSCI Could Shake Up the Intelligence Community's Whistleblowing System*, JUST SECURITY (Dec. 17, 2021).

At first glance, we might think that whistleblowers will play an even smaller role in identifying problems with national security algorithms and reporting those problems to appropriate officials because the waste, fraud, abuse, or incompetence will often be hidden in code. Indeed, it seems likely that the nature of the double black box likely will affect the types of actors who engage in whistleblowing and leaking, though it may not affect the overall volume of this activity. In particular, the types of government employees who decide to blow the whistle or leak information about ill-conceived or poorly tested national security AI will be more likely to have a technical background than those who have tended to serve as whistleblowers in the past. Cyber experts and computer scientists will find themselves in the best position to identify and disclose what they see as government abuses in the technology space. They will be most able to flag concerns that the government has trained its systems on poor-quality data, or ignored flaws or high failure rates during testing, or used a system in the real world that produced unexpected harm or failed to self-neutralize as expected.

The government should encourage AI whistleblowing activity, as it is in the government's best interests to have its own employees surface ineffective or dangerous AI tools before it tries to put those tools to use. After all, the IC itself recognizes that whistleblowing, done responsibly, helps to ensure that the government remains an ethical workplace and allows government officials and Congress to take appropriate action to correct wrongdoing.[146]

This is not to say that only those with technological backgrounds will be tempted to whistle-blow or leak. Other officials who have access to policies or operations that involve national security AI but who are not technologists may still leak information about those activities, though they seem likely to do so on the basis of observed outcomes (such as accidents that produce physical harm) or on the basis of policy discussions about whether to use particular high-risk tools, rather than on pieces of code. Further, interagency rivalries may prompt whistleblowing or leaks. A national security official from an agency that opposes the use of a particular AI system might decide to leak the fact of use to a journalist in the expectation that publicity about that system will lead the government to abandon its use.[147] As with all leaks, the public will confront the persistent conundrum that leaking classified

---

[146] Off. of the Dir. of Nat'l Intel., *What Is Whistleblowing?*

[147] *See* Jon. D. Michaels, *Of Constitutional Custodians and Regulatory Rivals: An Account of the Old and New Separation of Powers*, 91 N.Y.U. L. Rᴇᴠ. 227 (2016) (discussing how interactions of "rivalrous" bureaucratic actors can affect agency behavior).

information is generally unlawful, even though a particular leak may seem legitimate because it reveals that the government is using a system that itself is producing an illegal or immoral outcome.

Journalists will play a critical role in helping the public understand the problematic and positive uses of national security AI. Both mainstream and technology journalists have written extensively about nonclassified AI, cyber tools, and companies' recommendation algorithms, even though the systems are complicated and invisible to the naked eye. And national security journalists are always interested in important warfighting and intelligence developments, in both the United States and in adversary and allied states.

One possibility is that journalists will start to use large language models and other AI-based tools to identify otherwise hard-to-find connections within publicly available data. In a range of court cases beginning in the 1970s, the U.S. government argued that certain items of seemingly innocuous information—such as fees that the CIA paid to outside lawyers—could be combined into something that would reveal classified information.[148] The most recent executive order on classification specifically envisions this as a proper ground for classification. Section 1.7(e) states, "Compilations of items of information that are individually unclassified may be classified if the compiled information reveals an additional association or relationship that: (1) meets the standards for classification under this order; and (2) is not otherwise revealed in the individual items of information."[149] One critique of this "mosaic theory" was that it required speculation built on speculation, including speculation that an adversary would be able to compile and make these complicated connections. Today, however, the prevalence of AI tools makes this theory less speculative: AI systems are excellent at finding connections among millions of data points. Thus, journalists may be able to use AI tools to more easily piece together unclassified pieces of data, garnering greater insights into sensitive government activities, including—ironically—the classified use of AI tools.

Journalists may also use FOIA to try to obtain access to government algorithms or policies related to the use of AI. Whether they will be successful is unclear: recall *New York Times* journalist Christopher Chivers's largely unsuccessful efforts to access information about himself in DHS's

---

[148] *See* David Pozen, *The Mosaic Theory, National Security, and the Freedom of Information Act*, 115 YALE L.J. 628, 638–41 (2005).

[149] E.O. 13526, § 1.7(e).

traveler databases (discussed in Chapter 2). One question is whether algorithms themselves are "agency records" subject to FOIA in the first place.[150] Assuming they are "records," requesters will still need to argue that such algorithms do not fall into one of the national security exemptions, such as Exemption 1 for information that is properly classified to protect national security and Exemption 3, which covers information prohibited from disclosure by another law (such as information pertaining to NSA's functions or CIA's intelligence sources and methods).[151] One researcher found that the CIA denied several FOIA requests for source code, including code for a system used to train drone pilots. The CIA stated that it would neither confirm nor deny that it had relevant records (which is known as a Glomar response).[152] Another researcher requested source code related to XKeyScore, a program related to an NSA surveillance system; NSA, too, gave a Glomar response.[153]

The federal FOIA statute is not the only AI-relevant law: *Wired Magazine*'s reporters used state and local government freedom of information acts to uncover significant problems in Palantir's algorithmic policing product and its ineptitude at fixing the problems once identified.[154] The reporters noted that state FOIA laws "make[] it possible to peer inside the company's police-related operations in ways that simply aren't possible with its national security work."[155] Journalism like this presumably can stimulate national security reporters to start digging to explore Palantir's work in the national security space (which is extensive). In general, journalists and other members of the public will continue to face an uphill climb in trying to use FOIA to obtain information about national security AI—but they should and undoubtedly will continue to try.

---

[150] Katherine Fink, *Opening the Government's Black Boxes: Freedom of Information and Algorithmic Accountability*, INFO., COMM. & TECH (May 30, 2017) (noting that Treasury's and the Social Security Administration's FOIA regulations indicate that computer software and source code do not constitute "records"). A survey of various agencies' FOIA officers indicated that the officers had different views about whether computer code was a "record." In some FOIA cases, agencies did turn over source code for their systems, including models to measure pollution, heat indices, and annual percentage rates of charge. *Id.*

[151] U.S. Dep't of Justice, *Statutes Found to Qualify Under Exemption 3 of the FOIA* (Dec. 2016).

[152] Fink, *supra* note 150.

[153] *Id.*

[154] Mark Harris, *How Peter Thiel's Secretive Data Company Pushed into Policing*, WIRED (Aug. 9, 2017).

[155] *Id.* (describing Palantir's product as a "Facebook of crime that's both invisible and largely unaccountable to the citizens whose behavior it tracks").

As this chapter makes clear, there are substantial steps that some of our traditional secrecy surrogates can take to test the government's development and use of national security AI to make sure that the tools are effective, legal, and justifiable. None of these steps will comprehensively address our double black box problem—nor could they. The national security ecosystem is too complex and entrenched for that. But these steps, taken together, would contribute to building the public's, Congress's, and the Executive's own confidence in these systems, which will play a critical role in U.S. national security in the coming decade. Further, there are other types of secrecy surrogates who can build on these checks. The next chapter takes up questions about how they, too, can help.

5

Using Nontraditional Checks

A. Introduction

As Chapter 1 discussed, we tend to assume that the only actors who have access to government secrets are executive officials (including whistleblowers and leakers), members of Congress (and some of their staff on the intelligence, armed services, and foreign affairs committees), and federal judges who sit on the FISC or occasionally hear criminal cases that implicate classified evidence or civil cases that involve state secrets. As a result, we often assume that those actors are the only ones who are positioned to track secret government activity and assess whether that activity comports with our public law values.

In fact, other types of actors have access to secret U.S. government information and activities, including foreign allies that are U.S. partners in NATO or the Five Eyes alliance,[1] some U.S. state and local officials, and certain companies, including technology companies and defense contractors. These three categories of actors have specific expertise about new threats and targets. They have access to information or infrastructure that the federal government needs to execute its national security mission. And they often have legal or political commitments not to reveal the information (through nondisclosure agreements, contracts, or other information-sharing arrangements). From this perch, they can assess whether the U.S. government is acting lawfully and, in some settings, can challenge unlawful actions. They can assess whether U.S. policies are effective and sensible and they may have incentives to urge the government to change unsound policies. Further, their presence behind the curtain of secrecy provides a setting in which the United States may need to explain and justify the decisions that it makes. We can find examples of these checks in the cyber, electronic surveillance, and counterterrorism space—which means it is worth considering whether we

---

[1] The Five Eyes intelligence alliance, which cooperates on signals intelligence, is made up of the United States, the United Kingdom, Canada, Australia, and New Zealand.

will see (or can stimulate the operation of) similar checks in the national security AI (NSAI) space.

In the AI setting, NATO allies are likely to have some visibility into the types of tools the U.S. military is developing, acquiring, or deploying. By virtue of the U.S. need for battlefield interoperability, these allies can influence—though not necessarily dictate—what types of NSAI the United States ultimately adopts. States and localities are less likely to have direct access to information about the federal government's NSAI tools and systems. However, these actors have begun to adopt laws that implicate unclassified uses of AI, including limits on the use of facial recognition software. These restrictions may impact the types of tools that companies produce and that the federal government adopts. States and localities can also serve as canaries in the coal mine, serving as a valuable source of information about what American citizens do and do not want their governments to do with AI.

Technology companies have a complicated role to play: they are at the leading edge of developing advanced AI and so will play a key role in shaping the tools that the government uses. This means that companies can—and often will—drive technological developments forward quickly, to stay ahead of the competition and make money. But this also means that companies could slow the development of NSAI tools that they believe are illegal or immoral.

Finally, the public has a role to play in unpacking the double black box. Members of civil society, including nongovernmental organizations and think tanks, can use FOIA to obtain information that was formerly classified, ask hard questions of the government, and write or speak about what they learn. The public also can pressure Congress and the Executive when journalists report on activities that do not comport with our public law values. Further, academic researchers can advance public knowledge about AI reliability, safety, and explainability and propose industry-wide ethical guidelines that may influence how government officials and defense contractors perceive their own (classified) work. The public can thus work to peel back the curtain of secrecy using lawful tools and, even absent classified information, can articulate its views about unclassified AI systems that may have classified analogues behind that curtain.

These "nontraditional" surrogates that are poised to provide checks on the Executive need not themselves act in a manner that is consistent with the public law values that we expect from the U.S. government.[2] For instance,

---

[2] Ashley Deeks, *Secrecy Surrogates*, 106 VA. L. REV. 1395, 1453–54 (2020).

technology corporations are often not transparent in their activities—and generally are not legally required or expected to be. Fortunately, though, foreign (democratic) allies and U.S. states and localities face expectations that they will embody some set of public law values by virtue of being representative governments, even though their polities differ from the U.S. polity as a whole. Actors that are themselves committed to public law values may be more attractive and effective as secrecy surrogates, because they are more likely to be attuned to whether the Executive is practicing these values and be more familiar with the underlying mechanisms that advance or inhibit such values.[3]

B. Foreign Allies

Other than Congress, foreign allies are perhaps the group best positioned to urge the U.S. government to act lawfully, effectively, and with justification. Friendly foreign governments with advanced military and intelligence services interact frequently with their U.S. counterparts. To the extent that the United States wants or needs to work with these foreign partners to accomplish its military, counterterrorism, or intelligence goals, these partners have leverage over and may serve to constrain U.S. actions.[4] These checking mechanisms do not require formal international agreements between the United States and another state; indeed, they frequently arise in the absence of such mechanisms.

Thinking about foreign governments as surrogates for the U.S. polity in relation to secret government operations may seem counterintuitive.[5] After all, foreign partners have distinct foreign policy and national security interests that do not fully align with those of the United States. They have legal and political duties to their own citizens, and sometimes their legal obligations impose higher or lower standards than U.S. law does. But they often have incentives to prod the U.S. Executive to adhere to its own public law values, and they have leverage over the Executive: the ability to share or withhold intelligence or to grant or withhold consent to use their territory, airspace,

---

[3] *Id.*

[4] *See* Ashley Deeks, *Checks and Balances from Abroad*, 83 U. CHI. L. REV. 65, 68 (2016) ("If . . . one recognizes that US national security increasingly relies on relationships with foreign partners, then the idea that the executive responds to foreign critiques and concerns to enable ongoing partnerships has bite.").

[5] Deeks, *supra* note 2, at 1463.

or cyber infrastructure for military, counterterrorism, or cyber operations. They benefit when, in joint operations, the U.S. Executive acts competently (because it enhances their own security) and lawfully (as it minimizes the likelihood that they will find themselves facing adverse parliamentary or judicial oversight). When foreign allies themselves take seriously public law values, including the need to ensure that their partners adhere to the law and justify their decisions, they can serve as useful secrecy surrogates.

These actors have served as checks in a number of classified settings before. The U.S. intelligence community, which is constrained by specific domestic and international laws, often works with the intelligence services of other states, each of which has its own legal obligations. A foreign intelligence service "can impose forms of discipline or structural limits on the activities of its counterparts, particularly when it implements its own domestic and international legal obligations," and can affect how the United States "conducts activities such as interrogation, detention, targeted killings, and surveillance; the amount and type of intelligence the [United States] receives; and, less tangibly, the way in which the [United States] views its own legal obligations."[6] Today, the United States undertakes robust intelligence sharing and classified operations with foreign allies not only in traditional military settings but also in the cyber, elections, and counterterrorism contexts.[7]

Allies such as the United Kingdom and Australia have increasingly regulated their own intelligence communities and militaries, imposing greater oversight and approval mechanisms.[8] Where allies have more (or just different) constraints on their behavior, the United States may need to conform its behavior to those other constraints as well as the laws and regulations that directly apply to it. For example, the United Kingdom cooperated with the United States on some detention operations in Iraq and Afghanistan.[9] After U.S. detainee abuses came to light, the United Kingdom's Intelligence and Security Committee in Parliament conducted an investigation. Its report suggests that U.K. forces, which bore more stringent human rights obligations than U.S. forces did, repeatedly imposed informal legal

---

[6] Ashley Deeks, *Intelligence Communities, Peer Constraints, and the Law*, 7 HARV. NAT'L SECURITY J. 1, 4 (2016).

[7] Deeks, *supra* note 2, at 1446.

[8] Deeks, *supra* note 6, at 19.

[9] The United States has imposed similar constraints on allies, such as limiting the use by the Israeli government of certain intelligence and weapons. *See, e.g.*, Int'l Comm. of the Red Cross, *Humanitarian, Military, Technical and Legal Challenges of Cluster Munitions* 14 (2007) (discussing a secret agreement between the United States and Israel outlining restrictions on Israel's use of cluster munitions).

constraints on U.S. troops as those troops interrogated detainees.[10] This included seeking "humane treatment assurances"—assurances that the United States would not subject the detainees being interrogated to torture or cruel, inhuman, or degrading treatment—before the United Kingdom would provide intelligence to the United States about a detainee.[11]

Peer constraints abound in the context of military coalitions. Consider NATO's operations in Kosovo in 1999, which involved air strikes on Yugoslav and Serbian forces. During those operations, "the byzantine American procedures for approving targets needed to be replicated by every NATO government and its lawyers."[12] That is, each target that NATO bombed had to meet the highest common denominator of acceptability among twenty-eight NATO states. A state that interpreted LOAC targeting rules particularly narrowly could "turn off" a proposed target that did not comply with that narrow interpretation.[13]

These examples illustrate not only that the United States and its close allies cooperate on sensitive operations but also that those allies have opportunities and incentives to explore why the United States believes that certain actions are legal. Additionally, allies can press the United States about the effectiveness or wisdom of using particular tools and the reliability of its intelligence. And they can force the United States to justify why and how it is choosing to undertake a particular course of conduct, while allowing the operations to remain secret.[14] Further, if one ally experiences aggressive oversight from outside actors such as parliamentarians or independent commissions, that outside actor's oversight can affect the way in which the United States operates.[15] In a few cases, foreign prosecutors and courts attempted to hold their own officials accountable for counterterrorism actions that their officials took in partnership with the United States.[16] Of course, there may be cases in which an ally faces limitations on serving as a robust check on the Executive, including when the ally worries that it will lose access to U.S. intelligence and cooperation if the United States begins to view it as a difficult partner. Further, some allies have insufficient intelligence capabilities to be

---

[10] Deeks, *supra* note 6, at 29.

[11] *Id.* at 29–30.

[12] JACK GOLDSMITH, POWER AND CONSTRAINT: THE ACCOUNTABLE PRESIDENCY AFTER 9/11, 132 (2012).

[13] Deeks, *supra* note 6, at 32.

[14] *Id.* at 27–28; Deeks, *supra* note 2, at 1449.

[15] Deeks, *supra* note 6, at 27–28.

[16] *Id.* at 16–18.

able to detect flaws in U.S. analysis or conclusions—though even these allies still can ask probing questions about the intelligence on its face.[17]

From these past examples of military and intelligence cooperation, we can extrapolate how these "peer constraints" might operate in the NSAI setting and how U.S. allies could enhance the U.S. military's and intelligence community's compliance with public law values. Both sets of U.S. agencies are likely to engage their counterparts on current and future uses of NSAI tools.[18] Allies can enhance the U.S. government's compliance with international law, because allied officials represent policy and legal experts with whom the United States can discuss difficult questions about, for example, the laws of armed conflict (LOAC). Working out how autonomous machine learning systems can comply with rules such as distinction and proportionality is a complicated legal and technical issue, one that discussions with peer militaries might elucidate. Further, an ally could refuse to cooperate with the U.S. military if U.S. AI systems violate those rules or if the systems are so opaque that it is impossible for the ally to have confidence that the system is law-compliant.

Peer states can also impose physical restrictions on U.S. operations that involve systems they think may be unlawful.[19] For example, if the United States embedded autonomous command and control into its nuclear launch systems located in Europe, host states that believed such systems were unlawful or unwise could pressure the United States to reverse such a decision—or even deny the United States consent to use such systems on their soil. Or allies could decide that the United States was not permitted to launch fully autonomous lethal weapons systems from their territory or use them in joint operations with those allies. NATO as an institution, which possesses large quantities of useful military data, already may condition its data-sharing on the ways in which member states use that data.[20]

---

[17] Deeks, *supra* note 2, at 1465.

[18] National Security Commission on AI, 2020 First Quarter Recommendations 11 n.5 (Mar. 2020) (recommending the use of the Five Eyes "as a vehicle for beginning to expand and institutionalize allied cooperative planning, data sharing, procurement, and interoperability for AI-enabled warfighting and intelligence efforts"). And the U.S. military has engaged its NATO allies on accelerating the use of AI in military operations. U.S. Dep't of Defense, *DoD Announces U.S. Representative to NATO Defence Innovation Accelerator for the North Atlantic (DIANA) Initiative* (Feb. 6, 2023).

[19] Deeks, *supra* note 6, at 30 (describing United Kingdom refusal to allow United States to use U.K. airbases for rendition flights).

[20] NATO, *Summary of NATO's Data Exploitation Framework Policy* (Dec. 9, 2022).

Second, allies can serve as a check on the quality and effectiveness of U.S. NSAI systems by refusing to cooperate with the United States if they are concerned that the U.S. systems are technologically or morally unsound. Those allies will themselves confront the difficulty of penetrating U.S. algorithmic black boxes, however.

Third, allies might force the United States to explain and justify its choice to use a specific NSAI system—and explain and justify the decisions or recommendations that emerge from that system as well. The United States might well offer those explanations in an effort to persuade allies to conduct joint operations using those AI tools. Assume, for example, that the United States detained someone during a joint operation with the United Kingdom on the basis of a machine learning recommendation. U.K. forces might insist on understanding the parameters and confidence levels of that machine learning algorithm before being willing to participate in the person's interrogation or to share information about the person with U.S. forces. These measures would not necessarily preclude the United States from using such machine learning systems, but they would add friction to their use, especially where the systems lacked explainability features or had not yet proven reliable over time.

To some extent, these "secrecy surrogates" already exist wherever the United States seeks to cooperate with democratic peers (such as those in NATO, the Five Eyes, or AUKUS—a trilateral partnership among the United States, the United Kingdom, and Australia).[21] But there are affirmative steps that the United States—and these democratic peers—can take to enhance the potential for these positive checks to function.

First, the United States could increase its exchanges about AI strategies and technological developments with close allies such as the Five Eyes. Greater interactions offer greater chances for detailed conversations about national security AI tools and therefore greater opportunities to press the United States to explain its choices. Members of the U.S. Congress in 2023 proposed legislation that would mandate that the Defense Department create a working group with its Five Eyes partners with the goal of enhancing interoperability and possibly data-

---

[21] Patrick Parrish & Luke Nicastro, *AUKUS Pillar 2: Background and Issues for Congress*, CONG. RES. SERV. (June 20, 2023) (describing AI and autonomy as part of the AUKUS security pact's cooperation activities). DOD also created an "AI Partnership for Defense," in which it works with allies to "talk through how we can turn our commitment to responsible AI into a reality." U.S. Dep't of Defense, Remarks by Deputy Secretary of Defense Kathleen H. Hicks, *The State of AI in the Department of Defense* (Nov. 2, 2023). As of March 2022, there were sixteen countries in the Partnership.

sharing.[22] A former DOD official noted that the draft bill's repeated references to "testing and evaluation" were particularly important, because machine learning algorithms are notoriously opaque, "so the allies need a common, robust approach to ensuring they actually work and that each others' AIs can be trusted."[23]

NATO, too, seems to be an obvious forum in which the United States should discuss legal, technical, and ethical challenges and even share code, data, or algorithms. There is some suggestion in the media that this is happening already.[24] As the foremost military alliance of democratic states, NATO members have cooperated in the cyber setting, including by establishing frameworks to conduct joint offensive cyber operations.[25] This by definition requires NATO allies to share basic capabilities, allowing the alliance to operate as a "gut check" on each member state behind the curtain of secrecy. NATO can also serve as a forum in which to discuss and agree on ethical principles at a more granular level than we have seen in broader multilateral forums such as the UN Convention on Certain Conventional Weapons meetings. Further, NATO could agree to take some uses of NSAI off the table or agree collectively not to purchase certain types of AI (such as those that lack adequate testing, evaluation, and verification).

Another way the United States could take advantage of this democratic alliance is to robustly participate in testing AI projects in NATO's newly created data sandbox. The NATO Communications and Information Agency built a "Data Science and AI Sandbox" that will allow member states to use large data sets and high-performance computing to train AI models in a classified setting.[26] According to a recent report, "the Allies have expressed their willingness to participate in AI collaborative computing environment,

[22] Rep. Mike Gallagher, Press Release, Gallagher, Khanna Introduce Five AIs Act to Advance Development of AI Within Five Eyes (Nov. 21, 2023).

[23] Sydney Freedberg Jr., *AI For Five Eyes? New Bill Pushes AI Collaboration with UK, Australia, Canada, New Zealand*, BREAKING DEFENSE (Nov. 22, 2023).

[24] Maggie Gray & Amy Ertan, *Artificial Intelligence and Autonomy in the Military*, NATO CCDCOE (2021) ("While approaches and perspectives differ across the Alliance, there is a significant amount of intra-Alliance cooperation taking place, in which member states pool their resources to develop and secure AI-enabled and autonomous military [technology].").

[25] Shannon Vavra, *NATO Cyber-Operations Center Will Be Leaning on Its Members for Offensive Hacks*, CYBERSCOOP (Aug. 30, 2019) (noting that NATO is "working on pooling member nations' offensive cyber capabilities"); Maiike Machiels, *Active Cyber Defense and NATO*, ATLANTIC FORUM (Nov. 1, 2023) (describing the new Cyber Command Centre and "NATO's newfound ability to interfere directly with adversaries' operations, manipulate infrastructure through malware, shut off power networks, and stop an attack before it happens").

[26] NATO, *The NCI Agency's New Data Science and AI Tool Receives Security Accreditation* (Aug. 12, 2023).

although some of them have limited resources and expertise."[27] Although the United States, as the military with the most advanced AI capabilities, might be tempted to view this sandbox as unlikely to enhance those capabilities, it should treat efforts here as a way to advance both its allies' AI capabilities and a welcome opportunity to explain and justify various AI systems and processes that it brings to the table. It should also include its lawyers in these conversations.

We might think that the U.S. government would not want any additional oversight or fetters on its development of NSAI. But cooperation with allies along the lines discussed here will allow the United States to build confidence about its choices not only internationally but also domestically by pointing to peer engagement and cooperation. Where the United States really needs cooperation from an ally and seeks to use systems in which AI plays an obvious role, it will face pressure to disclose, explain, and justify its technological, legal, and strategic choices. Foreign allies thus can advance our public law values.

C. U.S. States and Localities

Since September 11, 2001, U.S. states and localities have assumed a more prominent role in U.S. counterterrorism activity. And since the growth of hostile cyber operations in the mid-2010s, state and local actors have increasingly worked with the federal government to help defend against threats to elections, hospitals, and other critical infrastructure. As a result, the federal government has necessarily had to provide security clearances to various state and local counterparts so that it can share sensitive information with them. During these exchanges, local officials have the chance to ask about the substance of the classified information and the level of certainty that the federal government has about it.[28] In some cases, local officials may challenge the federal government's assertions of fact and law, as they did in certain terrorism investigations.[29] Likewise, "[i]n the cyber setting, local governments have shown some appetite for challenging the federal government's current approach to legal norms for cyberspace," breaking

---

[27] Jan Hodicky, Volkan Kucuk & Orzuri Rique, *M&S Support to Operationalization of NATO Principles of Responsible Use of AI* 7-3, NATO (2022).
[28] Deeks, *supra* note 2, at 1442.
[29] *Id.*

with the federal government to sign on to restrictive international principles.[30] As Matt Waxman has noted, "some friction between intelligence
agencies at various levels of government resulting from these distinctive institutional perspectives may be useful for combating the 'groupthink' and
politicization of intelligence that can occur within entirely unified structures.
. . . [E]ven when they cooperate, they provide localized feedback based on
contextualized experience and community reactions to federal initiatives."[31]
That is, they can help advance public law values in the federal government.

U.S. states and local governments may play two distinct roles in shaping
the federal government's use of NSAI. These roles are slightly different from
the "secrecy surrogate" role that they have played in the cyber and counterterrorism setting. Here, they will help set the conceptual and tangible
boundaries of NSAI through the regulatory choices they make. In so doing,
they may effectively shrink the size of the double black box by reducing the
number of AI tools the federal government chooses to adopt, even if state
actions do not reduce the box's opacity.

First, the regulatory choices that states and localities make about AI systems in the non-national security setting may inform and influence the type
of AI systems that the federal government understands to be acceptable in
the national security space. Consider, for example, deepfakes. A range of
U.S. states have enacted or are poised to soon enact laws that regulate or prohibit the use of deepfakes, including in political advertising.[32] If a critical
mass of states effectively bars the use of deepfakes in elections, that signals
that many U.S. citizens believe that deepfakes should not be used to influence
or deceive voters. Though that sentiment does not automatically translate
into a view that the CIA and DOD should not use deepfakes to influence
foreign elections, it surely raises questions about whether the U.S. public
would support such activities. Regulations that restrict law enforcement's
use of machine learning–driven predictive policing may serve a similar purpose.[33] To date, only a few states have banned its use, though the technology

---

[30] *Id.* at 1444.

[31] Matthew Waxman, *National Security Federalism in the Age of Terror*, 64 STAN. L. REV. 289, 333
(2012).

[32] Scott Brennan & Matt Perault, *The State of State Technology Policy*, UNC CTR. FOR TECH. POL'Y
(2023) (stating that Minnesota, Michigan, and Washington have limited the use of deepfakes in political advertising and predicting that in 2024 more states will pass laws on the use of deepfakes in
elections).

[33] Kristi Sturgill, *Santa Cruz Becomes the First U.S. City to Ban Predictive Policing*, L.A. TIMES
(June 26, 2020); Keith Burbank, *Oakland 1st to Ban Predictive Policing, Biometric Surveillance Tech*,
BAY CITY NEWS (Jan. 15, 2021).

has garnered attention and criticism.[34] Further, the European Union's AI Act bans investigations based exclusively on predictive policing systems, which might create an impetus for more U.S. localities to take similar steps.[35] Whether or not they do, federal national security agencies should pay attention to state and local treatment of civilian AI tools that have national security equivalents, and they should treat those regulations as useful indications of what forms of AI the U.S. public does and does not support.

Second, regulations on the state and local level will affect the federal government's ability to acquire and use certain data, including data that national security agencies might otherwise use to train AI systems. For example, states have limited the federal government's use of driver's license data.[36] State and local laws may affect the availability of commercial data too. Federal homeland security and intelligence agencies today purchase commercially available data on American citizens.[37] If California, say, allows consumers to prevent companies from sharing their data with third parties (as California law currently does), there will be less data in the buckets of data that the federal government buys.[38] Eleven other states have enacted consumer privacy laws, some of which permit citizens to demand that companies delete their data.[39] Until citizens choose to do so in large numbers, the effect of state and local privacy laws on federal practices will be modest, but the example illustrates how state approaches to AI and data may inform federal ambitions. Further, states such as California have considered requiring companies that are developing "consequential" AI products to conduct impact assessments and incorporate administrative and technical safeguards.[40] Though California's proposed law would not implicate national security directly, some companies covered by that law might also perform classified work for the federal government and may—deliberately or incidentally—integrate their unclassified legal obligations into their classified work. In sum, through a variety of avenues, state and local laws and practices

[34] Matthew Guariglia & Jason Kelley, *Cities Should Act NOW to Ban Predictive Policing ... and Stop Using ShotSpotter, Too*. ELEC. FRONTIER FOUND. (Oct. 2, 2023).

[35] Luca Bertuzzi, *AI Act: EU Policymakers Nail Down Rules on AI Models, Butt Heads on Law Enforcement*, EURACTIV (Dec. 12, 2023).

[36] JAMES BAKER, THE CENTAUR'S DILEMMA: NATIONAL SECURITY LAW FOR THE COMING AI REVOLUTION 111 (2020).

[37] Kevin Collier, *U.S. Government Buys Data on Americans with Little Oversight, Report Finds*, NBC NEWS (June 13, 2023).

[38] California Consumer Privacy Act of 2018.

[39] BLOOMBERG LAW, *Which States Have Consumer Data Privacy Laws?* (Nov. 27, 2023).

[40] Itsiq Benizri et al., *A Comparative Perspective on AI Regulation*, LAWFARE (July 17, 2023).

may—over time—influence the size and shape of the U.S. government's national security black box and the Executive's perception of what tools will be easier or harder to defend in the public arena. State and local governments should be attuned to this avenue of influence.

D. Technology Companies

Companies, too, have a potential role to play in reducing the opacity of the double black box and advancing U.S. public law values, but that role will be a complicated one. Tech companies will serve as a major source of AI systems for the national security agencies, but they have mixed incentives to help ensure that the government acts lawfully and effectively in this space. This section explains how companies will be embedded in the government's AI ecosystems and then discusses ways in which companies may advance or defeat public law values.

It is clear that the military already relies heavily on the private sector as a source of AI tools and expertise. As the Defense Science Board stated, "Opportunities exist for DoD to enhance mission performance by employing autonomy at rest and autonomy in motion, both supporting human-machine collaboration. The commercial sector is a lucrative source of both basic capability and best practices relevant to many such opportunities."[41] In September 2023, the Defense Department entered into a $250 million contract with Palantir to research and develop AI and machine learning technology.[42] The Defense Intelligence Agency's Missile and Space Intelligence Center signed a $63 million contract in November 2023 with SOSi, a machine learning company.[43] DOD awarded a $100 million ceiling production contract with Teleidoscope to make and install an AI-powered airspace monitoring system.[44] And in December 2023, the National Geospatial Agency director announced a request for proposals worth a "significant" amount of money for a project that would "leverage industry analytics and

---

[41] Ruth David & Paul Nielsen, *Summer Study on Autonomy* 6, DEF. SCI. BD. (May 1, 2016).

[42] Lizette Chapman, *Palantir Wins $350 Million AI Deal with US Defense Department*, BLOOMBERG (Sept. 27, 2023).

[43] Lisa Daigle, *AI & ML Contract for Defense Intelligence Signed by SOSi*, MIL. EMBEDDED SYS. (Nov. 6, 2023).

[44] U.S. Dep't of Defense, *DOD Will Deploy AI-Enabled Detection System to Monitor D.C. Airspace* (Aug. 28, 2023).

automation in areas of national security interest."[45] This list just scratches the surface of AI-related private sector contracts with U.S. national security agencies.

Some of the AI tools that the private sector is selling to the government are based on tools developed for commercial sales. As Michael Horowitz notes, "Given that innovation in the underlying science comes from private industry and universities, rather than from classified military research . . . , a wide range of actors have access to information on technology breakthroughs. If commercially-driven AI continues to fuel innovation, and the types of algorithms militaries might one day use are closely related to civilian applications, advances in AI are likely to diffuse more rapidly to militaries around the world."[46] A UN report concurs: "Traditionally, peaceful applications of defence technologies were 'spun off' to the civilian sector. Today, many private sector advanced tech developments are 'spun on' to the defence sector."[47] There is an advantage to this public/private overlap within what we might call "common use companies": the government will incidentally benefit from the feedback about accuracy and reliability that private sector customers provide to AI companies that are selling similar tools to both the private and public sectors.

Some of the government's AI tools are likely bespoke, however, and will not benefit from this "coincidental" oversight. As Horowitz writes, "While the basic science underlying AI is applicable to both civilian and military purposes, it is plausible that the most important specific military uses of AI will not be dual use."[48] He further notes, "When technologies only have military applications, the number of potentially interested actors are limited, as are the net resources available for investment. Military-only applications also make inventions more likely to diffuse slowly, due to secrecy."[49] This means that incentives for U.S. defense contractors (for whom the government is by far the largest customer) to provide effective, pressure-tested intelligence and defense AI tools may be reduced compared to settings in which the "common use companies" are selling similar products to a broad set of customers.

---

[45] Jaspreet Gill, *NGA Eyes Imminent, "Significant" Contracts for Commercial GEOINT Object Detection, Analytics*, BREAKING DEFENSE (Dec. 12, 2023).

[46] Michael Horowitz, *Artificial Intelligence, International Competition, and the Balance of Power*, 1 TEX. NAT'L SECURITY REV. 36 (2018).

[47] *See* UNIDIR, *The Weaponization of Increasingly Autonomous Technologies* 5–6 (2017).

[48] Horowitz, *supra* note 46.

[49] Michael Horowitz, *AI and the Diffusion of Global Power*, CTR. FOR INT'L GOVERNANCE INNOVATION (Nov. 16, 2020).

In either case, the important role for tech companies in the national security AI ecosystem means that some companies will have access to classified programs that the government is pursuing, and it means that these companies can influence—positively or negatively—the government's approach to national security AI.

On one hand, these companies could help ensure that the government's AI systems are lawful, effective, and justifiable. Most of the big technology companies, which are "common use," have established public law values-enhancing corporate principles. The policies cite many of the same norms that the U.S. government's do: transparency, accountability, robustness, fairness, and explainability. One reason why the Defense Department may be careful to refer to safety principles in its various AI policy documents is to signal not only to its allies but also to U.S. technology companies and their employees that DOD is an acceptable client.[50]

In implementing those principles, the companies already have affected U.S. national security operations by declining to participate in certain activities that they found legally or morally problematic.[51] News reports from 2013 suggest that Apple and Twitter/X were very slow to agree to cooperate with the government on its secret warrantless electronic surveillance, even when those programs were based on a statute.[52] Google in 2018 decided not to renew its contract with DOD to analyze drone surveillance footage out of concern that the project violated internationally accepted norms.[53] The following year, Microsoft employees petitioned their CEO to cancel a contract with the U.S. Army for augmented-reality headsets because it would turn war into a "simulated video game."[54] In 2020, after Microsoft, Amazon, and IBM came under pressure from civil rights advocates, the companies announced that they would not sell facial recognition software to police departments.[55]

---

[50] I thank Chris Mesarole for this point.

[51] *See generally* Jennifer Fan, *Employees as Regulators: The New Private Ordering in High Technology Companies*, 2019 UTAH L. REV. 973, 973 ("As high technology companies work in areas that increasingly have moral and ethical implications, such as the use of technology for military drones among other areas, employees who have become concerned with either the directions or current practices of their companies are taking action.").

[52] *See* Barton Gellman & Laura Poitras, *U.S., British Intelligence Mining Data from Nine U.S. Internet Companies in Broad Secret Program*, WASH. POST (June 7, 2013).

[53] Daisuke Wakabayashi & Scott Shane, *Google Will Not Renew Pentagon Contract That Upset Employees*, N.Y. TIMES (June 1, 2018).

[54] Tony Romm & Drew Harwell, *Microsoft Workers Call for Cancelling Military Contract for Technology That Could Turn Warfare into a "Video Game"*, WASH. POST (Feb. 22, 2019).

[55] Lauren Feiner & Annie Palmer, *Rules Around Facial Recognition and Policing Remain Blurry*, CNBC (June 12, 2021).

(Though it did not state that it would extend this rule to the federal government, IBM decided to leave the industry entirely.)[56] And Alphabet is training Claude—its rival to ChatGPT—on "constitutional values" drawn from the Universal Declaration of Human Rights and Apple's data privacy rules.[57] These examples illustrate that corporate employee activism may shape government adherence to public law values in its AI use, as well as government access to particular AI-related products. The way that tech company employees respond to particular decisions by their companies to provide AI tools to the government—and the way that customers and advocates respond to and motivate the companies to act—should inform how U.S. national security agencies think about and decide to use specific AI systems.

On the other hand, there are reasons to be skeptical that companies will play a consistently positive role in prompting national security agencies to act lawfully, effectively, and justifiably.

First, notwithstanding a range of public statements from leading AI companies about their willingness to be regulated, their CEOs appear to believe that self-regulation is the preferred outcome.[58] Although President Biden persuaded seven big AI companies to sign commitments to (among other things) perform internal and external security testing before releasing models; establish cybersecurity and insider-threat safeguards to protect model weights; facilitate third-party reporting of vulnerabilities; and watermark products as AI-generated, these commitments are flexible and largely track steps that the companies already were taking.[59]

Second, the leaders of companies such as OpenAI and Palantir appear committed to charging forward with new products, regardless of possibly existential risks.[60] Some AI companies are specifically posturing themselves as key partners for the U.S. government in its "existential battle with China."[61]

---

[56] *Id.*

[57] Stephen Nellis, *Alphabet-Backed Anthropic Outlines the Moral Values Behind Its AI Bot*, REUTERS (May 9, 2023). When asked about the UDHR, Claude replied, "I place a high value on upholding the principles enshrined in the UDHR as part of my ethical training."

[58] Tom Wheeler, *The Three Challenges of AI Regulation*, BROOKINGS INST. (June 15, 2023).

[59] White House, *Fact Sheet: Biden-Harris Administration Secures Voluntary Commitments from Leading Artificial Intelligence Companies to Manage the Risks Posed by AI* (July 21, 2023); Kevin Roose, *How Do the White House's AI Commitments Stack Up?*, N.Y. TIMES (July 22, 2023).

[60] Ross Andersen, *Does Sam Altman Know What He Is Creating?*, ATLANTIC (July 24, 2023); Alexander Karp, *Our Oppenheimer Moment: The Creation of A.I. Weapons*, N.Y. TIMES (July 25, 2023).

[61] Gerrit De Vynck, *Some Tech Leaders Fear AI. ScaleAI Is Selling It to the Military*, WASH. POST (Oct. 22, 2023) (describing Scale, a company founded "to help other companies organize and label data to train AI algorithms" as "aggressively pitching itself as the company that will help the U.S. military in its existential battle with China, offering to help the Pentagon pull better insights out of

And even if some large companies refuse to sell AI tools to the government, smaller companies almost certainly will seek to backfill those contracts.

Third, even companies that have signaled that they intend to be cautious about their work with the military have taken steps in practice that raise questions about their commitments. OpenAI's ethics policy originally contained a prohibition on using ChatGPT for "weapons development" and "military and warfare" purposes, but the company later narrowed that language to enjoin only the use of ChatGPT to "develop or use weapons" without publicly announcing the change.[62] There have been a spate of reports that AI companies such as Microsoft, Twitter/X, and Amazon's Twitch have laid off their ethical AI teams, further complicating the idea that those companies will help advance public law values.[63]

Fourth, the companies could be careless or untruthful about the training data they use, misrepresent the efficacy and reliability of their systems, unintentionally embed biases in their systems, or resist sharing their data or algorithms with the government—and thus exacerbate the double black box problem, including for actors inside the U.S. government.[64] The Pentagon's Chief Digital and AI officer described the process he had seen to date as reflecting the latter: "We're just getting the end result of the model-building— that's not sufficient. . . . They're saying: 'Here it is. We're not telling you how we built it. We're not telling you what it's good or bad at. We're not telling you whether it's biased or not.'"[65] Which outcome obtains moving forward depends on what behaviors the Executive is willing to tolerate, on whether

the reams of information it generates every day, build better autonomous vehicles and even create chatbots that can help advise military commanders during combat").

[62] Sam Biddle, *OpenAI Quietly Deletes Ban on Using ChatGPT for "Military and Warfare"*, INTERCEPT (Jan. 12, 2024); Sam Biddle, *Can the Pentagon Use ChatGPT? The Pentagon Won't Answer*, INTERCEPT (May 8, 2023) (discussing OpenAI, Google, and others).

[63] Rebecca Bellan, *Microsoft Lays Off an Ethical AI Team as It Doubles Down on OpenAI*, TECHCRUNCH (Mar. 13, 2023) ("Teams like Microsoft's ethics and society department often pull the reins on big tech organizations by pointing out potential societal consequences or legal ramifications. Microsoft perhaps didn't want to hear 'No,' anymore as it became hell bent on taking market share away from Google's search engine."); Gerrit De Vynck & Will Oremus, *As AI Booms, Tech Firms Are Laying Off Their Ethicists*, WASH. POST (Mar. 30, 3023) ("[I]t's now going to be tough for people to believe any ethics team within a Big Tech company is more than just an ethics-washing operation.").

[64] *See* Cade Metz et al., *How Tech Giants Cut Corners to Harvest Data for A.I.*, N.Y. TIMES (Apr. 6, 2024).

[65] *See, e.g.*, Katrina Manson, *Pentagon Urges AI Companies to Share More About Their Technology*, BLOOMBERG (Sept. 29, 2023). *See also* K. Sabeel Rahman, *Reconstructing the Administrative State in an Era of Economic and Democratic Crisis*, 131 HARV. L. REV. 1671, 1678 (2018) (noting that outsourcing can diminish democratic accountability, rendering the operations "less scrutable, accountable, and effective").

Congress decides to legislate standards for national security AI, and on the extent to which other actors (U.S. states, whistleblowers, and civil society) check the companies.

Corporate whistleblowers can position companies to better serve as secrecy surrogates. (Corporate leakers may serve a similar function to whistleblowers, though they would not be protected from retaliation by the company.) Whistleblowers inside companies that hold contracts with U.S. national security agencies can, like government whistleblowers, identify violations of public law values in products that the U.S. government intends to use. However, if they do not use the statutory whistleblower pathways created for the intelligence community, they face the possibility of being prosecuted. To date, a few whistleblowers have revealed what they viewed as problematic practices within tech companies, but they did not reveal classified information. Though not related directly to the development of AI tools, a prominent Facebook whistleblower, Frances Haugen, filed a complaint with the SEC and shared thousands of documents reflecting that the company was aware of the harm its products caused to society.[66] Haugen received a "hero's welcome" in the media and Congress.[67] Subsequently, in March 2024, a Microsoft staffer warned federal regulators at the Federal Trade Commission, as well as members of Congress, about flaws in Copilot Designer (an AI-based image-generation tool) that allowed users to create abusive and violent content.[68] It seems likely that more such examples will follow.

Governments themselves are attuned to the value of data-, cyber-, and algorithm-related whistleblowing. Some states (including New York) recently have enhanced their whistleblower protections.[69] At the federal level, the Consumer Financial Protection Bureau (CFPB) has created a process by which technology workers can blow the whistle when they discover misconduct within the CFPB's mandate.[70] The agency encourages "engineers, data scientists and others who have detailed knowledge of the algorithms and

---

[66] Reed Albergotti, *Frances Haugen Took Thousands of Facebook Documents: This Is How She Did It*, WASH. POST (Oct. 26, 2021).

[67] Hannah Bloch-Wehba, *Can Whistleblowing Save Tech?*, LAWFARE (Apr. 17, 2023).

[68] Jackie Davalos, *Microsoft Staffer Warns Regulators About Harmful AI Content*, BLOOMBERG (Mar. 6, 2024).

[69] Debevoise & Plimpton LLP, *Cybersecurity and AI Whistleblowers: Unique Challenges and Strategies for Reducing Risk* (Nov. 2, 2021).

[70] Consumer Fin. Protection Bd., *CFPB and Federal Partners Confirm Automated Systems and Advanced Technology Not an Excuse for Lawbreaking Behavior* (Apr. 25, 2023).

technologies used by companies and who know of potential discrimination or other misconduct within the CFPB's authority to report it."[71]

The possibility that individuals who work for government contractors may blow the whistle on problematic corporate approaches to AI illustrates how two different sets of secrecy surrogates (states and companies) may interact to affect the government's AI activity, at least that which is not classified. As one law firm noted, "(1) the rise of internal company disputes over cybersecurity and AI, (2) expanding whistleblower protections, (3) the prospect of significant awards and (4) the media's interest in these kinds of disputes due to the public's suspicion that companies are not doing enough in cybersecurity and AI to protect consumers point to a likely significant increase in the number of data-related whistleblowers in the coming years."[72] These laws and policies may encourage corporate whistleblowing about data, cyber, and algorithmic problems generally, though they likely will have at best a limited effect on national security whistleblowing because of the classified nature of many national security algorithms. Corporate national security whistleblowers will have to employ the IC whistleblower statutory framework if they wish to stay within a safe harbor.

Some scholars have proposed that Congress enact new whistleblowing protections for individuals who identify prohibited algorithmic practices.[73] Sonia Katyal, for example, notes that "whistleblowing has been shown to be particularly effective in situations . . . where companies are increasingly relying on internal systems of self-regulation and trying to address the importance of combating bias. Here, particularly given the internal nature of AI, there is even more of a necessity to integrate a culture of whistleblower protection."[74] Congress should consider ways to encourage corporate employees working on classified AI projects to use the statutory whistleblowing regime to report when those projects appear to involve illegality, fraud, or abuse, including through the use of *qui tam* tools.[75] Further, DOD and the intelligence

---

[71] *Id.*

[72] Debevoise & Plimpton LLP, *supra* note 69 (noting that "cyber- or AI-related concerns are often technical in nature and may require expertise to properly evaluate").

[73] MILES BRUNDAGE & SHAHAR AVIN, THE MALICIOUS USE OF ARTIFICIAL INTELLIGENCE: FORECASTING, PREVENTION, AND MITIGATION 56 (2018); Deven Desai & Joshua A. Kroll, *Trust But Verify: A Guide to Algorithms and the Law*, 31 HARV. J.L. & TECH. 1, 43 (2017).

[74] Sonia K. Katyal, *Private Accountability in the Age of Artificial Intelligence*, 66 UCLA L. REV. 54, 128 (2019).

[75] *See generally* Sean Farhang, *Public Regulation and Private Lawsuits in the American Separation of Powers System*, 52 AM. J. POL. SCI. 821 (2008) (noting that legislatively created private rights of action reflect legislative desire to surface information about wrongdoing held by private actors without cost to public fisc).

community themselves should ensure that their whistleblowing regimes are easy for contractors to use to report AI-related problems, particularly classified ones. This may be a particularly promising avenue by which to identify national security AI tools that are ineffective or unlawful, because those individuals in a position to blow the whistle will have technical skills and access to the algorithms and data at issue.[76]

Beyond whistleblowers, there may be ways to channel corporate profit motives into activities that could enhance national security AI's accuracy. Google's former CEO, Eric Schmidt, has argued that governments should require advanced AI models "to be evaluated by government-certified private testing companies," where those companies would "compete for dollars and talent."[77] If we are concerned that the government's AI tools may become so sophisticated that the average engineer may not fully understand the tools' capabilities, having expert companies—whose skills will have been honed by private sector competition and who are "incentivized to out-innovate each other"[78]—looking over the government's shoulder at its classified, high-risk AI tools will provide quality control. Indeed, the government could build into its national security AI-related contracts a requirement that its AI vendors employ such certified private testing before providing the tool to the government.

It is clear that the U.S. government and companies will have a complex relationship when it comes to AI. As I have written about the role of cybersecurity companies, in some cases

> their interests will align with the public's interest in executive adherence to public law values such as accuracy, transparency, reason giving, and legality. Both tech companies and the public benefit when the intelligence community collects accurate intelligence and produces solid analyses. The companies enhance their bottom line and their reputation when reliable government information facilitates their ability to make accurate cyber attack attributions and effectively defend their customers against cyber attacks. Indeed, tech companies receive a direct reward for serving as

---

[76] *See* Hannah Bloch-Wehba, *The Promises and Perils of Tech Whistleblowing*, 118 Nw. L. Rev. 1503 (2024) ("Secrecy, however, begets leaks, and leaks have become the de facto source of crucial information for lawmakers, regulators, and the public. Today, whistleblowing is an important part of broader efforts to bring accountability and transparency to the tech industry.").

[77] Eric Schmidt, *How We Can Control AI*, Wall St. J. (Jan. 26, 2023).

[78] *Id.*

secrecy surrogates that demand quality intelligence and press the government for context and justifications.[79]

The same should hold true for AI-related cyber activities, particularly where the public is paying attention to the relationships between companies and the military and intelligence agencies. Kristen Eichensehr has postulated a model in which technology companies "will fight against or resist governments when the companies perceive themselves to be and can credibly argue that they are protecting the interests of users against governments."[80] In contrast, those companies will not resist government efforts to conduct national security or law enforcement operations, for example, when the companies assess that there is "an alliance between users and governments."[81] This suggests that "common use" companies will remain sensitive to the perceptions of their users and structure their behavior in response to those perceptions.

E. The Public

This brings us to the final set of nontraditional (or perhaps the most traditional!) checks on government secrecy: the public. Individuals, interest groups, and academic researchers have the ability to pressure other actors that serve as checks on the Executive—Congress, companies, journalists, states and localities—and even the agencies themselves in ways that may reduce the size of the double black box and enhance compliance with public law values.

The range of avenues that these groups could pursue is diverse, with costs running from very expensive to free. At the costly end, U.S. states should empower academic researchers by funding AI-focused labs that can pressure-test the ethics and functionality of various AI tools in a setting that is not driven by profit motives.[82] Although these tools will presumably be unclassified, there may be important overlaps between unclassified AI tools and

---

[79] Deeks, *supra* note 2, at 1459–60.

[80] Kristen Eichensehr, *Digital Switzerlands*, 167 U. PA. L. REV. 665, 704 (2019).

[81] *Id.* at 705.

[82] Grace Ashford, *Hochul to Propose A.I. Research Center Using $275 Million in State Funds*, N.Y. TIMES (Jan. 8, 2024) ("'Industry is moving so quickly—they don't actually have time to think about the long-term future for where this technology is going. That is the role of academia,' Dr. Wing said, adding that researchers would also be able to take up ethical questions that those in industry might have less incentive to consider.").

classified ones, such that research about the former will inform the latter. At the less costly end, individuals can use tools such as social media campaigns to communicate their views to both the government and to tech companies about AI tools that are proving to be harmful or otherwise inconsistent with the public law values discussed in this book.[83] Groups such as Human Rights Watch and the Electronic Frontier Foundation are carefully watching how national security agencies appear to be buying and using AI tools. But these campaigns will be particularly powerful when they cross the political spectrum, perhaps drawing on bipartisan skepticism about the societal benefits of large technology companies. Think tanks or foundations could even convene a broad range of academic researchers, ethicists, lawyers, and futurists to imagine different possible uses of NSAI (even assuming many of the actual uses remain secret) and collect data about how the participants view those different imagined uses.

The government should pay close attention to public or expert views that begin to coalesce around the propriety of using particular categories of unclassified AI tools, as these views will help forecast how the public would react to various classified AI forms and products if those tools ultimately came to light. Chapter 1 showed that some parts of the government were surprised at the public's reaction when some of the "war on terror" measures came to light. The government has the opportunity now to consider how to draw on what is known about public sentiment to inform its AI-related decisions behind the veil of secrecy.

In James Madison's view, representative democracy works best when elected officials "refine and enlarge the public views, by passing them through the medium of a chosen body of citizens, whose wisdom may best discern the true interests of their country."[84] Asking elected officials (and career bureaucrats) to pay careful attention to the views and sentiments of

---

[83] *See* Mariano-Florentino Cuellar & Aziz Huq, *The Democratic Regulation of Artificial Intelligence* 27, KNIGHT FIRST AM. INST. (2022) (urging "a search for ways in which the wider rank and file of citizens can better understand the moral and political choices embedded not just in code but in the design choices of AI systems"); Rahman, *supra* note 65, at 1704 (noting that "the capacity for civil society groups, social movements, and constituencies on the ground to influence policymaking institutions depends crucially on the ways in which these groups are able to target and participate effectively in political institutions"). The U.K. Parliament has urged the U.K. Ministry of Defence to monitor or poll public attitudes toward the use of autonomous weapons systems. UK House of Lords, *Proceed with Caution: Artificial Intelligence in Weapon Systems* 3–4 (2023).

[84] THE FEDERALIST NO. 10, at 66 (James Madison) (Clinton Rossiter ed., 1961).

informed members of the public need not undercut the idea that we need elected officials and executive experts to process and filter those public views as they build NSAI. But the government should treat public views as important inputs to NSAI today. In the longer term, the public will be the ultimate judge of whether the United States took the right approach to NSAI.

6

The Hurdles to International Regulation

A. Introduction

As this book has demonstrated, democratic states such as the United States will confront the problem of the double black box first and foremost in their domestic sphere, where constitutions, statutes, regulations, and judicial decisions set out rules for the government's activities.[1] But interactions among states also will affect the U.S. approach to its own national security AI (NSAI). In being affected by other states, the United States is hardly an outlier. First, states will care about what types of NSAI other states are developing; what a state's adversaries are doing will affect what tools the first state deems "necessary" to pursue. A state might not be inclined to allow a military system to operate in a fully autonomous mode, but could learn that its adversary has done so to great effect and may be driven to do so itself. These tensions are spawning what some term an NSAI arms race.[2] Second, what a state's ally is doing will affect the interoperability of the two states' militaries. Third, if a state makes an international commitment to take some NSAI tools off the table or to interpret existing international law to prohibit certain activities, this will reduce the size of that state's domestic double black box. A number of states and nongovernmental experts perceive that certain NSAI tools pose a risk so great that they have called for binding international agreements to manage those risks—though those agreements have not yet emerged.[3]

There are real risks that some states may use NSAI tools in ways that are dangerous to international peace and security or are unethical, even if the

---

[1] This chapter draws from Ashley Deeks, *National Security AI and the Hurdles to International Regulation*, Lawfare Paper Series (Mar. 2023).

[2] Richard Walker, *Germany Warns: AI Arms Race Already Underway*, DW (June 7, 2021) (German foreign minister warning of AI arms race); Special Competitive Studies Project, Mid-Decade Challenges to National Competitiveness (Sept. 2022) (describing the "race for actionable insight in an information-rich and geopolitically-competitive world").

[3] *See, e.g.*, GA Res. 78/241 (Dec. 28, 2023) (stressing the urgent need for states to address concerns posed by lethal autonomous weapons and asking the Secretary General to submit a report on ways to address those concerns).

United States is not one of them. In general, international agreements can help improve strategic stability and protect individual rights. This is why scholars and some states have considered—and advocated for—international regulation of AI.[4] Various scholars and policy experts have drawn analogies between nuclear arms control and international efforts to regulate high-risk NSAI, including lethal autonomous weapons systems (LAWS) and uncontrolled AI systems. They use these analogies to show that even when very powerful national security tools are at stake, states sometimes agree to limit their own use of those tools and develop verification mechanisms to enforce those limits.

Although this nuclear arms control analogy may be normatively appealing, it is flawed. There are good reasons to be skeptical about the prospects of a robust, multilateral international agreement containing rules that implicate a state's development of NSAI.[5] The threat posed by NSAI seems less tangible and, for now, less existential than nuclear weapons. The geopolitics among leading NSAI states are very strained, and their development and use of AI is a closely guarded secret. And nuclear weapons themselves are different from NSAI systems in salient ways.

There is a better analogy to be made, one that can more accurately predict what will happen in international discussions about NSAI: efforts to regulate hostile cyber operations (HCO). Identifying good analogies and avoiding bad analogies lets us focus on the most fruitful pathways by which to shape behavior, while minimizing time spent on projects that face limited chances of success. Because HCO and NSAI share important features, state efforts to identify certain HCO as internationally impermissible suggest several features about efforts to regulate NSAI internationally. Specifically, those efforts suggest that (1) a binding global agreement containing new rules about NSAI will be beyond reach unless and until there is a major crisis; (2) basic agreement about how existing international law applies to NSAI may be possible, though subject to contestation; (3) close allies can do useful work to set guardrails around certain uses of NSAI, at least among themselves; (4) there may be very narrow areas in which the United States, Russia, and China might agree not to deploy NSAI; and (5) much of the work to sketch out expectations about how states generally should and should not

---

[4] *See, e.g.,* ICRC Position on Autonomous Weapons (May 12, 2021); Rebecca Crootof, *The Killer Robots Are Here: Legal and Policy Implications*, 36 CARDOZO L. REV. 1837 (2015).

[5] *See* Yahli Shereshevsky, *International Humanitarian Law-making and New Military Technologies*, 104 INT'L REV. RED CROSS 2131, 2138 (2022).

use NSAI will be done unilaterally, in the form of government statements, sanctions, and criminal prosecutions.

B. The International Risks Posed by National Security AI

Chapter 2 described some of the current U.S. uses of national security AI and the possible risks those systems present. But it is worth revisiting what types of NSAI tools could be used across state borders and pose the kinds of risks that are stimulating calls for international regulation. There are at least three categories of NSAI risks that states and other actors are concerned about. First, they worry about effects from NSAI tools that may result in *harm to people*. Machine learning algorithms may be directly or indirectly implicated in a decision to use force against or detain someone. That is, the algorithm might produce a recommendation that a human decision maker acts on, or the algorithm might be deployed in a weapons system that undertakes the act itself. These acts of killing or detention might take place during an international armed conflict, but could also take place at an international border, during a peace enforcement operation, or by a law enforcement official domestically against a foreign national. States might also use NSAI in their covert actions, such as by launching a swarm of microdrones equipped with facial recognition software to assassinate a political enemy inside another state. Or a state might deploy an NSAI system that unexpectedly goes haywire during an armed conflict. Perhaps most alarmingly, states may build machine learning tools into their nuclear command and control systems; those tools may wrongly predict that an attack is coming and lead to an inadvertent use of nuclear weapons.

Second, NSAI may lead a *government to deploy force in a way that is unintended or is based on flawed premises* because another actor interfered with the NSAI. Consider a deepfake image that purports to show a foreign leader in a secret cabinet meeting, instructing his defense minister to launch a hail of ballistic missiles at the neighboring state the next day. It is not hard to see how that image, sent by a malicious state or nonstate actor to the neighboring state, might lead to exchanges of force.[6] Or consider the use of machine learning to autonomously penetrate another state's military systems and

---

[6] *See, e.g.,* Sarah Kreps & Richard Li, *Cascading Chaos: Nonstate Actors and AI on the Battlefield,* BROOKINGS INST. (Feb. 1, 2022).

escalate cyber operations (discussed in Chapter 3).[7] Because many NSAI tools today are brittle, they provide a broad surface area for others to attack.

Third, and relatedly, powerful NSAI tools could fall into the *hands of non-state actors.* Consider potent drone swarms in the hands of the Houthis, a rebel group in Yemen, who have shown a persistent willingness to launch explosive aerial drones against Saudi oil refineries and both aerial and underwater drones against international shipping.[8] These attacks are sophisticated and pernicious, and they are not yet enabled by machine learning. Adding AI tools to the mix will produce attacks that are more efficient and lethal.[9] Nonstate actors will also be able easily to access and deploy AI-enabled cyber and misinformation tools, including deepfakes, and will attempt to hack a state's NSAI systems.[10]

Although not complete, this list highlights the types of risks that states and experts have suggested that states should regulate internationally. Some proposals focus on broad swaths of NSAI, emphasizing the need to preserve accountability and human judgment in national security activities generally. Others focus on what they perceive as the riskiest type of NSAI: lethal autonomous weapons systems. Within these proposals, some worry about the effects of AI tools; other worry about the fact of using the tools at all.

C. How Much Can International Law Help?

As a result of the risks that states will use accident- or hacking-prone NSAI in military conflicts or in other ways that impose significant, adverse effects on foreign states or their nationals, various actors have urged states to use international law to mitigate those risks. There is some agreement that existing bodies of international law apply to NSAI, just as those rules apply to any area of state activity.[11] But *how* those bodies of international law apply to

---

[7] Ashley Deeks, *Will Cyber Autonomy Undercut Democratic Accountability?*, 96 INT'L L. STUD. 646 (2020).

[8] REUTERS, *Yemen's Houthis Claim Drone Attack on Refinery in Saudi Capital* (Mar. 22, 2022); Omar Tamo & Mohammed Hatem, *Houthis Target Aramco Sites in Saudi Arabia Using Drones*, BLOOMBERG (Mar. 19, 2022).

[9] Kreps & Li, *supra* note 6.

[10] *Id.* ("In contested Jammu and Kashmir, Indian authorities have cited militant groups using fake videos and photos to provoke violence to justify restricting internet services.").

[11] Guiding Principles affirmed by the Group of Governmental Experts on Emerging Technologies in the Area of Lethal Autonomous Weapons Systems (Annex III), CCW/MSP/2019/9 ("International humanitarian law continues to apply fully to all weapons systems, including the potential development and use of lethal autonomous weapons systems.").

NSAI tools is contested, and the rules themselves are often general enough that they provide only limited constraints. If states agree to new binding international rules that regulate the use of certain NSAI systems and then comply with those rules, it would take the risks of certain harmful uses of AI off the table. This would narrow the size of the national security black box. Further, a state that undertakes in-depth exchanges with allies about its NSAI to improve interoperability may produce slightly more transparency around the algorithmic black box than a state that operates unilaterally, because the former type of state will be pressed to explain its algorithmic tools to actors outside its executive branch.

Since 2013 or so, states, scholars, and nongovernmental organizations have developed proposals for international agreements or coalitions to regulate AI or for the creation of international organizations to serve as a focal point for international discussions to address AI risks. The highest-profile proposal is an effort to ban the use of autonomous weapons that can select and engage targets without meaningful human control.[12] (A few scholars have been skeptical about the prospects for a new international agreement on autonomous weapons—a skepticism that has proven prescient.)[13] Other proposals, which tend not to distinguish among particular types, users, or uses of NSAI, urge states to create NSAI-focused international organizations to set standards for states' use of NSAI; or to require AI systems to have kill switches; or to require that states make all of their AI systems traceable back to them.[14] Although some of the proposals' authors recognize the difficulty of achieving these types of agreements, authors often analogize to nuclear arms control to show why and how this type of regulation—which would limit states' flexibility in a very strategic and sensitive area—might be achievable. This section pushes back on those purported parallels, arguing that nuclear arms control agreements do not help us forecast the ways in which state efforts to regulate NSAI are likely to unfold—and that undue attention to nuclear arms control regimes diverts our attention from more promising areas of progress.

---

[12] HUMAN RTS. WATCH, *Killer Robots: Negotiate Treaty in New Forum* (Nov. 10, 2022).

[13] *See* Kenneth Anderson & Matthew Waxman, *Law and Ethics for Autonomous Weapons Systems* 20–22, HOOVER INST. (2013) (evincing skepticism about treaties that regulate or prohibit autonomous weapons).

[14] *See, e.g.,* SIMON CHESTERMAN, WE, THE ROBOTS? 197, 208 (2021); Defense Innovation Board, *AI Principles: Recommendations on the Ethical Use of Artificial Intelligence by the Department of Defense* (Oct. 2019) (identifying traceability as a principle).

1. Existing Proposals to Regulate National Security AI

Some actors have proposed ambitious concepts for regulating NSAI systems on an international scale.[15] Often these proposals are vague in content, indiscriminate in the type of NSAI they hope to reach, and light on details about how states could agree on new rules. For instance, Oren Etzioni and Nicole DeCario propose that AI in all its forms (including robotics, autonomous systems, and embedded algorithms) must be "accountable, interpretable and transparent" and urge states to ban fully autonomous offensive weapons. In addition, they want all AI systems to have "an impregnable off switch."[16] In their view, these goals are achievable because a wide range of states, including the United States, China, and forty others, have agreed on high-level AI-related principles such as "upholding human rights and values," "ensuring fairness," and "limiting harmful uses of AI."[17] However, there is a vast chasm between achieving (costless) agreement on very abstract principles and persuading states to agree (at a high cost) to only use AI systems that have impregnable "kill switches" embedded in them.

Others have offered more detailed—though equally ambitious—proposals. John Allen and Darrell West note that after World War II the United States, the U.S.S.R., China, France, Japan, and others were concerned about the strategic stability and ethical challenges posed by nuclear, chemical, and biological weapons and concluded a range of treaties to constrain the use of these tools.[18] Drawing parallels with the threats that AI poses, they urge the United States to "reach treaties with allies and adversaries that provide reliable guidance for the use of technology in warfare, create rules on what is humane and morally acceptable, outline military conduct that is unacceptable, ensure effective compliance, and take steps that protect humanity."[19] Specifically,

---

[15] Governments such as the United States and the United Kingdom have established policies governing their own development and use of some autonomous weapons or systems. *See, e.g.,* DOD Directive 3000.09: Autonomy in Weapons Systems (Jan. 25, 2023) (United States) and U.K. Ministry of Defence Joint Doctrine Publication 0-30.2, Unmanned Aircraft Systems (Jan. 15, 2018) (United Kingdom). Those policies reflect domestic commitments and do not necessarily reflect expectations about how other states will act.

[16] Oren Etzioni & Nicole DeCario, *We Have the Basis for an International AI Treaty*, THE HILL (July 17, 2019).

[17] *Id. See also* Jessica Cyssins Newman, *AI Principles in Context*, ASIA SOCIETY (Aug. 20, 2020) ("The partial international consensus of AI principles indicates significant common ground and potential . . . alignment on international agreement.").

[18] John Allen & Darrell West, *It Is Time to Negotiate Global Treaties on Artificial Intelligence*, BROOKINGS INST. (Mar. 24, 2021).

[19] *Id.*

Allen and West argue that states should "incorporate ethical principles such as human rights, accountability, and civilian protection in AI-based military decisions"; "keep humans in the loop with autonomous weapons systems," including missile launches, drone attacks, and large-scale military actions; keep AI algorithms out of nuclear operational command and control systems; "agree not to steal vital commercial data or disrupt power grids, broadband networks, financial networks, or medical facilities on an unprovoked basis through conventional digital attacks or AI-powered cyber-weapons"; and "develop effective oversight mechanisms to ensure compliance with international agreements," including periodic site inspections.[20]

Some of Allen and West's proposals on their face would raise concerns within the U.S. Defense Department, which generally does not construe human rights rules as applicable to international armed conflicts and which sees one advantage of autonomous weapons systems as avoiding the need to keep humans in the loop. But there are more serious challenges to the proposal as well. Allen and West are optimistic about achieving these goals because states already have agreed to support the Global Partnership on AI and because NATO members have started to consult about norms and policies on AI and other new technology. But they fail to explain why we should be confident that states can move from agreeing to high level AI-focused principles (such as "fairness" and "security") to agreeing to the very constraining rules they propose.[21] They also fail to explain why Russia and China would be willing to adhere to their proposed guardrails for military action. They simply point out that the stakes for inaction are high.

Simon Chesterman bears down on two core concerns about NSAI and proposes that states develop an international institution—modeled after the International Atomic Energy Agency (IAEA)—to manage those two risks.[22] Chesterman believes that it is necessary to establish red lines to prohibit (1) weaponized AI (that is, LAWS that lack meaningful human control), and (2) the "development of AI systems posing a real risk of being uncontrollable or uncontainable."[23] He would also require that "the conduct of AI systems remain[] traceable back to an entity with a presence in at least one state."[24]

---

[20] *Id.*

[21] There may be some reason for optimism that NATO states can make progress among themselves in agreeing on more detailed policies and practices for using NSAI, but those policies would not be highly constraining and would not apply directly to a broad swath of states.

[22] CHESTERMAN, *supra* note 14, at 209–17.

[23] *Id.* at 213.

[24] *Id.* at 197, 208.

Putting aside the challenge of developing a new international organization, the idea that states will agree to "mark" every AI system they use seems unlikely, particularly for intelligence agencies that will use such systems to conduct clandestine surveillance or covert action.

The most detailed proposal for regulating one subset of NSAI comes from Human Rights Watch (HRW). HRW asserts that fully autonomous weapons will be unable to comply with core law of armed conflict principles; will create an "accountability gap" that renders it difficult to hold anyone accountable for war crimes committed while using an autonomous weapon; and will undermine principles of humanity because the weapons are unable to show compassion or respect human dignity.[25] HRW also worries about an arms race and proliferation to nonstate actors. HRW and Harvard Law School's International Human Rights Clinic therefore proposed a new treaty that would require states to maintain "meaningful human control" over the use of force and ban the development and use of weapons systems that autonomously select and engage targets.[26] Similarly, the International Committee for the Red Cross (ICRC) advocates for "new legally binding rules" that would ban autonomous weapons systems that are unpredictable or that target humans, and it wants states to regulate other autonomous weapons systems by limiting the situations in which they could be used and requiring effective human supervision.[27] The ICRC's approach is more measured and plausible than the other proposals discussed here, but it still seeks new, widely binding international rules.

Each of these proposals is too vague, too ambitious, or both. There are of course excellent reasons to want to avoid strategic instability among the United States, China, and Russia or runaway autonomous systems that wreak havoc on the battlefield. But proposals that call on states to conclude agreements with their adversaries that "create rules on what is humane and morally acceptable, outline military conduct that is unacceptable, [and]

---

[25] Bonnie Docherty, *The Need for and Elements of a New Treaty on Fully Autonomous Weapons*, HUMAN RTS. WATCH (Feb. 20, 2020); HUMAN RTS. WATCH, *Losing Humanity: The Case Against Killer Robots* 46 (2012). *See also* Darrell West & Jack Karsten, *It's Time to Start Thinking About Governance of Autonomous Weapons*, BROOKINGS INST. (May 10, 2019) (calling for "meaningful" international governance of autonomous weapons, including regulations requiring transparency in technology performance; maintaining human-in-the-loop systems; and regulating technology transfers to prevent malicious use of advanced technology).

[26] Docherty, *supra* note 25.

[27] ICRC Position, *supra* note 4. For a helpful analysis of this proposal, see Rebecca Crootof, *Changing the Conversation: The ICRC's New Stance on Autonomous Weapons*, LAWFIRE (May 24, 2021).

ensure effective compliance"[28] without articulating what those rules and structures would look like and why states such as China, Russia, and the United States have sufficient incentives to reach such agreements are wildly optimistic. The next section analyzes a common source of that optimism.

2. Justifying Optimism Through Nuclear Arms Control Analogies

Several advocates and scholars who have proposed regulations on NSAI are optimistic about the prospect of achieving multilateral agreement because states have come together before to regulate weapons and weapon systems. There are a significant number of arms control agreements that regulate or constrain the deployment of national military means of destruction, including nuclear weapons and powerful conventional weapons. Some of those agreements restrict states parties from deploying particular weapons or forces to certain locations;[29] others set limits on the number of armaments that a state party may have.[30] Some ban certain weapons entirely,[31] while others restrain development.[32] Many of the regimes establish monitoring and verification tools or bodies.[33] Verification requires cooperation, reciprocal access, and some level of informational transparency from the inspected state.[34]

Those who advocate for regulating NSAI draw analogies to a wide range of weapons bans and regulations, including conventional weapons such as blinding lasers, antipersonnel land mines, and cluster munitions. Two

---

[28] Allen & West, *supra* note 18.

[29] Treaty on Principles Governing the Activities of States in the Exploration and Use of Outer Space, including the Moon and Other Celestial Bodies (Outer Space Treaty), Jan. 27, 1967, 18 UST 2410 (1967); Antarctic Treaty, Dec. 1, 1959, 12 UST 794, 402 UNTS 71, 19 ILM 860 (1980); Treaty on Conventional Forces in Europe (O.S.C.E. Doc. CFE-1.E) (1990) [hereafter CFE Treaty].

[30] Treaty on the Limitation of Anti-Ballistic Missile Systems and the Interim Agreement on Certain Measures with respect to the Limitation of Strategic Offensive Arms (SALT I) (1972) (imposing limitations on the number of ICBM and SLBM launchers); Treaty Between the United States of America and the Russian Federation on Further Reduction and Limitation of Strategic Offensive Arms (START II), signed at Moscow on Jan. 3, 1993; New START Treaty, signed at Prague on Apr. 8, 2010.

[31] Treaty on the Prohibition of Nuclear Weapons, UN Doc. A/CONF.229/2017/8, UN Doc. CN.476.2017.TREATIES-XXVI-9 (2017); Convention on the Prohibition of the Development, Production, Stockpiling and Use of Chemical Weapons and on their Destruction, 1342 UNTS 137 (1983).

[32] Comprehensive Nuclear Test-Ban Treaty, Doc. A/50/1027 (1996).

[33] *See, e.g.,* the Comprehensive Test Ban Treaty Organization; Open Skies Consultative Commission. These include technical (i.e., satellite) and nontechnical verification tools, such as human observation, tagging and sealing items, installing sensors, environmental sampling, and overflights.

[34] Office of Scientific and Technical Information, Dep't of Energy (slide 13).

scholars have examined these precedents and identified a range of factors that make a ban on a given conventional weapon likely to succeed, including the ineffectiveness of the weapon, its inherently indiscriminate nature, and the existence of other means to accomplish the same military objective.[35] Applying those factors to LAWS, each concludes that major military states are unlikely to agree to ban LAWS—a conclusion that is surely correct.

Nevertheless, scholars continue to argue that a different body of arms control—nuclear arms control—should serve both as a model for regulating AI and as a cause for optimism. Because adversarial (and friendly) states were able to come together to negotiate binding international rules to regulate the most physically and strategically powerful weapon ever created, the argument goes, we should be confident that states can come together to negotiate binding rules for potent, risky, and (perhaps) existentially destabilizing NSAI systems.

Early nuclear arms control agreements grew out of a near catastrophe. During the 1962 Cuban Missile Crisis, Soviet Communist Party Chairman Nikita Khrushchev authorized Soviet forces to use nuclear weapons stationed in Cuba against the United States if the United States invaded.[36] Because the United States in fact contemplated such an invasion, the United States and the Soviet Union came close to nuclear war.[37] In the aftermath, President Kennedy, who feared that up to twenty-five countries would have nuclear weapons by 1975, agreed with the USSR and the United Kingdom to begin negotiations on a comprehensive test ban treaty.[38] Within two months, they had negotiated the Limited Nuclear Test Ban Treaty, which prohibited nuclear testing in the atmosphere, in outer space, or under water.[39] By 1965, they had begun to negotiate what became the Nuclear Non-Proliferation Treaty (NPT), pursuant to which all states parties would work to prevent nuclear proliferation; all would share the benefits of peaceful uses of nuclear energy; and the nuclear weapons states would work to eliminate their

[35] Crootof, *supra* note 4, at 1884–92; Sean Watts, *Autonomous Weapons: Regulation Tolerant or Regulation Resistant?*, 30(1) TEMP. INT'L & COMP. L.J. 177, 178 (2016).

[36] JAMES BAKER, THE CENTAUR'S DILEMMA: NATIONAL SECURITY LAW FOR THE COMING AI REVOLUTION 192 (2020).

[37] GRAHAM ALLISON, ESSENCE OF DECISION: EXPLAINING THE CUBAN MISSILE CRISIS (2d ed. 1999). For a brief history of arms control, see Rose Gottemoeller, *U.S.-Russian Nuclear Arms Control Negotiations—A Short History* (May 2020).

[38] U.S. Dep't of State, Office of the Historian, *The Limited Test Ban Treaty, 1963.*

[39] Treaty Banning Nuclear Weapons Tests in the Atmosphere, No. 6964, signed at Moscow on Aug. 5, 1963; Outer Space Treaty, *supra* note 29.

nuclear weapons. Additional nuclear arms control treaties followed in the 1970s and 1980s.

A range of writers have found the parallels between nuclear arms control and AI regulations compelling.[40] Some draw *inspirational* parallels to the nuclear arms control regime, using it as evidence that adversaries can reach international agreements even on weapons that are fundamental to their national security. Others draw *structural* parallels, using the structures and organizations created by nuclear arms control treaties as guideposts for proposed AI regulation.

Scholars have invoked nuclear arms control as evidence that states sometimes find it in their national interests to curtail the use of powerful military tools. Chesterman notes, "[I]t may be asked whether states would ever willingly give up weapons that might provide a military advantage. Yet, in additional to the limits on nuclear weapons, that is precisely what states have done in respect of chemical and biological weapons, as well as more recent limitations on blinding weapons."[41] Likewise, James Baker points to U.S.-USSR nuclear negotiations to conclude that agreement "is sometimes possible at moments of great, even greatest, tension."[42]

Others look to nuclear treaties for structural ideas. Because states like the United States, Russia, and China appear to have a considerable lead on developing NSAI, some view the "have/have not" approach contained in the NPT as a useful model. For instance, Douglas Frantz proposes that states should agree to a "grand bargain," pursuant to which they would share the beneficial uses of AI while accepting universal safeguards to prevent its misuse.[43] James Baker points to the NPT's "have nots" construct as a potential model for states that wish to renounce certain weapons that employ AI, such as

[40] Joseph Nye draws high-altitude parallels between nuclear arms control and cyber, including the ideas that continuing technological change complicates early efforts to establish strategy; that strategies for new technologies will lack adequate empirical content; that new technologies raise new issues in civil-military relations; that civilian uses of the technology complicate the development of a national security strategy; and that it is important to involve the military in international contacts. Joseph Nye, *Nuclear Lessons for Cyber Security?*, 5 STRATEGIC STUD. Q. 18 (Winter 2011).

[41] CHESTERMAN, *supra* note 14, at 213. The ban on chemical weapons might offer a basis for slightly more optimism than the nuclear analogy does, because chemical weapons often are produced using dual-use materials and yet the ban has been relatively successful. However, states generally understood that chemical weapons were difficult to control on the battlefield and might affect their own troops. *See* Watts, *supra* note 35, at 178–79. The same is not manifestly true for AI systems.

[42] BAKER, *supra* note 36, at 202. *See also* Kenneth Payne, *Artificial Intelligence: A Revolution in Strategic Affairs?*, 60 SURVIVAL 7 (2018); Matthijs Maas, *How Viable Is International Arms Control for Military Artificial Intelligence? Three Lessons from Nuclear Weapons*, 40 CONTEMP. SECURITY POL'Y 285, 303 (2019).

[43] Douglas Frantz, *We've Unleashed AI. Now We Need a Treaty to Control It*, L.A. TIMES (July 16, 2018).

weapons that do not maintain a human in the loop.[44] Baker also suggests that, as state leaders did in the nuclear setting, "policymakers might wish at some point to consider numeric limits on LAWS and other AI systems."[45]

Others believe that the IAEA—the premier international organization that works on nuclear issues—is a useful model for an international organization that can address the risks of AI. Chesterman proposes that states create an "International Artificial Intelligence Agency" (IAIA).[46] He treats nuclear regulation as an illuminating parallel because nuclear power has enormous potential for both good and ill and because, as with nuclear weapons, some states possess advanced AI and others do not.[47] The IAEA treaty promoted peaceful uses of nuclear energy while constraining its military uses, set safety standards for civilian uses of nuclear energy, and empowered the Agency to establish and administer safeguards and conduct field inspections in non-nuclear weapons states to ensure that states do not divert nuclear materials to military purposes.[48] Chesterman's IAIA would set standards regarding meaningful human control of NSAI and require states to prevent AI systems from being deployed in a manner that cannot be traced back to a legal person.[49]

Scholars like Chesterman and Baker recognize that there are differences between nuclear arms control regimes and the scenarios that NSAI tools present today. For example, Baker concedes that AI is not a weapon but a collection of technological capacities and that, unlike with nuclear weapons, governments do not have a monopoly over its production and use—facts that will make it harder to regulate NSAI.[50] Nevertheless, Baker concludes that "the nuclear regime seems the most apt to AI because of the potential impact of AI to transform the national security landscape, as nuclear weapons did before."[51] As a result, Baker considers that states might establish limits or prohibitions on the number of human-out-of-the-loop weapons

---

[44] BAKER, *supra* note 36, at 204.

[45] *Id.* at 197.

[46] CHESTERMAN, *supra* note 14, at ch. 8. *See also* Brad Smith, *The Need for a Digital Geneva Convention*, Microsoft (Feb. 14, 2017) ("While there is no perfect analogy, the world needs an organization that can address cyber threats in a manner like the role played by the International Atomic Energy Agency in the field of nuclear non-proliferation.").

[47] CHESTERMAN, *supra* note 14, at 197.

[48] Statute of the International Atomic Energy Agency (1956), art. III.A.

[49] CHESTERMAN, *supra* note 14, at 216.

[50] BAKER, *supra* note 36, at 186, 192.

[51] *Id.* at 187.

applications, systems connected to cyber or nuclear weapons, or the deployment of AI systems into space or critical infrastructure.[52]

Although one can extract broad lessons from sixty years of nuclear arms control, there are critical differences between nuclear weapons and NSAI systems that undercut the value of the analogy and show why states currently lack incentives to negotiate binding international agreements to regulate NSAI systems. The next section discusses those differences.

3. The Flaws in Nuclear Arms Control Analogies

Nuclear weapons and AI systems differ in ways that will make it much harder for states to reach multilateral agreement about NSAI regulation.

a. Agreement/disagreement on the object of regulation

When the United States and the Soviet Union came to the negotiating table in 1963, there was little disagreement about the object of potential regulation. When negotiating the Limited Test Ban Treaty, which prohibited certain "nuclear weapon test explosions," states did not even define the term, suggesting that its meaning was clear. The fact that relevant states agreed on the kind of weapon about which they were negotiating eliminated ambiguity and closed off one door to "cheating," because states parties could not plead that they did not understand the parameters of the treaty.

In contrast, AI systems themselves are not weapons; machine learning and other types of AI algorithms serve as software in certain weapons and decision-making systems. There is debate about what set of AI systems gives rise to strategic concerns and sharp disagreement even about the NSAI tool that states, nongovernmental organizations, and scholars are most focused on: LAWS. For several years, discussions in the Convention on Certain Conventional Weapons' Group of Government Experts were bogged down in uncertainty about which systems to focus on and what terms such as "meaningful" or "effective" human control meant.[53] The United States defines a weapon as fully autonomous if, when activated, it "can select and engage targets without further intervention by a human operator."[54] The

---

[52] *Id.* at 204.
[53] Frank Sauer, *Autonomy in Weapons Systems: Playing Catchup with Technology*, ICRC Humanitarian Law & Policy (Sept. 29, 2021).
[54] DOD Directive 3000.09, *supra* note 15.

U.K. Ministry of Defence emphasizes the high level of sophistication of the weapon, including its ability to perceive, understand "intent," and decide.[55] China defines LAWS very narrowly as indiscriminate, lethal systems that lack human oversight and cannot be terminated.[56] A lack of clarity about the scope of what an agreement covers will naturally make states that take seriously their international obligations wary of joining that agreement.[57]

In addition, autonomy is not binary. Unlike a weapon that either is or is not powered by nuclear fission, autonomy exists on a sliding scale. States will gradually increase the level of autonomy in weapons systems, making it hard (certainly for observing states) to determine when a system is operating in fully autonomous mode.[58] Further, machine learning in weapons means that the capabilities of the weapon will change over time, unlike the fixed nature of a nuclear weapon. Attempting to regulate a complex tool that will appear in a wide range of weapons looks very different from efforts to regulate a specific, concrete weapon whose effects are well-understood, as nuclear weapons are.[59]

b. Publicity/secrecy of development and use

The United States used two nuclear weapons in 1945. Russia tested its first weapon in 1949,[60] the United Kingdom in 1952,[61] and China in 1964.[62] As Chesterman notes, nuclear weapons are "expensive to build and difficult to hide."[63] Indeed, most nuclear weapons states want other states to know that they possess the weapons, since the primary goal of nuclear weapons is to deter conflict and the weapons' "first use."

NSAI systems are easier to build than nuclear weapons, though advanced autonomous weapons still require sophisticated computer scientists and high quantities of data and computing power.[64] But NSAI systems are simple

---

[55] U.K. Ministry of Defence Joint Doctrine Publication 0-30.2, *supra* note 15.

[56] Statement of the Chinese Delegation at the Thematic Discussion on Conventional Arms Control (Oct. 2019).

[57] *See generally* Oona Hathaway, *Do Human Rights Treaties Make a Difference?*, 111 YALE L.J. 1935 (2002).

[58] Anderson & Waxman, *supra* note 13.

[59] PAUL SCHARRE, ARMY OF NONE 341–43 (2018).

[60] William Burr, *U.S. Intelligence and the Detection of the First Soviet Nuclear Test, September, 1949*, Nat'l Security Archive (Sept. 22, 2019).

[61] THE MANCHESTER GUARDIAN, *A New Method—Or a New Bomb* (Oct. 4, 1952).

[62] Lyndon B. Johnson, Statement by the President on the First Chinese Nuclear Device (Oct. 16, 1964).

[63] CHESTERMAN, *supra* note 14, at 223.

[64] SCHARRE, *supra* note 59, at 332.

to hide. Although Russia, China, and the United States intend to build advanced NSAI for use in conflict, it is very unclear what the state of AI is in those states, or in states that have been less public about their interest in NSAI. Is there currently an equality of arms? Have some states secretly achieved production of effective, fully autonomous weapons systems? It is not clear to the public and may not be clear to adversarial states themselves.

In August 2022, China announced that it was stopping all dialogue with the United States on major issues, including military relations, though conversations resumed in 2023.[65] And U.S.-Russia relations are near an all-time low in the wake of Russia's February 2022 invasion of Ukraine. This means that these states are going to be particularly secretive about the progress they are making on NSAI systems; discussions between them about AI tools would be particularly fraught because conversations could reveal developments that each state wishes to keep concealed. This radical difference between the publicity of nuclear weapons and the secrecy of NSAI development further renders the analogy inapt: if states cannot discuss what systems they have, they cannot discuss what aspects are most risky and potentially worth regulating.

This secrecy leads to a related problem: counting what could be limited and verifying whether states have used those tools. A range of arms control agreements limited the number of weapons that states were permitted to develop or retain. In the Anti-Ballistic Missile (ABM) Treaty, for example, the United States and USSR agreed to limit the numbers of ABM launchers and interceptor missiles and to only deploy them in certain locations. The Conventional Armed Forces in Europe Treaty established a military balance among two groups of states (NATO states and Warsaw Pact members) in the European area by creating equal ceilings for major weapons and equipment systems and required states parties to notify each other of the maximum levels of their holdings of equipment covered by the treaty.[66] In short, many arms control agreements involve a quantitative approach to weapons and weapon systems.

In contrast, AI will prove ubiquitous in weapons systems[67] and is not subject to being counted,[68] even if states can define the precise effects that

---

[65] NPR, *China Halts Climate and Military Dialogue with the U.S. over Pelosi's Taiwan Visit* (Aug. 5, 2022).

[66] CFE Treaty, *supra* note 29, arts. IV, VII.

[67] SCHARRE, *supra* note 59, at 352.

[68] Frank Sauer, *Stepping Back from the Brink: Why Multilateral Regulation of Autonomy in Weapons Systems Is Difficult, Yet Imperative and Feasible*, 102 INT'L REV. RED CROSS 235 (2020) (suggesting that states focus on the functional capabilities of certain AI systems rather than their

they wish to restrain. Further, it will be very difficult to tell when a system with autonomous capabilities has in fact operated in autonomous mode.[69] For example, news reports indicate that government-backed forces in Libya deployed a military drone that attacked enemy forces in its civil war.[70] However, experts have not been able to confirm whether the system actually operated autonomously.[71] Restrictions on nuclear weapons, incendiaries, and blinding lasers work better because it is relatively simple to know whether an actor has used them. Because of NSAI's ubiquity and the difficulty in ascertaining whether a system was in "autonomous" mode in a given situation, it will prove very hard to create a verification regime by which states parties can identify each other's NSAI systems and confirm each other's compliance with the rules.[72]

c. Visceral/speculative nature of threat

Finally, the visceral nature of a nuclear explosion brought into sharp relief the existential damage that nuclear weapons could wreak and sobered adversaries enough to bring them to the negotiating table. As Paul Scharre notes, "[S]tates often may not fully understand how terrible a weapon is until they see it on the battlefield."[73] No such operation has occurred (yet) with NSAI systems. Even Chesterman, who is reasonably optimistic about the ability to regulate NSAI, concedes that absent a threat that reveals the "visceral evidence of its destructive power," reaching international agreement about how to regulate AI will be difficult.[74] (He nevertheless insists that states should create a global institution to deal with it "in a hurry."[75])

The United States, Russia, and China have all made public statements reflecting their views that it is critical to win the "AI race." In this view, the cost of failing to develop such systems is, for now, much higher than the (still

---

number, especially a system's ability to target humans vice materiel). The same is true for cyber exploits, which are possible because of flaws in code, with their numbers nonfixed and almost unknowable. Nathaniel Fick & Jami Miscik, *Confronting Reality in Cyberspace: Foreign Policy for a Fragmented Internet* 35, COUNCIL ON FOREIGN REL. (July 2022).

[69] Robert Trager, *Killer Robots Are Here—And We Need to Regulate Them*, FOREIGN POL'Y (May 11, 2022); SCHARRE, *supra* note 59, at 354.

[70] Maria Cramer, *A.I. Drone May Have Acted on Its Own in Attacking Fighters, U.N. Says*, N.Y. TIMES (June 3, 2021).

[71] *Id.*

[72] SCHARRE, *supra* note 59, at 352.

[73] *Id.* at 344.

[74] CHESTERMAN, *supra* note 14, at 223; Sauer, *supra* note 68 (noting that the concept of "weapon autonomy" is "elusive and hard to conceptualize").

[75] CHESTERMAN, *supra* note 14, at 223.

theoretical) risk of doing so. Some people envision AI weapons as more reliable than human-manned weapons, while others envision them as "rogue
robot death machines killing multitudes," but it is hard to know which vision
is more accurate.[76] The lack of visceral evidence of the harm that risky NSAI
can produce means that the impetus that drove adversaries to reduce the risk
of nuclear war is absent today for states that are developing NSAI.[77]

If there is a useful parallel to be drawn with nuclear arms control, perhaps it is this: it took from 1945 until 1963 for states to conclude a binding
international agreement related to nuclear weapons, even though ideas for
how to regulate those weapons materialized as early as late 1945. The United
States, the USSR, and a handful of other states continued to produce nuclear weapons to gain military advantage and counter the risks posed by
adversaries, and it took a crisis—the Cuban Missile Crisis—to persuade the
major players to come to the table and begin negotiations in earnest. It may
take that long and require a real crisis before states take a similar international approach to NSAI. In the meantime, there is another area of national
security that offers stronger predictive analogies to NSAI: hostile cyber
operations.

D. A Better Analogy: Hostile Cyber Operations

There are fruitful analogies to be drawn between states' bilateral and multilateral efforts to regulate hostile cyber operations (HCO) and what may
work or fail in the efforts to regulate NSAI.[78] Tracing the trajectory of cyber-
related efforts can help us predict the trajectory of AI-related efforts and
identify what factors must change on the ground if states want to successfully
regulate NSAI.[79]

---

[76] SCHARRE, *supra* note 59, at 347.

[77] One exception may be the incident in which Russian Lt. Col. Petrov, who in 1983 received an
automated alert about incoming U.S. ballistic missiles and, rather than accept the computer's output,
correctly concluded that the computer had made a mistake. This visceral example of how reliance on
automation could have led to nuclear war presumably accounts for the U.S. decision not to employ
AI in nuclear command and control systems. Sydney Freedberg Jr., *No AI For Nuclear Command &
Control: JAIC's Shanahan,* BREAKING DEFENSE (Sept. 25, 2019).

[78] Indeed, states are likely to deploy autonomy in some of their cyber operations, perhaps even
sooner than they deploy tangible autonomous weapons. Difficulty in regulating HCO could be
compounded by the use of autonomy therein, and vice versa.

[79] *See* Crootof, *supra* note 4, at 1884–92; Watts, *supra* note 35, at 178.

HCO are digital operations by a state or nonstate actor that "disrupt, deny, degrade, manipulate, or destroy" a target's computer networks or information resident in those networks.[80] The operations sometimes produce tangible effects, but more often do not. Readers will be familiar with some of the dozens of high-profile HCO that have taken place in the last decade: North Korea's HCO against Sony, China's hack of OPM and theft of twenty-two million records of federal employees, Russia's interference with the 2016 U.S. elections, the U.S. operation against the Internet Research Agency before the 2018 mid-term elections, and Iran's wiping of data on thirty thousand computers at the Saudi Aramco oil company.

This section first describes why there is an apt analogy between HCO and NSAI. It then details the arc of transnational efforts to regulate HCO, an arc that carries lessons for NSAI regulation.

1. Why the Analogy Works

HCO bear important similarities to NSAI, including the fact that both are used by a wide range of states; that the tools are dual-use and built by both states and private actors; that states disagree about which regulations would be in their interest; and that the nature of the tools makes it complicated to verify norm compliance.

a. Broad range of users

Numerous and varied states and nonstate actors have access to HCO and NSAI tools. For both sets of tools, a small set of states has the most advanced technologies. Unlike with nuclear weapons, however, many other actors operate in this space.[81] A greater number of states will need to be part of negotiations about regulation; the polydimensional nature of geopolitics among states such as Russia, China, Iran, Israel, and the United States will make those negotiations even more complicated. States that lack cyber and AI tools (and expect to be victims of such tools) are often interested in regulating or banning these tools,[82] but regulation without agreement from the major state players has limited value. Further, nonstate actors have

---

[80] Memorandum for Chiefs of the Military Services, *Joint Terminology for Cyberspace Operations* 3 (n.d.).

[81] *See* Fick & Miscik, *supra* note 68, at 35.

[82] SCHARRE, *supra* note 59, at 347.

aggressively developed and used HCO against states and private entities, including to solicit ransoms from hospitals, cities, and schools. Determining the level of obligation that a state has to suppress HCO by nonstate actors within its territory poses an additional difficulty—as would determining a state's obligation to suppress hostile private uses of NSAI.

b. Dual-use nature of the tools

"Dual use" tools usually refer to tools that have both military and civilian applications, such as the electric grid. Both cyber and NSAI tools are clearly dual use. Cyber connectivity has brought about untold advantages in both the civilian and military realms. Early signs suggest that machine learning algorithms can be used for good in improving healthcare and addressing the effects of climate change, just as militaries will use those algorithms to enhance their decision-making.[83]

Even in the national security space, each of these tool sets has beneficial uses that are not adversarial, but instead enhance compliance with existing international rules. For instance, the United States might undertake a cyber operation against a suspicious foreign company to assess whether the company is trading with North Korea and thus violating a UN sanctions regime. We might think of that cyber operation as advancing overall compliance with internationally agreed rules. But observing that operation from the outside, it would be difficult to know whether the United States was surveilling for compliance reasons or stealing that company's trade secrets. Likewise, a state might develop an AI tool that allows a machine to "perceive, decide, and act more quickly, in a more complex environment,"[84] with the goal of using it for commercial airline safety, but it could also be used to exert air dominance over an adversary. This means that it will be hard to regulate the military uses of the tools without regulating the civilian uses and potentially surrendering the benefits of the latter.[85]

Further, unlike with nuclear weapons, the private sector plays a critical role in developing cyber and AI tools, including defenses against them. In the United States, private companies control most of the infrastructure across which cyber operations transpire. Because the private sector will develop some of the key tools that states then will adopt, regulating the production

---

[83] Rob Toews, *These Are the Startups Applying AI to Tackle Climate Change*, FORBES (June 20, 2021).

[84] National Security Commission on AI, Final Report at 22 (Mar. 19, 2021).

[85] BAKER, *supra* note 36, at 204.

of those tools in a way that preserves their benefits is more complicated than regulating systems (such as nuclear weapons) that states alone develop and deploy.

c. Misalignment of regulatory interests

In explaining his skepticism in 2011 about the prospects for cybersecurity treaties, Jack Goldsmith explained that Chinese and U.S. regulatory interests did not align.[86] The United States might welcome a ban on cyberattacks against civilian targets because it generally does not conduct HCO against those targets, it has a wide range of civilian infrastructure that poses an attractive target for adversaries, and the U.S. military uses civilian networks to conduct much of its business. China, in contrast, has more secure civilian networks; its military does not use those networks; and it perceives itself as having weaker traditional military capabilities that it wants to counteract by sitting inside U.S. civilian networks.[87] These same postures seem to still exist in 2024, though China likely now feels that it has improved its conventional military strength relative to the United States. As a result, there still seems to be little common ground for an agreement between the United States and China on cyber rules. China and Russia, which are more likeminded, have concluded a bilateral cybersecurity agreement not to conduct cyberattacks against each other, but it is unclear whether they are complying with that agreement.[88]

Another source of disagreement about what to regulate stems from divergent value systems between democracies and nondemocracies. There are certain targets, such as another state's voting machines, against which democracies would probably not conduct HCO, largely as a matter of principle and ethics. However, nondemocratic adversaries have shown that they do not view foreign elections as off limits. Other examples include operations against healthcare systems and water systems.[89] It has therefore proven

---

[86] Jack Goldsmith, *Cybersecurity Treaties: A Skeptical View* 4–5, HOOVER INST. (Mar. 9, 2011). *See also* Ashley Deeks, *Moving Forward on Cyber Norms, Domestically*, LAWFARE (July 10, 2017).

[87] Goldsmith, *supra* note 86, at 5. *See also* Watts, *supra* note 35, at 184–85.

[88] Olga Razumovskaya, *Russia and China Pledge Not to Hack Each Other*, WALL ST. J. (May 8, 2015); Yuxi Wei, *China-Russia Cybersecurity Cooperation: Working Towards Cyber-Sovereignty*, U. WASH. (June 21, 2016).

[89] National Cyber Awareness System, Alert, *North Korean-Sponsored Cyber Actors Use Maui Ransomware to Target the Healthcare and Public Health Sector* (July 7, 2022) (assessing that North Korean state-sponsored cyber actors attacked U.S. health care organizations); Joby Warrick & Ellen Nakashima, *Foreign Intelligence Officials Say Attempted Attack on Israeli Water Utilities Linked to Iran*, WASH. POST (May 8, 2020) (discussing attacks by Iranian hackers on Israeli water systems).

difficult to identify a category of targets that all states could agree not to attack.

NSAI presents a similar misalignment of regulatory interests. Although China and Russia would presumably prefer not to face U.S. LAWS on the battlefield or deepfakes intended to sow chaos inside their regimes, they may view the cost of forgoing those tools as too high. In addition, Russia and China exercise tighter control over their press and publics and can control public reactions to deepfakes better than the U.S. government can.

Further, there are certain types of NSAI systems that democracies would avoid developing or using because the systems risk failing to comply with the laws of armed conflict.[90] Because Russia understands this, it may conclude that developing LAWS that are not restrained by the laws of armed conflict will produce a battlefield advantage for it. Indeed, Russia's renewed aggression and war crimes in Ukraine illustrate a lack of interest in complying with international law more generally, so any purported Russian commitment today to only deploy NSAI that complies with international law would not be credible. In short, with both HCO and NSAI, Russia and China likely do not perceive the benefits of regulation in the same way that the United States (and its allies) may.

d. Verification challenges

Even if there were an identity of interests among the United States, China, and Russia about which cyber and NSAI systems to regulate, the incentives to regulate would still be very weak because states will be unable to develop a credible verification regime for the misuse of either set of tools. The development of both cyber and NSAI tools are generally closely held secrets. Reports about state-sponsored uses of cyber tools are now prevalent, but in most cases the actor conducting the HCO wishes to remain obscured. Some victim states have become more skilled at attributing those attacks, but doing so is complicated, and the states accused of committing the HCO generally deny them.[91]

The extent of a state's NSAI tools likewise is generally treated as top secret. Some uses of military AI by Russia, China, and the United States have appeared in the press, but most of the programs will remain hidden, because each state wants to protect its technical advances from theft and keep its

---

[90] *See* Anderson & Waxman, *supra* note 13, at 19.
[91] Kristen Eichensehr, *Cyberattack Attribution as Empowerment and Constraint* 2, HOOVER INST. (Jan. 15, 2021).

adversaries guessing about its capabilities. As a result, even discussing with adversaries the possibilities of certain kinds of risks from NSAI operations and options for verification could reveal information to those adversaries about the extent of a state's NSAI development.

Further, both cyber and NSAI tools are essentially invisible, and the effects a given tool will have are not patently obvious (unlike, say, a missile). A potential victim may detect a cyber intrusion but not be able to determine whether that intrusion is facilitating an act of espionage (which might not violate an international agreement) or an HCO (which might). For NSAI tools, the level of autonomy inside a given system will be very difficult for opponents to detect without capturing and reverse-engineering the algorithm.[92] The intangibility of these tools contributes to the verification problems. Indeed, each state must contend not only with its own black box challenges but also with the black box nature of its adversaries' NSAI.

2. The State of International Cyber Discussions

These four similarities between cyber and NSAI tools suggest that international efforts to regulate these tools will take similar paths.[93] Indeed, some cyber and NSAI tools may soon merge, with states increasingly turning to autonomous cyber tools to accomplish their national security goals.[94] Since 2007 or so, many scholars have proposed that states negotiate cyber treaties to suppress HCO.[95] With a few exceptions, those calls have tapered off, as states have shown little appetite for developing new binding international law on state cyber operations.[96] This section identifies seven distinct types

---

[92] Crootof, *supra* note 4, at 1891.

[93] HCO and NSAI have differences. First, nongovernmental organizations have been more assertive in calling for bans on one type of NSAI (LAWS); they have not done so for cyber tools, presumably because LAWS are more likely to result in civilian death and raise harder ethical questions. Additionally, it is harder to conceptualize weapons autonomy than it is to conceptualize what the effects of HCO look like, since states have experienced many HCO.

[94] For a discussion of autonomy in cyber operations, see Chapter 3.

[95] *See, e.g.,* Duncan Hollis, *Why States Need an International Law for Information Operations,* 11 Lewis & Clark L. Rev. 1023 (2007); Louise Arimatsu, *A Treaty for Governing Cyber-Weapons: Potential Benefits and Practical Limitations,* 2012 4th International Conf. on Cyber Conflict.

[96] There are two notable exceptions. First, Microsoft continues to urge states to conclude a "Digital Geneva Convention," pursuant to which states would agree not to conduct cyberattacks on civilians and critical infrastructure during peacetime. *See* Brad Smith, *The Need for a Digital Geneva Convention,* Microsoft (Feb. 14, 2017). Second, in 2024 an Ad Hoc Committee in the United Nations finished negotiating a UN Convention Against Cybercrime that addresses cybercrimes by

of international activities that states (and nonstate actors) have undertaken in the past fifteen years to clarify what set of rules or norms do or should apply to operations in cyberspace.[97] Tracing these efforts leads to three conclusions: (1) that a binding multilateral agreement about *new* HCO rules has proven elusive; (2) that the level of specificity of a proposed norm decreases as the number of states backing that norm increases; and (3) that progress on establishing uniform expectations of state behavior in conducting cyber operations has been modest.

a. Application of existing international law

In 2003, the UN Secretary General established a group of governmental experts (GGE) to "consider existing and potential threats in the sphere of information security and possible cooperative measures to address them."[98] The GGE began as a group of fifteen state experts and ultimately grew to twenty-five experts. From 2004 to 2021, the GGE assessed these threats and agreed on a number of conclusions and recommendations, which the UN General Assembly then adopted.[99] In 2013, the GGE concluded, "International law, and in particular the Charter of the United Nations, is applicable and is essential to maintaining peace and stability and promoting an open, secure, peaceful and accessible [information and communications technologies (ICT)] environment."[100] Two years later, the GGE agreed more specifically that international legal rules related to the threat or use of force, nonintervention, human rights, armed conflict, and the norms that flow from sovereignty applied to ICT.[101]

However, in 2016–17, the GGE failed to achieve consensus on a new report when some members of the group sought to include specific references to "self-defense" and "international humanitarian law" (IHL), which would have put more meat on the bones of the 2015 report.[102] In 2021, the GGE reached agreement—a bit obliquely—about the applicability of those

nonstate actors, but does not reach a wide range of HCO committed by states. *See* UN Office of Drugs and Crime.

[97] *See* Martha Finnemore & Duncan Hollis, *Constructing Norms for Global Cybersecurity*, 110 AJIL 425, 428 (2016).

[98] GA Res. 58/32 (Dec. 18, 2003).

[99] UN Office for Disarmament Affairs, Developments in the field of information and telecommunications in the context of international security.

[100] GA Res. A/68/98 (June 24, 2013).

[101] GA Res. A/70/174 (July 22, 2015).

[102] Michael Schmitt, *The Sixth United Nations GGE and International Law in Cyberspace*, JUST SECURITY (June 10, 2021).

provisions to cyber operations.[103] The Group "reaffirmed the commitment of States" to "the settlement of international disputes by peaceful means in such a manner that international peace and security and justice are not endangered; refraining in their international relations from the threat or use of force against the territorial integrity or political independence of any State, or in any other manner inconsistent with the purposes of the United Nations; . . . and nonintervention in the internal affairs of other States."[104]

This statement includes language drawn from Article 2(4) of the Charter prohibiting the use of force, but it does not specifically refer to language in Article 51 on the inherent right of self-defense. In a later paragraph, the report subtly recalls "that the Charter applies in its entirety" and notes "the inherent right of States to take measures consistent with international law and as recognized in the Charter."[105]

The 2021 GGE report was similarly delicate about IHL. Instead of directly stating that IHL regulates states' cyber activities during armed conflict, the report notes "that international humanitarian law applies only in situations of armed conflict." The report further "recognised the need for further study on how and when these principles apply to the use of ICTs by States."[106]

In short, states, by supporting the GGE's reports, have generally recognized that important bodies of existing international law apply to cyber operations, just as those bodies of law apply to other state operations. However, the fact that the GGE—a relatively small group of twenty-five states—could only obtain consensus by treading very softly around the concepts of self-defense and IHL suggests that not all states have fully bought into the applicability of those concepts. Indeed, some uncertainty remains about whether China actually agrees that IHL applies in cyberspace.[107] Further, the GGE report leaves unresolved questions about *how*, precisely, IHL applies to cyber operations. Pushing beyond this existing high-level affirmation that certain existing bodies of international law apply seems like a Sisyphean task. Indeed, significant uncertainty remains (even among close allies) about how cyber operations map onto the rule against "intervention in the internal affairs of

---

[103] Report of the Group of Governmental Experts on Advancing Responsible State Behaviour in Cyberspace in the Context of International Security.
[104] *Id.*, ¶ 70.
[105] *Id.*, ¶ 71(e).
[106] *Id.*, ¶ 71(f).
[107] Binxing Zhang, *Cyberspace and International Humanitarian Law: The Chinese Approach, in* Asia-Pacific Perspectives on International Humanitarian Law (Suzannah Linton et al. eds., 2019); Xixiong Huang & Yaohui Ying, *The Application of the Principle of Distinction in the Cyber Context: A Chinese Perspective*, 102 Int'l Rev. Red Cross 335 (2020).

other states," which is the kind of cyber activity that occurs much more often than resort to force or armed conflict.

These discussions have been fraught for all of the reasons set out in the prior section: the broad range of states affected by HCO (as authors, victims, or bystanders); the dual-use nature of the tools; and a misalignment of regulatory interests. These discussions were not intended to set the groundwork for negotiating a new treaty, so issues of verification were not squarely presented.

b. Multilateral norms

The GGE discussions produced another outcome in 2015: eleven nonbinding norms of responsible state behavior in cyberspace.[108] In 2021, the GGE revisited those norms, adding commentary about what the norms mean and how states could comply with them.[109]

Some of the eleven norms are very vague (e.g., prevent harmful cyber practices, consider all relevant information when trying to attribute a cyber incident, respect human rights on the internet).[110] A few are more concrete, including the norms that states should not knowingly allow their territory to be used for internationally wrongful cyber acts; conduct or knowingly support cyber activity contrary to their obligations under international law that intentionally damages or impairs critical infrastructure that provides public services; or harm the information systems of emergency response teams.[111] Those norms are laudable, if still quite general, but states are a long way from converting them into binding rules, either through treaty negotiations or by consistent state practice done out of a sense of legal obligation.[112] Nevertheless, they will serve as a placeholder for continued interstate discussions about cyber issues.

c. Mini-lateral norms

Some states have tried to achieve greater agreement about appropriate international cyber behavior through discussions within smaller groups of like-minded states. These groups start with a clearer alignment of regulatory interests than broader groups such as the GGE and can have more

---

[108] Report of the Group of Governmental Experts, *supra* note 103 (norm 13(f)).
[109] Schmitt, *supra* note 102.
[110] Report of the Group of Governmental Experts, *supra* note 103 (norms 13(a), (b), and (e)).
[111] A/70/174, *supra* note 101.
[112] A few provisions listed as norms may already be international legal rules.

frank conversations with each other about tools, threats, and strategies. As a 2022 think tank report put it, "Norms are more useful in binding friends together than in constraining adversaries."[113] Of course, the states agreeing on mini-lateral norms are less likely to be adverse to each other. These norms are unlikely to suppress or deter operations by adversaries against the norm-adopting states. Nevertheless, the hope is that by showing how "responsible states" behave and how these norms enhance political and economic stability, other states eventually will join the original norm adopters, giving added weight to the norm. In some cases, these mini-lateral norms are even sharper, containing an implicit warning that the states articulating the norms plan to enforce those norms against norm violators.[114] These "mini-lateral" efforts have taken several forms.

On several occasions, NATO member states have affirmed that certain types of HCO could constitute "armed attacks" that would trigger the mutual defense provision of the North Atlantic Treaty.[115] NATO states have thus put other states on notice that NATO members reserve the right to treat certain high-impact HCO as triggering the right of self-defense under the UN Charter. In addition, NATO issued a communiqué in 2021 that criticized Russia's "attempted interference in Allied elections and democratic processes; . . . widespread disinformation campaigns; malicious cyber activities; and turning a blind eye to cyber criminals operating from its territory."[116] That document also called on China to "act responsibly in the international system, including in the space, cyber, and maritime domains."[117] Through these statements, NATO states condemned the use of ransomware, virtual currency to launder ransoms, disinformation against other states, and interference with other states' elections. However, NATO's statements stopped short of asserting that Russia's and China's actions violated existing rules of international law, which suggests that even NATO views these concepts as nascent.

Other examples of mini-lateral efforts to identify and condemn certain types of HCO have taken the form of joint attributions.[118] One of the

---

[113] Fick & Miscik, *supra* note 68, at 35.

[114] The 2022 Brussels Summit Communique from NATO contained such a warning in a paragraph about cyber threats to the alliance. *See* NATO, Brussels Summit Communique (June 14, 2021), ¶ 32 ("If necessary, we will impose costs on those who harm us. Our response need not be restricted to the cyber domain.").

[115] Maggie Miller, *NATO Members Agree to New Cyber Defense Policy*, THE HILL (June 14, 2021).

[116] NATO Communique, *supra* note 114.

[117] *Id.*

[118] For a list of collective cyber attributions, see Yuval Shany & Mike Schmitt, *An International Attribution Mechanism for Hostile Cyber Operations*, 96 INT'L L. STUD. 196, 211 (2020).

earliest joint attributions took place in April 2018, when the United States and the United Kingdom released a "joint technical alert" about malicious cyber activity by the Russian government.[119] The attributing governments accused Russian state-sponsored actors of extracting intellectual property, among other things.[120] In July 2020, the United States, the United Kingdom, and Canada publicly accused Russian intelligence services of targeting organizations involved in developing COVID vaccines.[121] In July 2021, an even larger group of actors—the United States, Canada, Japan, Australia, New Zealand, the United Kingdom, NATO, and the European Union—attributed to China a "broad array of malicious cyber activities," including a hack that compromised over one hundred thousand Microsoft Exchange mail servers.[122]

These acts reflect efforts to publicly articulate what smaller groups of states see as unacceptable categories of HCO. There is reason to be skeptical that statements like these will affect the behavior of "out-group" states, at least in the medium term. Nevertheless, the United States and a range of its partners appear to have concluded that establishing these guideposts will be fruitful in the longer term, even if adversaries do not immediately accept those guideposts.[123]

d. Bilateral agreements

In addition to discussions with allies, the United States (and a few of its partners) have sought or concluded very narrow bilateral agreements with adversaries to confirm that certain types of cyber operations should be off limits. Most notably, the United States and China agreed in 2015 "that neither country's government will conduct or knowingly support cyber-enabled theft of intellectual property, including trade secrets or other confidential business information, with the intent of providing competitive advantages to

---

[119] U.S. Embassy, *Joint U.S.-UK Statement on Malicious Cyber Activity Carried Out by Russian Government* (Apr. 16, 2018).

[120] *Id.*

[121] National Cyber Security Centre, *Advisory: APT29 Targets COVID-19 Vaccine Development* (July 16, 2020).

[122] Kristen Eichensehr, *United States Joins with Allies, Including NATO, to Attribute Malicious Cyber Activities to China*, 115 AJIL 715–21 (2021) [hereafter Eichensehr, *United States Joins*]; John Hudson & Ellen Nakashima, *U.S., Allies Accuse China of Hacking Microsoft and Condoning Other Cyber Attacks*, WASH. POST (July 19, 2021); Kristen Eichensehr, *Cyberattack Attribution and International Law*, JUST SECURITY (July 24, 2020) [hereafter Eichensehr, *Cyberattack Attribution*] (discussing "internationally coordinated attributions of the WannaCry attack to North Korea, the NotPetya attack to Russia, and October 2019 cyberattacks on Georgia to Russia").

[123] Fick & Misick, *supra* note 68, at 53.

companies or commercial sectors."[124] The agreement initially was seen as a positive step; many now view it as a minor success that reduced such operations for a period of time but ultimately failed.[125] China concluded a similar agreement with the United Kingdom, and later joined a Group of Twenty agreement on a norm against cyber-enabled theft of intellectual property.[126]

In June 2021, the United States sought Russia's agreement to cease particular types of HCO. President Biden reportedly presented to Russian President Vladimir Putin a list of sixteen specific types of critical infrastructure that should be "off limits to attack" by cyber or any other means, including the energy sector and water systems.[127] Biden stated that he and Putin agreed to "task experts in both of our countries to work on specific understandings about what's off limits."[128] In July 2021, Biden reportedly warned Putin that he must halt the ransomware attacks against the United States that were emanating from Russia.[129] Although a prominent Russia-based ransomware group went offline shortly thereafter, it subsequently reappeared.[130]

These examples reflect both that the United States sees value in engaging directly with its most assertive adversaries in cyberspace and that the likelihood of durable agreement is very limited. We might expect continued efforts on this front, however, because of the lack of satisfactory alternatives.

e. Unilateral declarations

The most detailed views about what types of HCO should be off limits to states and nonstate actors have emerged from unilateral statements by government officials.[131] Indeed, even scholars who were optimistic in the early 2010s about the prospects for multilateral cyber regulation have turned their sights on a more modest goal, calling on states to articulate their views about cyber operations publicly in the hope that these statements can play a "constitutive role" in developing new norms.[132]

---

[124] White House, *Fact Sheet: President Xi Jinping's State Visit to the United States* (Sept. 25, 2015).
[125] Fick & Miscik, *supra* note 68, at 37.
[126] *Id.*
[127] Biden Administration, The President's News Conference in Geneva, Switzerland (June 16, 2021).
[128] *Id.*
[129] David Sanger & Nicole Perlroth, *Biden Warns Putin to Act Against Ransomware Groups, or U.S. Will Strike Back*, N.Y. TIMES (July 9, 2021).
[130] Eichensehr, *United States Joins, supra* note 122.
[131] Deeks, *supra* note 86.
[132] Martha Finnemore & Duncan Hollis, *Beyond Naming and Shaming: Accusations and International Law in Cybersecurity*, 31 EJIL 969 (2020); Kristen Eichensehr, *The Cyber-Law of Nations*, 103 GEO. L.J. 317, 360–61 (2015).

In recent years, government officials have made four primary types of statements: interpretations of the international rules that apply to HCO; articulations of new norms that try to place certain types of HCO off limits; attributions of HCO to foreign actors; and submissions to international organizations or other multilateral bodies to explicate legal positions. The United States took the lead in making the first three of these types of unilateral declarations, but other states have followed suit.[133]

For example, in 2016, then State Department Legal Adviser Brian Egan argued that "States should publicly state their views on how existing international law applies to State conduct in cyberspace to the greatest extent possible in international and domestic forums."[134] To that end, he described how the United States applies concepts from the laws of armed conflict (such as "attacks") to cyber operations and how it views the principle of "non-intervention" as applying in the cyber setting, specifically noting that manipulating another country's election results would violate that rule.[135] Egan also proposed four nonbinding (though detailed) norms, including that a state should not conduct or support cyber-enabled theft of intellectual property or conduct online activity that intentionally damages critical infrastructure.[136]

Since then, state officials from France, the United Kingdom, the Netherlands,[137] Germany,[138] New Zealand,[139] and Estonia,[140] among others, have set out their states' perspectives on how international law applies to cyber operations and sometimes also identified specific norms that they think should shape states' behavior.[141] Estonia, for instance, has spelled out how it interprets the international rule of "due diligence" and, more prescriptively, has argued for the concept of "collective countermeasures" to support states affected by HCO.[142] States have been explicit that they intend these

---

[133] For a discussion of why states issue these statements, see Shereshevsky, *supra* note 5, at 2131, 2150.

[134] Brian Egan, *International Law and Stability in Cyberspace*, 35 Berkeley J. Int'l L. 169 (2017).

[135] *Id.*

[136] *Id.*

[137] Michael Schmitt, *The Netherlands Releases a Tour de Force on International Law in Cyberspace*, Just Security (Oct. 14, 2019).

[138] German Federal Government, *On the Application of International Law in Cyberspace* (Mar. 2021).

[139] Michael Schmitt, *New Zealand Pushes the Dialogue on International Cyber Law Forward*, Just Security (Dec. 8, 2020).

[140] Michael Schmitt, *Estonia Speaks Out on Key Rules for Cyberspace*, Just Security (June 10, 2019).

[141] For a fuller list of state comments on this issue, see Inter-American Juridical Committee, *International Law and State Cyber Operations* (Nov. 1, 2020); CCDCOE, *National Positions*.

[142] Schmitt, *supra* note 140.

public statements to help develop settled expectations about how states should behave in cyberspace.[143]

States that are victims of HCO sometimes unilaterally attribute those HCO to other states, generally critiquing the underlying HCO as inconsistent with "responsible state behavior" in cyberspace. As Mike Schmitt notes, "Only with such specificity will condemnation yield meaningful normative value."[144] However, many attributions do not specifically charge that the HCO violated international law.[145] In perhaps the most dramatic unilateral response to date to an HCO, the government of Albania terminated diplomatic relations with Iran and ordered Iranian staff to leave Albania after accusing Iran of an HCO that "threatened to paralyse public services, erase digital systems and hack into state records [and] steal government intranet electronic communication."[146]

Finally, many states have submitted documents to multilateral bodies such as the Convention on Certain Conventional Weapons (CCW), the UN GGE, and the Organization of American States. These multilateral processes have served a forcing function, stimulating states to develop agreed positions that are often more detailed—and more focused on legal issues—than other unilateral government statements.[147]

f. Indictments

The sixth set of tools that a few states have deployed to shape international cyber behavior are criminal indictments. Most prominently, the United States has indicted a range of Chinese, Russian, and Iranian officials under U.S. law for undertaking HCO. In 2016, the Department of Justice indicted an Iranian linked to the Iranian Revolutionary Guard Corps with hacking the control system of a New York dam.[148] In July 2021, the United States indicted three Chinese security officials for a broad hacking scheme to steal the data of companies, universities, and government entities

---

[143] Egan, *supra* note 134. *See also* Josh Gold, *The Five Eyes and Offensive Cyber Capabilities: Building a "Cyber Deterrence Initiative"*, NATO CCDCOE (2020) (concluding that recent statements by the Five Eyes states aim "to further enforce and strengthen the UN cyber stability framework through the collective imposition of real-world costs to states which violate the norms and principles of that framework").

[144] Schmitt, *supra* note 140.

[145] Eichensehr, *Cyberattack Attribution*, *supra* note 122.

[146] Reuters, *Albania Cuts Iran Ties Over Cyberattack, U.S. Vows Further Action* (Sept. 7, 2022).

[147] Thanks to Kristen Eichensehr for suggesting this point.

[148] U.S. Dep't of Justice, *Seven Iranians Working for Islamic Revolutionary Guard Corps-Affiliated Entities Charged for Conducting Coordinated Campaign of Cyber Attacks Against U.S. Financial Sector* (Mar. 24, 2016).

abroad.[149] The U.S. government alleged that Chinese officials stole trade secrets, technologies, data, and personal information, including to benefit research and development work in China.[150] Even though these indictments are tools of domestic law, they signal the indicting state's view that the underlying cyber activity must be condemned and, where possible, punished.

Scholars and government officials have debated whether such indictments are valuable for this purpose.[151] Jack Goldsmith and Robert Williams conclude that the U.S. indictments have failed to deter HCO and make the United States look toothless.[152] Garrett Hinck and Tim Maurer argue that these indictments can help disrupt operations, pressure states to refrain from future HCO, and support the emergence of norms.[153] The U.S. Department of Justice clearly believes that the indictments have value, because it continues to issue them. Nevertheless, this tool can do modest work, at best, to structure behavior on the international plane.

g. Nonstate processes

Although this book is largely focused on states (and the United States in particular), nonstate actors have developed a range of processes intended to flesh out the contents of international cyber rules or help states achieve some consensus around such rules. Most prominent is the *Tallinn Manual,* through which a group of nonstate experts set forth their views on the current state of international law applicable to cyber operations. (The third iteration of this process is underway, with the goal of revising prior chapters and incorporating the recent statements and practice of states.)[154] More recently, the Oxford Process attempted to identify and clarify specific cyber norms at a higher level of specificity than other projects.[155] Oxford Statements to date have addressed the obligation to refrain from HCO against the healthcare sector and foreign elections. In addition, certain experts have established

---

[149] Devlin Barrett, *U.S. Charges Chinese Security Officers with Hacking,* WASH. POST (July 19, 2021).

[150] U.S. Dep't of Justice, *Two Chinese Hackers Working with the Ministry of State Security Charged with Global Computer Intrusion Campaign Targeting Intellectual Property and Confidential Business Information, Including COVID-19 Research* (July 21, 2020).

[151] *See* Garrett Hinck & Tim Maurer, *What's the Point of Charging Foreign State-Linked Hackers?,* LAWFARE (May 24, 2019).

[152] Jack Goldsmith & Robert Williams, *The Failure of the United States' Chinese-Hacking Indictment Strategy,* LAWFARE (Dec. 28, 2018).

[153] Hinck & Maurer, *supra* note 151.

[154] TALLINN MANUAL 2.0 ON THE INTERNATIONAL LAW APPLICABLE TO CYBER OPERATIONS (Michael Schmitt ed., 2d ed. 2017).

[155] Oxford Process on International Law Protections in Cyberspace (May 2020).

nongovernmental "Track 1.5" or "Track 2" dialogues with China and Russia on cyber issues.[156]

In general, exercises like this, in which academic and other experts publish detailed views on the existing doctrine or proposed norms or discuss those norms with nonstate counterparts who understand the thinking of foreign government officials, do some work to inform state views, especially where state lawyers lack the legal experience necessary to advise their governments.

h. Cyber crisis?

Having reviewed the tools that states have used to date, one is left with the impression that it may take a true cyber crisis to illustrate to all states the costs of having no binding rule precluding HCO against a hugely valuable or interconnected target, such as a major stock exchange or a nuclear command and control system.[157] Although HCO to date have produced significant financial, privacy, and security costs, those costs have not proven shocking or insurmountable. Current trends suggest that, absent a catastrophic shock to the international system, it will be hard to make concrete progress on reining in HCO.

Ultimately, the international problems posed by misuse of AI systems are more like those posed by HCO than by nuclear weapons. As a result, a clear understanding of efforts at international cyber norm-setting helps us forecast where AI regulation is likely to head and where U.S. efforts may prove more or less successful. The tools discussed previously have moved the needle a bit, but genuine and broad multilateral agreement on new norms against certain HCO has proven elusive. The most fruitful articulations about how international law applies to HCO or what specific targets should be off limits occur in small, like-minded groups or when states present their views unilaterally. Indeed, the level of specificity with which states propose norms is inversely proportional to the number of states that have evidenced support for that norm. Even then, there is little empirical evidence to suggest that these statements (rather than other motivations) that have led adversary states to forgo specific targets, though we have—to date—avoided a genuine cyber catastrophe.

---

[156] For a description of Track 1.5 dialogues, see Jennifer Staats et al., *A Primer on Multi-Track Diplomacy: How Does It Work?*, U.S. INST. OF PEACE (July 31, 2019); Jason Healey et al., *Confidence-Building Measures in Cyberspace* 9 n.25, ATLANTIC COUNCIL (Nov. 2014).

[157] *See, e.g.*, Fick & Miscik, *supra* note 68, at 5.

E. International Norm-Setting for National Security AI: The (Slow) Way Ahead

International cyber discussions—which have been happening for a decade longer than AI discussions—offer a useful roadmap for how international AI discussions are likely to play out. We can already see parallels between the processes. At bottom, it is improbable that a broad new international agreement on regulation of NSAI—at least an agreement that includes major military powers—will emerge unless and until a major crisis occurs.[158] Instead, the way ahead is likely to include high-level agreement about the applicability of existing international law; some limited, relatively general multilateral norms; more specific mini-lateral norms and processes; unilateral statements of policy; and some use of domestic law to try to shape the behavior of foreign actors.

The pressures to regulate NSAI will vary by type. For instance, human rights groups may apply intense pressure on states to regulate facial recognition software—first domestically and then internationally. Or we might see particular emphasis in keeping NSAI out of nuclear command and control systems. In contrast, states may face little pressure to regulate forms of NSAI that will be useful to enhance intelligence analysis and decision-making, either because those uses seem less risky or because outside actors understand that they would be unlikely to succeed in demanding regulation. The very heterogeneity of NSAI systems and risks, like those of HCO, strengthens the analogy between HCO and NSAI and further illustrates how different these systems are from nuclear weapons.

1. Application of Existing International Law

To date, the most significant interstate discussions about NSAI have taken place among a group of governmental experts (GGE) under the auspices of the CCW. Those discussions, which began in 2014 and operate by consensus, have focused on whether and how the use of LAWS can comply with the

---

[158] Liis Vihul, *International Legal Regulation of Autonomous Technologies*, CTR. FOR INT'L GOVERNANCE INNOVATION (Nov. 16, 2020). For views of what such a regime could look like, see Crootof, *supra* note 4, at 1897 (concluding that "an ideal international legal regime [for autonomous weapons systems] would consist of a framework convention and a thorough collection of associated additional protocols, supplemented by domestic law and other sources of informal governance mechanisms"); ICRC Position, *supra* note 4.

existing laws of armed conflict.[159] In 2019, the GGE adopted eleven "guiding principles," intended to shape the work of the GGE moving forward.[160] Most of the principles reaffirmed that existing international law applies to LAWS when used during armed conflict. For instance, the principles assert that states using LAWS must comply with the rules of distinction, proportionality, and precautions in attack through a responsible chain of command, and cannot use LAWS that would cause unnecessary suffering.[161] There is disagreement, however, about how to define autonomous weapons systems, how existing law regulates the use of those systems, and whether there is a need for additional international law in this area.

It is unclear whether states will be able to develop new international law in this forum. In 2022, Russia refused to allow the GGE to formally operate and then obstructed informal substantive discussions.[162] Even before that, eighteen days of discussion in 2021 failed to produce substantive consensus about a way ahead. Some states are seeking a ban on LAWS. But the United States, Russia, Australia, the United Kingdom, Canada, Japan, and other major military states are unlikely to join such a ban. It is possible that the GGE will continue to pursue a "best practices" document, but that is more likely to contain voluntary norms than binding international law. As occurred in cyber discussions, states began by examining existing international law and concluded that it applied to the use of a subset of NSAI (i.e., LAWS), but had difficulty agreeing on the details of how it applies. These difficulties result from the elements discussed previously in section C: it is hard to achieve a consensus definition of the tool to be regulated; states have different perspectives about whether existing law applies and whether it provides adequate guidance in specific situations; states have misaligned regulatory interests; and the major state developers of LAWS would be deeply suspicious of their adversaries' purported commitments to comply with any agreed legal norms.

---

[159] UN Office of Disarmament Affairs, *Timeline of LAWS in the CCW.*

[160] Report of the 2019 session of the Group of Governmental Experts on Emerging Technologies in the Area of Lethal Autonomous Weapons Systems, CCW/GGE.1/2019/3 [hereafter 2019 GGE Report], ¶ 17.

[161] *Id.,* ¶ 17(a), (d), (h).

[162] Ousman Noor, *Discussions at UN on Autonomous Weapons Systems Blocked by Russia, but States Indicate Way Forward,* STOP KILLER ROBOTS (Mar. 15, 2022).

2. Multilateral Norms

CCW participants have also attempted to develop "good practices" for using LAWS, which states may apply voluntarily. For example, the GGE has discussed good practices in the conduct of legal reviews of weapons,[163] and various groups of states have put forward "principles" and "good practices" documents that provide greater specifics than the "eleven principles" discussed above. In March 2022, Australia, Canada, Japan, Korea, the United Kingdom, and the United States submitted a document to the CCW that included principles related to human responsibility for the use of LAWS, human-machine interactions, and risk assessments (the latter two of which are not topics covered by international law).[164]

If NSAI negotiations proceed the way that cyber discussions have, we should expect to see continued discussions about norms, but it is not clear that a wide swath of states will be able to achieve agreement around a more detailed set of voluntary norms as long as their regulatory interests remain at odds.

3. Mini-lateral Norms

As with cyber, the "mini-lateral" group of NATO states have adopted a set of principles (the "Principles of Responsible Use for AI") to which they intend to adhere. Even here, though, the norms (at least those made public) are crafted at a high level of generality: lawfulness, responsibility and accountability, explainability and traceability, reliability, governability, and bias mitigation.[165] NATO subsequently established a Data and Artificial Intelligence Review Board to help operationalize the Principles of Responsible Use.[166] The member states surely will have more detailed conversations about military tools, requirements, testing, and verification than they would in a larger group, not least because they have an interest in facilitating the interoperability of their NSAI systems and understanding each other's redlines and risk tolerances. Indeed, two scholars have proposed that NATO states share

---

[163] 2019 GGE Report, *supra* note 160, at ¶ 18(c).
[164] Australia et al., *Principles and Good Practices on Emerging Technologies in the Area of Lethal Autonomous Weapons Systems* (Mar. 7, 2022), ¶¶ 16, 19–20.
[165] Zoe Stanley-Lockman & Edward Christie, *An Artificial Intelligence Strategy for NATO*, NATO (Oct. 25, 2021).
[166] *Id.*; NATO, *NATO's Data and Artificial Intelligence Review Board* (Oct. 17, 2022).

machine learning models with each other.[167] However, the secrecy of states' NSAI will prove a persistent hurdle to robust information sharing, even among close allies.

If NATO produces reasonable, detailed, public norms, certain other (non-NATO) states might agree to adhere to those norms, at least in conflicts with states that also have accepted those norms.[168] Further, NATO (or other mini-lateral groups such as the Five Eyes or the forty-six members of the Council of Europe) could announce certain specific norms that they will adhere to, regardless of what their adversaries do.[169] A possible parallel here is international humanitarian law: states have agreed that they will adhere to certain rules during armed conflict, even if their adversary fails to do so.[170] Possible norms include requiring LAWS to "check in with a human operator at regular intervals after deployment and to shut down or self-destruct if it did not receive reiterated approval to continue"; committing not to develop LAWS that possess a significant amount of destructive power; or limiting LAWS use to stationary or defensive purposes.[171]

The United States has developed a ten-point political declaration related to the military use of AI, and, as of September 2024, it has persuaded fifty-five states to endorse it.[172] The declaration includes provisions urging states to "ensure that senior officials effectively and appropriately oversee the development and deployment of military AI capabilities with high-consequence applications," "ensure that military AI capabilities are developed with methodologies, data sources, design procedures, and documentation that are transparent to and auditable by their relevant defense personnel," and "ensure that the safety, security, and effectiveness of military AI capabilities are subject to appropriate and rigorous testing and assurance within their well-defined uses and across their entire life-cycles," and, for self-learning

---

[167] Edward Christie & Amy Ertan, *NATO and Artificial Intelligence*, in ROUTLEDGE COMPANION TO ARTIFICIAL INTELLIGENCE AND NATIONAL SECURITY POLICY (Scott Romaniuk & Mary Manjikian eds., 2021).

[168] For related ideas, see Michèle Flournoy & Anshu Roy, *NATO Must Tackle Digital Authoritarianism*, JUST SECURITY (June 29, 2022); Martijn Rasser, *The American AI Century: A Blueprint for Action*, CTR. FOR NEW AM. SECURITY (Dec. 17, 2019); Ashley Deeks, *An International Legal Framework for Surveillance*, 55 VA. J. INT'L L. 291 (2015) (envisioning in-group commitments).

[169] *See* National Security Commission on AI, Interim Report 72 (Nov. 2019) (discussing a Five Eyes "Technical Cooperation Program" that is focused on AI applications for allied militaries).

[170] *See* U.S. DEP'T OF DEFENSE, LAW OF WAR MANUAL (2016), § 3.6.3 (indicating that application of the laws of war does not legally depend on reciprocity).

[171] Crootof, *supra* note 4, at 1900; *see also* ICRC Position, *supra* note 4.

[172] U.S. Dep't of State, *Political Declaration on Responsible Military Use of Artificial Intelligence and Autonomy* (Jan. 12, 2024).

or continuously updating military AI capabilities, ensure that critical safety features have not been degraded.[173] The document is notable in that it includes a greater level of substantive detail than other AI-focused political commitments. However, the document is not legally binding and China, Russia, and Israel, among other AI leaders, have not signed on.[174] Those states that have signed on might consider making joint attributions and levying joint critiques of uses of military AI that they identify as problematic, as has happened in the cyber setting.

4. Bilateral Agreements

Even if there is little chance that the United States will achieve very narrow binding legal commitments from Russia and China related to NSAI, there is near-consensus that it is important to keep open bilateral discussions on NSAI. Though they lack the formal imprimatur of government conversations, Track 1.5 and 2 dialogues on NSAI safety and security have taken place between U.S. and Chinese (nongovernmental) experts for years, with the goal of increasing understanding between the United States and China about each other's approach to these issues and avoiding unintended escalation.[175]

Apart from those bilateral conversations, the United States could offer to negotiate with Russia and China to establish limits on use of AI systems in nuclear command, control, and communication systems, a highly sensitive situation in which machine learning errors could prove even more catastrophic than human errors.[176] President Biden reportedly raised this possibility with Chinese President Xi Jinping in November 2023, but China was not prepared to agree to do more than continue to discuss the topic.[177] A very narrow context such as this one might overcome the challenges found elsewhere in NSAI discussions because there could be clear agreement about the object of regulation, a threat that is very easy to envision, and an alignment

---

[173] *Id.*

[174] *Id.*

[175] Andrew Imbrie & Elsa Kania, *AI Safety, Security, and Stability Among Great Powers* 4, CTR. FOR SECURITY & EMERGING TECH. (Dec. 2019).

[176] Allen & West, *supra* note 18 (arguing that states should "agree not to have AI algorithms within nuclear operational command and control systems").

[177] David Sanger & Katie Rogers, *Biden-Xi Talks Lead to Little but a Promise to Keep Talking*, N.Y. TIMES (Nov. 15, 2023).

of regulatory interests among adversaries, though verification would remain difficult.

Even if the United States and China cannot reach a binding agreement on any AI uses, there are historical examples of nonbinding arrangements between adversaries that might serve as useful models for a way ahead. In 1991, for example, the United States and the U.S.S.R. made parallel, nonbinding declarations about their policies toward nuclear sea-launched cruise missiles.[178] Pursuant to the declarations, each side would specify the number of missiles deployed, with a cap of 880; would not deploy missiles equipped with more than one nuclear weapon; and would exchange additional information about capabilities, among other things. They used this format because they did not want to commit to verification measures but did want to create certain guardrails around missile deployment and use.[179] Although numerical caps on the number of AI-enabled weapons systems would not make sense for the reasons discussed previously, the United States and China could attempt to develop parallel, nonbinding declarations about the internal processes their governments use to approve autonomous systems, their policies about deactivating any deployed autonomous systems that begin to act unpredictably, or the auditability of their systems. This could set basic guardrails around military AI use, reduce inadvertent escalation, and possibly set the stage for future binding agreements.

5. Unilateral Declarations

As with cyber norm development, many of the near-term developments in NSAI norms likely will come in the form of unilateral declarations of policy or allegations that another state is engaged in irresponsible behavior.[180] This might include positive statements about how states intend to develop and deploy NSAI, such as a commitment not to use deepfakes in a way that could lead to an armed conflict. The United States and the United Kingdom have both issued one or more policy statements about how they intend to use and

---

[178] United States and U.S.S.R. Declarations of Policy Concerning Nuclear Sea-Launched Missiles (July 31, 1991).

[179] U.S. Senate, Capability of the United States to Monitor Compliance with the START Treaty 8, S. Rep. 102-431 (Sept. 29, 1992) ("The United States insisted that limitations on sea-launched cruise missiles (SLCMs) should not be . . . subject to START's verification provisions.").

[180] See Anderson & Waxman, supra note 13, at 23.

not use autonomous military tools.[181] Or, just as India and China have formally adopted "no first use" policies for nuclear weapons, a state could announce that it would not direct LAWS against other states that have not first deployed their own LAWS. Using unilateral declarations, states may also condemn certain adversarial acts. For instance, if Iraq detected with confidence that Turkey had deployed an autonomous loitering weapon that targeted civilian infrastructure, it could issue a public statement condemning the operation and explaining why it was confident that the system had operated autonomously. Or a state that captured another state's NSAI system could post the code of that system, just as the United States has posted samples of North Korean and Russian malware.[182]

6. Indictments

Finally, it is conceivable that states will use their domestic criminal laws in the future to sanction those engaged in perceived misuses of NSAI. A state might, for example, initiate a war crimes prosecution against a foreign military officer or commander who deploys a LAWS that targets a group of the state's civilians. Or imagine that a foreign official deploys a deepfake that leads the United States to take kinetic action against another state. Perhaps the U.S. Justice Department could charge the individual with conspiracy to commit fraud against the United States, as the United States did when it charged Russia hackers who attempted to interfere with the 2016 U.S. election.[183] Such prosecutions would only come after the fact but could signal an individual state's condemnation of a particular use of NSAI that harmed its citizens.

---

[181] *See, e.g.,* DOD Directive 3000.09, *supra* note 15; Intel.gov, Principles of Artificial Intelligence Ethics for the Intelligence Community; U.S. Dep't of Defense, DOD Adopts Ethical Principles for Artificial Intelligence (Feb. 24, 2020). In addition, the National Security Commission on AI produced several detailed reports about AI policy and norms. *See* National Security Commission on AI. The U.K. Ministry of Defence has also produced an AI policy. *See* U.K. Ministry of Defence, *Ambitious, Safe, Responsible: Our Approach to the Delivery of AI-enabled Capability in Defence* (June 2022).

[182] Fick & Miscik, *supra* note 68, at 34.

[183] U.S. Dep't of Justice, *Grand Jury Indicts 12 Russian Intelligence Officers for Hacking Offenses Related to the 2016 Election* (July 13, 2018).

7. Nongovernmental Processes

As in the cyber context, the role of nonstate experts will be important. This is especially true because of the highly technical nature of AI and the need to include technical, policy, legal, and ethical perspectives when developing norms around NSAI. Actors such as the ICRC have offered specific proposals that, while likely too ambitious at this time, are helpful because they focus on specific contexts in which LAWS pose the greatest risk. To date, there have been limited conversations about NSAI outside the LAWS context, a gap that presents an opportunity for experts to help draw attention to other NSAI challenges.

Relatedly, as Chapter 5 discussed, companies (rather than states) may decline to produce certain types of NSAI and then explain why. Decisions by companies such as Microsoft, IBM, Google, and Amazon to constrain the sale of NSAI tools such as facial recognition technology have the potential to shape (and suppress) the use of NSAI by depriving states of easy access to some of those tools.[184] Some companies could decide not to sell their products to governments that will not adhere to certain AI-related commitments, though there are a range of ways for such governments to acquire those tools through third parties.

8. AI Crisis?

As with HCO, there is little reason for optimism about reaching a set of agreed voluntary norms around the development and use of NSAI in the medium term. There is a possibility, however, that a significant, unexpected, and lethal use of an NSAI system will focus the collective international mind on the need for certain agreed rules. Because the current state of play in NSAI development occurs behind tightly closed doors, it is hard to know whether, when, and how such an AI catastrophe might transpire—and whether we will even know that a given crisis was instigated by NSAI tools. But if it is clear that NSAI caused the crisis, the event, like the use of nuclear weapons in World

---

[184] Newman, *supra* note 17, at 5 ("Microsoft, Amazon, and IBM all made announcements and pledges to stop selling facial recognition technology to police departments, either for a designated period of time or until a federal regulation is in place to help protect people's privacy and rights."). Google's AI Principles also state that the company will not help build weapons or surveillance technology that violates international norms or laws. Because these U.S. companies are multinational, their commitments will affect both the United States and other states.

War II, likely would be sufficient to alter the otherwise gloomy prognosis for rule-creation just outlined.

F. Conclusion

The weak forecast for a new international agreement on how to regulate the use of NSAI suggests that international norms will do little work to decrease the size of the double black box confronting democracies. Instead of new international norms, domestic constitutions, statutes, case law, and executive policies are more likely to do the important work of shaping how democracies use NSAI. This might take the form of detailed statutes about when states can use facial recognition software; when military and intelligence agencies may use deepfakes; or what level of testing and verification those agencies must conduct before deploying NSAI. In the United States, it might also take the form of judicial decisions requiring the executive branch to use only "explainable AI" when it uses NSAI in a way that affects U.S. persons.[185]

There are advantages to this domestically focused approach. First, the lack of clear guidance in existing international law may give states "the appropriate room required to experiment with potential alternative responses to the problems discussed. The laboratory of ideas of the different States . . . could suggest different solutions to these questions that over time could end in an international consensus."[186] We have begun to see a type of "international federalism"[187] and "Brussels effect" emerge with facial recognition software, for example, with the European Union and several U.S. states enacting or considering legislation to regulate or prohibit its use.[188]

Second, where legislatures or executives choose to act domestically, the depth of rule explication will likely be considerably greater than it would be

---

[185] Ashley Deeks, *The Judicial Demand for Explainable AI*, 119 COLUM. L. REV. 1829 (2019).

[186] John Bellinger & Vijay Padmanabhan, *Detention Operations in Contemporary Conflicts: Four Challenges for the Geneva Conventions and Other Existing Law*, 105 AJIL 201 (2011).

[187] Ashley Deeks, *Domestic Humanitarian Law: Developing the Laws of War in Domestic Courts, in* APPLYING INTERNATIONAL HUMANITARIAN LAW IN JUDICIAL AND QUASI-JUDICIAL BODIES: INTERNATIONAL AND DOMESTIC ASPECTS (Derek Jinks et al. eds., 2014).

[188] Clothilde Goujhard, *Europe Edges Closer to a Ban on Facial Recognition*, POLITICO (Sept. 20, 2022) (European Union considering ban); Rachel Metz, *First, They Banned Facial Recognition. Now They're Not So Sure*, CNN (Aug. 5, 2022) (describing state restrictions and some later reversals of those restrictions); Michael Berens, *One U.S. State Stands Out in Restricting Corporate Use of Biometrics*, REUTERS (Sept. 16, 2021) (noting that Illinois prohibits companies from using facial recognition software to identify and track people without their consent).

on the international stage. Third, such regulation could happen faster. In the cyber context, the U.S. Congress enacted statutes such as the 1986 Computer Fraud and Abuse Act and the 1986 Electronic Communications Privacy Act (and U.S. states enacted state laws) much earlier than states initiated international discussions about HCO.[189]

This is not to suggest that leaving domestic regulation to do all of the work will be satisfactory or easy. As earlier chapters of this book reveal, legislatures and even executive branch leadership face real hurdles to understanding these secret and highly technical tools and so will face genuine hurdles to producing meaningful constraints. Further, few national security issues make it into court, and thus few will face judicial review.

Ensuring executive compliance with public law values will require diligence by a wide range of actors. In the United States, we will need to rely on our traditional surrogates, including congressional committees that oversee the military and intelligence community. But we will also need to rely on our nontraditional "secrecy surrogates" as well: foreign allies, U.S. technology companies, and states and localities.[190] By virtue of how machine learning algorithms work, it will be critical to ensure early policy and legal input into whether to use a machine learning algorithm at all in a given national security operation, and what kinds of data, parameters, and factors that algorithm should contain (or avoid). Drawing from Lawrence Lessig's seminal early insight that "code is law," there is important work for lawyers to do to build legal guardrails into the code that becomes national security "law."[191] It can be done, but it will not be neat or easy.

---

[189] *See* Kristen Eichensehr, *Cyberwar and International Law Step Zero*, 50 Tex. Int'l L.J. 355, 362 and n.44 (2015).
[190] Ashley Deeks, *Secrecy Surrogates*, 106 Va. L. Rev. 1395 (2020).
[191] Lawrence Lessig, Code and Other Laws of Cyberspace (1999).

Conclusion

The Future of the Double Black Box

Recall the presidential briefing that this book opened with. The Secretary of Defense and the CIA Director were recommending that the President authorize a drone strike against a senior al Qaeda member based on a series of AI-produced predictions about the target's identity, his location, and the strike's political effects. The situation is a paradigmatic double black box. The public will have no visibility into the scenario, decision-making, or inputs. Further, not only the public but also DOD and CIA officials will have limited visibility into the workings of the algorithms delivering the recommendations and the autonomous systems that might help conduct the operation. Part I of this book demonstrated why this scenario challenges the public law values on which our government is built.

Part II identified and analyzed ways in which our current set of "secrecy surrogates," ranging from Congress to executive lawyers to whistleblowers to foreign allies to U.S. states, can do work behind the veil of secrecy to ensure the government is acting lawfully, effectively, and accountably. If we put the laws, policies, and actions proposed in Part II into effect, the Secretary of Defense and the CIA Director might be able to deliver a number of assurances to the President that would give her comfort in making the decision—and, more conceptually, would give the public, stuck outside of the double black box, greater comfort that U.S. national security operations are comporting with those values.

Imagine, for example, that the Secretary of Defense and the CIA Director could tell the President that the armed services and intelligence committees in Congress are regularly briefed on the training, testing, and use of these algorithms; that interagency policymakers and lawyers inside the Executive must sign off on their use; that surveys have revealed that the public supports the use of predictive algorithms in military settings under certain conditions; that senior Defense and State Department officials have had extensive discussions with NATO allies about what confidence levels targeting-related algorithms should require and detailed discussions about how to test them; that the Defense Department has a robust understanding of what training data its defense contractors used to train the systems and what bespoke data Defense Department officials used to fine-tune the models for targeting purposes; and that the two Cabinet members and the Defense Department's Chief Data and Artificial Intelligence Officer will hold themselves personally accountable for errors in framing the issue and data for the President. The U.S. officials making these consequential national security decisions, who are "traveling across obscured terrain with little to no ability to assess the powerful beasts that carry and guide" them, will have modestly tamed those beasts.[1]

Some may argue that the normative proposals identified in Part II are insufficiently robust to meet the tidal wave of AI-driven changes that they foresee. This book's goal was to focus primarily on procedural, rather than substantive, adjustments that would be achievable in the current domestic and international climate and would remain relevant regardless of how quickly technological changes come. Others may resist Chapter 6's pessimism about the prospects for robust international agreements among major AI powers that would slow or eliminate the development and use of the highest risk AI. That chapter is not intended to urge the United States and its allies to give up on international engagement with a shrug. After all, U.S. allies can join with the United States to condemn unacceptable uses of AI by adversaries and potentially impose economic costs when those uses occur. But that chapter is intended to highlight that effective international legal solutions to high-risk AI will be harder to achieve than domestic adjustments, even in today's sharply divided political environment in the United States.

As this book has shown, there is no single solution to the double black box dilemma. Each of the secrecy surrogates described herein has a role to play, and ideally their work will be overlapping and complementary. Chapter 5 highlights that even those for whom the double black box is the most opaque—the vast swathes of the American public who do not work inside the national security establishment—can affect what types of national security AI the government decides to adopt. Our job is to find ways to signal to and influence the surrogates about when, where, and how we want our national security agencies to use or disclaim AI tools.[2] A cynic might argue

---

[1] Richard Danzig, *Technology Roulette*, CTR. FOR NEW AM. SECURITY 16 (June 2018).

[2] DARRELL WEST & JOHN ALLEN, TURNING POINT: POLICYMAKING IN THE ERA OF ARTIFICIAL INTELLIGENCE 25 (2020) ("[O]ne crucial point to remember . . . is that there are particular ways

that the public will want those agencies to throw everything they can at U.S. adversaries, but that is not borne out in every historical case. Nor, to its credit, does that appear to be the U.S. government's approach to date. But the government must explain better how it is operationalizing its high-level principles as it embeds AI into its national security decision-making and activities.

At bottom, the Executive needs buy-in from Congress, the U.S. public, and U.S. companies in its AI-related national security choices: to maximize which companies will work with U.S. national security agencies, to garner support from allies and noncommitted states, and to avoid future backlash against overly aggressive national security activities. The struggle to look behind the curtain is part of our ongoing democratic experiment, and it is an eminently human struggle. As George Kennan wrote, "If the policies and actions of the U.S. government are to be made to conform to moral standards, those standards are going to have to be America's own, founded on traditional American principles of justice and propriety."[3] There is no one Platonic ideal of how to balance secrecy and transparency: we all must remain active participants in this shared project.

people can retain control . . . , [including through] public opinion that demands reasonable safeguards.").

[3] George Kennan, *Morality and Foreign Policy*, 64 FOREIGN AFF. 208, 214 (Winter 1985).

Index